HUNTSVILLE

Pictorial Research by Patricia H. Ryan

A touch of New Orleans or Mobile, the McGee Hotel built in 1877 on the corner of Jefferson and Clinton, was the prettiest hotel in Huntsville, until it burned down in 1924. Courtesy, Ernest C. Smartt

*Facing page
East Side Square in the late 1940s before parking meters were installed in 1949. Courtesy, Ernest C. Smartt*

American Historical Press
Sun Valley, California

HISTORIC
HUNTSVILLE

A City of New Beginnings

Elise Hopkins Stephens

Library of Congress Catalogue Card Number: 2002094841
ISBN: 1-892724-31-6

Bibliography: p. 234
Includes Index

Contents

For my two Huntsville sons,
James and Russell . . .
and Huntsville's two daughters,
Eleanor and Margaret

*Crew laying wire for
Huntsville's first electric
system, circa 1887–1890.
Courtesy, Huntsville
Madison Public Library*

A military reel at Huntsville appeared in Harper's Weekly in April 1864. Begun in 1857, the weekly was widely read in both parlors and army camps because of its extensive coverage of the Civil War. Courtesy, Mrs. W. Truman Ryan.

Acknowledgments

My thanks ...

To the Historic Huntsville Foundation for its support throughout this labor of love. This new edition owes much to the Foundation for allowing me to serve as editor of the *Quarterly* for almost 10 years. Thanks also to Heather Zeug and the American Historical Press. To Ed Starnes for allowing me to use his marvelous watercolors. To Daniel Little for his special photography. To Tom Carney of Old Huntsville Inc. for granting permission to use three volumes of the "Old Huntsville" photo collection on CD. To The Botanical Garden and the Convention and Visitors Bureau for photograph CDs. To EarlyWorks and families visiting for permission to photograph. To Larry Waldrup Photography. To interviewees Mayor Loretta Purdy Spencer, Lee Sentell and Judy Ryals of the Convention and Visitors Bureau, Brian Hilson of the Chamber of Commerce, Ralph Gipson of CityScapes and Sonnie Hereford, III, M.D. Thanks also to gatherers of material: Thomas Hutchens and Ranee Pruitt of the Public Library, Barbara Nash of the Chamber, Lucy Mize, Marion Conover and Adelene and Ted Bledsoe. A special thanks to Eleanor Hutchens, John Conover and David Bowman who read the final chapter and offered suggestions, all of which I did not take, of course.

To the many people who have opened their homes, sharing pictures, books, and reminiscences with me, especially Mrs. Bess Hay Bradley; Mrs. Ruth R. Jones and her son; Dr. John Rison Jones; Mr. Fred C. Monroe; Mr. and Mrs. Jack Hay; Mr. and Mrs. Walter Jackson;

Mr. and Mrs. Gene Paul King; Mr. and Mrs. Lawrence B. Goldsmith; Mr. and Mrs. James Reeves; Mr. and Mrs. Michael O'Reilly; and Mrs. Delia Jenkins. To Mr. and Mrs. Loran Hyden whose walls at "Wildwood" yielded up fresh, though long-hidden, Clay-Clopton material, which was most graciously given to the Friends of the Library for the Zeitler Room. To Harvie Jones for the loan of the Lillian Bone Paul Papers. To Trice Hinds for sharing his Grace Hinds, Lady Curzon, material with me and for other clippings he had saved. To Coy Michael for his Civil War expertise. To Mr. and Mrs. Wilson D. Smith, Jr. To Wenona Switzer for her Cobb family material. To Benjamin Franklin Johnson who shared his Huntsville childhood. To Dr. John McDaniel whose manuscript described the military's role at the arsenal and in the missile program. To Nancy Dickson, with whom I taught in Houston, Texas, in the early '60s and whose earlier experiences had included a Huntsville stint/sojourn in 1941-1942. When called upon, Nancy wrote marvelous recollections. To Henry and Marsha Marks and Dick Curtis for their support. To Suzanne Frew and Malcolm Tarkington for their photography.

To Donna Schremser and the entire staff of the Huntsville Public Library for their friendly encouragement and fellowship, especially Martin Towery, Patti Reny, Sara McDaris, Richard White, Lee Deal, Irene Charles, Kenny Michael, and Melodie Drewyor.

To the Heritage Room's Director, Anne White Thomas Fuller, goes a special thanks for letting me feel like one of the staff and always

helping me in her cheerful, efficient manner. Her sharp intelligence came into play more than once in aiding me to find the right word or book. To Ranee Pruitt, who didn't fuss when the table in the corner of the Zeitler Room grew steadily more cluttered and jammed with books and documents. To Barbara Farrington for assisting me so willingly.

To those who contributed so much to the store of Huntsville history and from whose works I have profited, especially the writings by Dr. Frances C. Roberts, James Record, Judge Thomas Jones Taylor, and Edward Betts. I am also most grateful to my colleagues Bill Stubno whose reading of my rough drafts was kindly, and Linda Bayer for sharing knowledge, material, and laughter with me.

To Dorothy Scott Johnson who read each chapter and offered material from her store of local lore and records. To Dr. John and Marion Conover who read and critiqued several chapters with me. To Joberta Wasson and Catherine Gilliam, who read the manuscript for historical accuracy.

To my good friend and colleague, Dr. Sarah Newman Shouse who originally was to co-author this book, my gratitude for her belief that I could do the job by myself and for always being there in case I couldn't.

To Dr. Eleanor Newman Hutchens whose love of Huntsville and the traditions of scholarship obliged her to comment freely upon the manuscript as it evolved. To Margaret Hutchens Henson for the warmth of her daily welcome to the Heritage Room.

Elise Hopkins Stephens

CHAPTER I

Squatters and Squires

The voices of the past are like leaves that settle to the ground. . . .They make the earth rich and thick, so that new fruit will come forth. . .
—Chief Dan George

There is an aristocracy of the spirit and the intellect that transcends the trappings of nationality, wealth, or the lineage of family—though these often underlie them. The land that became Huntsville in the Great Bend of the Tennessee River seems always to have attracted to it men and women who, awed by its beauty and bounty, have sought to preserve the one while savoring the other. First a hunting ground, they made of it a squatter's suzerainty that early yielded to a frontier squirearchy. Blended together, these elements made of their settlement a "Colonial Williamsburg" of the Alabama wilderness.

The land lay nestled in the elbow bend of the outreaching Tennessee. The surrounding mountains lifted upwards to 1,600 feet above sea level and were laced, like the veins on an elderly hand, by the blue waters of smaller rivers—the Elk and the Flint—and by countless creeks. Like a tipsy Dionysius, the Tennessee pitched a crooked course as it swerved down from Appalachian peaks, darting here and there, making its way southward. Toward the center of the river's dip into Alabama, near where it abruptly veered from its southerly journey and instead careened northwesterly, there would lie Huntsville. The weathered limestone and red clay soil lent a reddish hue to the river, but the blush left as it roared over ancient shoals, racing as though late for its rendezvous with the Ohio.

LeRoy Pope, the "Father of Huntsville," represented the squires in the state's first senatorial race, but when the squatters and squires squared off, Gabriel Moore trounced Royalist Pope by 1,966 votes to 528. Courtesy, Archives, Constitution Hall Park

Riverboats on the Tennessee transported passengers, cotton, livestock and manufactured goods into the interior. Steam-powered paddle-boats came into use after 1819. Courtesy, Old Huntsville Magazine *and Huntsville Madison County Public Library*

From mountain heights the land below appeared carpeted a deep, lush green. The "forest titans"—the cedars, oaks, walnut, hickory, and poplars—formed a "green cathedral" that had very little undergrowth and was open enough for a wagon to drive through. There were swamps and canebrakes, too, but they did not distract from the beauty of the place. So profuse was the generosity of the Great Bend that it became among the Creeks, Chickasaws, and Cherokees a vast hunting ground, not fought over but held in common.

With the advance of European exploration and claims to inland America in the 1700s, the Great Bend became a fighting issue. The Cherokees stood ready to protect it and fought the Iroquois, the Shawnees, the Creeks, the British and the Chickasaws for it. Similarly, the Chickasaws fought the Iroquois, the Shawnees, the Choctaws, the French and the Cherokees. Moving eastward from their Mississippi base, the Chickasaws established themselves along the Elk and Flint rivers and tried to push back from their village on Chickasaw Island (which later was renamed Hobbs Island) the westward-moving Cherokees.

The Indians' claim to the land of the Tennessee was authentic and had seemed ageless before the arrival of the Europeans. This was to change. The virgin land was claimed, competed for, and fought over by Spanish, French, and British gallants. Intrigues of international scale, involving first the Indians and then the rising new nation of Americans, were plotted in the royal chambers of Europe and wars were fought to determine whose land it would be. Even local legend and poetry depict the devastating effects of the white man's appearance. Huntsville's beloved Monte Sano—the protective mountain forming its northeasterly shoulder—so named by physician Thomas Fearn for its beneficience to health, is said to take its name from the clash between cultures. In one version of the legend, "Monte" is a beautiful Indian maiden betrothed to an Indian brave. A pale-faced stranger steals Monte's heart away. Whereupon the brave pleads, "Monte, say no" to the white man's charms. But Monte, as though a symbol of her people, succumbed to the advances of the white man, was beguiled by his promises, and then was left to pay the price.

This land, so prized by natives and nations alike, had naturally caught the wandering eye of America's frontiersmen and land speculators. The American Revolution had been fought to open America's inland garden to the seaboard-cramped colonials. Virginians, North and South Carolinians, Georgians, and then Tennesseans set their sights on the lower piedmont and Tennessee Valley, and a slew of land schemes surfaced.

Nothing became of one speculative venture in 1784 that called the Great Bend, Houstoun; so the state of Franklin, which was temporarily cut from North Carolina, sought in 1787 to take in the land at the Great Bend. Men whose names would be written large in Southern frontier history took the lead in these efforts: William Blount, John Donelson (said to have a "passionate lust" for land, and whose daughter Rachel inspired the same in Andrew Jackson), John Sevier, Joseph Martin, and Richard Caswell chief among them. In 1787 the Georgia legislature approved a plan proposed by Franklin's Governor John Sevier that 1,500 troops from Franklin would go forth and subdue the restless and warring Indians in Georgia's western back yard in return for bounty land in the Great Bend.

Time was running out on these expansionist schemes. A determined band of men who sweated their summer away in Philadelphia writing the Constitution of the United States behind close-shuttered windows, brought to light a document that would make Indian and territorial concerns a national rather than a state, local, or private matter.

But buccaneering efforts continued to jeopardize state and national interests. John Sevier, his appetite for land unsatiated, made a treaty with the great Creek Chief Alexander McGillivray (Hoboi Hili Miko—"Good Child King") in 1788 and even flirted with the Spanish, who were trying to hold on to their claims to Florida and Louisiana. In 1789, while Georgia still held claim to its western lands, its state legislature hastily sold vast tracts to the South Carolina, Virginia, and Tennessee Yazoo Companies. Amounting to about 20 to 25 million acres in all, the Tennessee tract, which included the Great Bend, covered three to four million acres and sold for only $46,000. This was a sell-out. Immediate protest swept over Georgia and up to the President of the new United States, George Washington, who issued a proclamation forbidding the settlement and removing any protection for settlers in the Yazoo areas.

This first Yazoo land scandal was followed in 1795 by another, even bigger boondoggle, Yazoo II. The Georgia legislature sold the whole of north Alabama for the sum of $60,000. Anger and revulsion swept Georgia as it was discovered that almost all the legislators had accepted bribes for their votes of sale. The next legislature rescinded the act in February 1796, declaring "null and void" the great giveaway that in all had exchanged 35 million acres for only $500,000. A public burning of the reprehensible act took place in an effort to purge the proud state of its weak moment. James Jackson, later governor of Georgia, fought four duels because the name "Yazoo" was mentioned in his presence, earning him the title of the "prince of duelists." Meanwhile though, hundreds of Yazoo claimants had pushed their way westward. Indeed a sales office as far north as Boston, Massachusetts, sold over $2 million in warrants. Land-hungry Americans purchased the warrants with the enthusiasm of modern-day lottery purchasers. But in this case, everyone expected to be a winner.

Funneling control of the western land into the hands of the federal government, in 1796 President Washington appointed Benjamin Hawkins as Indian agent to secure the Great Bend against incursion. In 1802 the federal government and the State of Georgia came to satisfactory terms. For $1.25 million Georgia ceded all her western land to the United States, and Congress took over settlement of the Yazoo claims. Congressional disputes over the validity of Georgia's repudiation and Congressional responsibility for paying the claims delayed organization of the Mississippi Territory which, until 1804, was to include all of the Great Bend. In *Fletcher v. Peck,* the United States Supreme Court in 1810 ruled that the Yazoo claims were valid, and between 1814 and 1815 Congress appropriated more than $4 million in scrip for the purchase of government land. The cure was almost worse than the disease.

All of the claims and counterclaims may have given the Indians in the Great Bend a few extra years of hunting and hoping, but their fate was inexorably sealed. Both the Chickasaws and the Cherokees, swayed by the white man's possessions and weakened by his liquor and disease, held claim to the land until cornered by the newcomer's cunning and power. Little by little, treaty by treaty, the Indians gave ground. Finally in 1805 the Chickasaws relinquished title and in January 1806 the Cherokees let go their claims as well.

And so it was that the Great Bend became an integral part of the frontier movement that swept across 19th-century America, leaving in its wake settlements that replaced Indian pastoral with American vitriol, so-called savagery with slavery, and pristine forests with short-leaf cotton fields. To the Great Bend came the Southern frontier in all its guises: rough and tumble, often drunk and boisterous, lonely to the extremes of homicide and suicide, and never far removed from the constant threat of death.

The most vibrant and volatile forces of 19th-century America intersected at the Big Spring in the Great Bend. John Hunt, in search of a new location for his family in the Mississippi Territory, came looking for the great limestone spring that the Indians spoke of. Accompanied by David Bean, (both most recently hailing from Tennessee), Hunt spent a night—in the fall of 1804—with Isaac Criner in his cabin at the Mountain Fork of the Flint River. Criner later recalled that Hunt and Bean were on their way to the Big Spring and that a fortnight later Bean came back, informing him that Hunt was going to settle at the spring.

All who have written of Huntsville and Madison County have been perplexed by the lack of information about John Hunt. Virgil Carrington "Pat" Jones, who researched old files for his Huntsville *Times* articles in the 1930s, described Hunt as a bearded Irishman who, having immigrated only a few years before, arrived at the Big Spring "standing five feet, ten inches in height, his 180 pounds. . .a mass of flexible steel." A recent history calling him "courageous and uneducated," also described Hunt as standing "six feet tall and weighing 180 pounds." Give or take a few inches, Hunt embodied the American frontiersman.

John Hunt's family, like many other Scotch-Irish, immigrated to Pennsylvania and moved down through Virginia's Shenandoah Valley into the Holston country of East Tennessee. John Hunt's family can be traced back to the early 1770s in Botetort County, Virginia. His family and the Henry Larkin family would intermarry and share fortunes there, later in a North Carolina and Tennessee settlement, and finally in the founding of Hunt's Spring.

Although Georgia ceded her western lands to the United States in 1804, this 1806 map illustrates the confusion over the validity of the two Yazoo swindles. Courtesy, Huntsville-Madison County Public Library

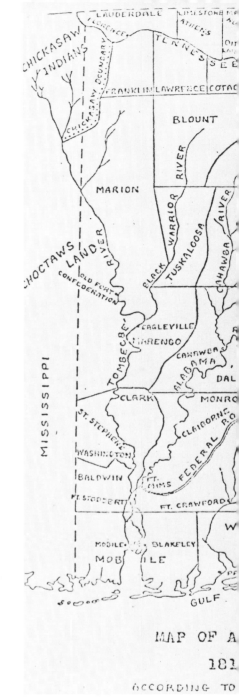

Hunt fought in the Revolution, but since he served as a private in a regiment not in the "Continental establishment" he received no pension. Hunt later became a captain of the militia of Hawkins County, North Carolina, and was first sheriff of that county, his term ending in 1790. In the 1790s he moved his family across the Clinch River into the Powell River Valley and built a home in what became Tazewell, Claiborne County, Tennessee. Hunt's house was used as the first courthouse, and he also served Claiborne county as the first sheriff. There the Hunts joined fortunes with the Acklen family from Virginia. The senior Acklen also served a term as sheriff and married one of Hunt's daughters. Their combined family strength was severely tested in 1796 and 1797, when the federal government sent troops threatening to enforce earlier Indian treaties and evict the settlers from their prospering farms. In his capacity as leader, Hunt wrote a letter of protest to Tennessee governor John Sevier. That letter reveals John Hunt's aspirations for land as well as what Dr. Frances Roberts calls his "frontier style" of writing.

The people on the north side of the Clinch River is to a man determined to stop them from running the line that governor Bount maid in his treaty with the Indians—Now we want to see if you can do nothing for us—we expect and hope that you will talk to the Commissioners whither or not the lines that was maid by Blount Shoud be the line now to be run—we want your excellency to give us youre advice and what is Best for us dow in thiss

This line would take our lands and living away from us—we bought our lands, paid deer for it, both by the sword propertity and money and to be turned off froom our lands and livings like a parcell of heathens will look very unhuman and I expect will cause a revelution But I would wich that might not be the case...

 I am with a steem your Sener friend and well wicher
John Hunt

This letter was written July 17, 1797. In November Sevier answered Hunt's letter and quieted his fears. Apparently Hunt did not move again until he brought his family in 1805 to live in the two-room cabin he had built by the spring that was to bear his name—and to establish his claim as founder of Huntsville.

A steady stream of other settlers followed. A community soon grew up around Hunt's Spring and out along the creeks and forks of the rivers, especially along the Flint. Most of these settlers had

An 1818 map shows the white man's advance across the red man's lands. Madison County later extended its eastern and southeastern boundaries to encompass even more Cherokee lands. Courtesy, Huntsville-Madison County Public Library

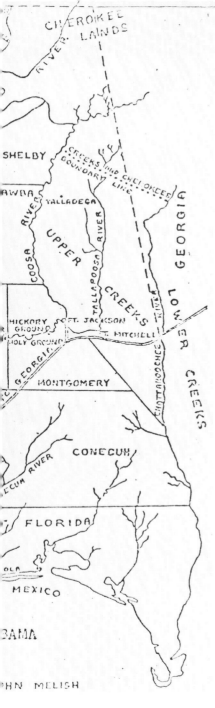

HN MELISH

already pushed back earlier wildernesses and had sown their wild oats. Many had fought in the Revolution a quarter of a century earlier. Most had tested their wit and their flintlocks against the Indians who by the late 18th century had become thoroughly aroused.

Between 1804 and 1809 the more than 5,000 people who made their homes in the Great Bend had one thing in common: they were all squatters. Whether they liked it or not, the land was free to be used and developed but not to be owned. Those who wanted to settle down, acquire land, purchase slaves, and pass that property on, as well as those who made land speculation their stock in trade, were impatient for the government to release the land for sale.

Huntsville historian Frances Roberts gives a breakdown on these early settlers. They were concentrated in seven population centers: Hickory Flat and Mountain Fork of Flint River, the "Three Forks of Flint," the Ryland—Brownsboro-Maysville area, Hunt's Spring south to Ditto's Landing, and along Aldridge's Creek, Hazel Green, Meridianville, and Indian Creek. Of 730 families, more than half wanted to buy government land at the two-dollar-an-acre price, on credit, when it became available. Twenty-three percent were slave-holders though there were only a few who owned more than ten. They were described by land surveyor Thomas Freeman as "quiet, peaceable, extremely industrious," unlike the typical "intruders on the public lands." They were overwhelmingly Southern, hailing from Tennessee, North Carolina, and Virginia. Besides building cabins, they improved the land, typically planting between ten and 60 acres of corn and smaller patches of cotton and tobacco. Corn mills quickly popped up all around the countryside and even a distillery was in the making. Intent upon building homes in the wilderness, these early settlers swapped skills, shared jobs, and pooled their resources.

On December 13, 1808, Robert Williams, governor of the Mississippi Territory, issued a proclamation creating Madison County. President James Madison hastily ordered a census taken and appointed persons to conduct land sales. On April 5, 1809, a presidential proclamation announced that the sale "shall be held at Nashville in the State of Tennessee, to commence on the first Monday in August One thousand eight hundred and Nine, and to continue for and during the three following weeks." Thus, the squatters, for a small fee, were at last given the opportunity to register as "tenants at will" with the right to purchase up to 360 acres. By October 1809 more than 24,000 acres had been purchased. Approximately 14 percent of the squatters bid on or

Brahan Springs was named for the receiver of public money at Huntsville. A public park now surrounds the Springs and the city's handsome Senior Center shares wooded acres with tennis courts, horseshoes and baseball diamonds, swings and picnic areas. Courtesy, Old Huntsville Magazine and Huntsville Madison County Public Library

purchased without contest the land they preempted. But by 1815 only 43 percent had purchased land in the county.

Since the land office was in Nashville, Tennessee, the squatters were at an immediate disadvantage in filing their claims. They also faced two more insidious threats: one was the jacking up of prices by the competitive bidding of a wealthier class of settlers intent upon establishing cotton culture on the valley flood plains and transforming a wilderness into a squirearchy. To be sure, there was enough land for squatters and squires. But the choicest parcels—especially those around the Big Spring—were bought up early. The other threat was their own westering instinct, a marvel to more settled generations. Some went so far as to accept the belief forwarded by a European university professor in the early 19th century who created "an ingenious device" trying to prove "that man, like the squirrel in a cage, is irresistibly impelled to step westward by the fact of the earth's rotation eastward."

The experience of Martin Cole, while singular, illustrates other problems experienced by simple, untutored frontiersmen. Cole, a poor farmer with a growing family, came to Madison County from South Carolina seeking a small tract of land that he could purchase. Upon looking over the land that was available, Cole chose the northeast quarter of Section 10 in Township 2 of Range One West. But when he went to enter his claim, being illiterate, he asked his neighbor and friend John Childers to examine the corners and give him the true numbers. As fate would have it, Childers was nearly as illiterate as Cole and the wrong quarter section was entered. Neither man caught the error, and Cole started clearing and seeding and cutting lumber on a lot that wasn't his. Great was his indignation and chagrin when a few months later the proper holder of a certificate for the land presented it and demanded Cole's removal. Cole then had to figure out where his land was. With the aid of a more literate friend, he located the tract—at least what he could see of it. Cole's land turned out to be a swamp, with only about ten acres above water and those not worth cultivating.

At the close of the War of 1812, Madison County land prices rose to new heights. What went for $2 an acre between 1809 and 1811 now sold for $20. Farm acreage near town sold for $100 per acre and prices on lots in town were exhorbitant. The southeast corner of the public square, which had sold for $715 in 1811, swelled to a selling price of $7,500 in 1818—with minimal improvements. The inflated land prices attracted thousands of settlers who were seemingly heedless of the landslide sure to follow. Huntsville stood on the threshold of expansion. The Creek land to the south was opened to purchase, and wealthy Georgians and Tennesseans, including Huntsville's own, again acquired vast acreage.

To facilitate this land orgy, the federal land office was moved from Nashville to Huntsville in 1811. Madison County gained another 174,000 acres through further Indian cessions. This land was sold at the Great Land Sales of 1818 and went at inflated prices that in many cases could not be paid in the years ahead, the purchase having been made on credit, with an easy down payment of one-fourth and four years to pay the balance.

John Coffee, next to Andrew Jackson the most admired of the Creek War heroes, became the surveyor general of the Huntsville Land Office. Having tramped over much of the land as a soldier, he was knowledgeable of the terrain. It was assumed that Coffee would use his position to help himself and his friends to locate and bid on the best land. In a letter dated September 28, 1817, Andrew Jackson wrote him: "let me see you as I pass. . .I have but little doubt, but something can be done at the sales—on which subject I wish to see you."

In "Articles of Agreement between John Coffee and his clerks," signed prior to the February sales date, Coffee's clerks agreed to pay him one-half the amount of "land, money, or other consideration" they received for "purchasing, locating, or giving information" to purchasers. They pledged to give no voluntary or gratuitous information.

John Coffee also joined with Andrew Jackson, James Jackson, John Childress, and John Donelson, all of the Nashville region, and with wealthy Philadelphia financiers to bid on and buy up the choicest land offered in the sale, including those improved by squatters who had been on the land as far back as 1809. The Tennesseans met stiff local competition in the bidding, sending prices up to as high as $78 per acre. Chief among the Huntsvillians to go toe-to-toe with the coterie was John Brahan, the receiver of public money at Huntsville. Carried away by the enthusiasm of the "chase," Brahan came away from the bidding with 44,677.96 acres, valued at $318,579.91. Fortunately, Brahan's down payment only amounted to $78,901.43—all of which he paid with government money. Something of a local hero for having stood up to the Nashvillians, nonetheless what Brahan did was careless if not criminal. When called upon to account for the public monies, Brahan naturally was some $80,000 short. Blaming his error on his effort to keep the land from being gobbled up by wealthy speculators whose intent was to resell at outlandish prices, the congressional committee investigating recommended that he not be prosecuted. Brahan was removed from his position and a local group of trustees—including Clement C. Clay, John

John Coffee was a bold surveyor of Mississippi Territory lands and a frontier entrepreneur instrumental in Huntsville's beginning. Courtesy, Archives, Constitution Hall Park

W. Walker, LeRoy Pope, and Obediah Jones, the new receiver—was assigned the task of supervising the transfer of 1,260 acres of Brahan's land, several Huntsville lots, and notes due him from the United States treasury to square the debt he owed the United States Treasury.

This pattern of exploitation and preferential treatment for the men of means, while more pronounced in 1818, had its beginning in the 1809 sales. Thomas Freeman, the surveyor of the Mississippi Territory, used his position to advise Nashvillians William P. Anderson and James Jackson of valuable land surrounding Hunt's Spring. John Coffee was then hired by those men to survey the site and represent them locally. LeRoy Pope and these men were the major purchasers of land around the Big Spring, and they instructed Coffee to "lay off the Town in such a manner, or such form as you and Major Walker, the agent of Colo. Pope, shall think proper." He was to be sure to "let the plan of the town be as dashing as possible and the ground on which it shall stand as eligible as may be." Coffee and Walker lobbied to get the new town—then named Twickenham—selected as the county seat, and they had to twist some arms to do it.

The methods of Coffee and Brahan were business as usual and accepted as manifestations of frontier opportunism. They were precursors of the Jacksonian spoils system. These two "red-blooded" Americans, like Andrew Jackson and John Hunt before them, embodied the squatter as sovereign and equal to the "blue bloods" of Virginia and Georgia. The history of Huntsville and Alabama was shaped in large part by the comingling and clash of squatters and squires. More than pride and progeny were at stake. Land and the political power to determine its uses were at issue as well. But even more important was this question: Was Alabama to be led by red-blooded or blue-blooded Americans?

Justice cannot be done the blue-bloods without resorting to genealogy and tracing them to Petersburg, Georgia, from whence they came—lock, stock, and sterling silverware. There in the tobacco town tucked snugly between the Broad and Savannah rivers, the future leaders of Huntsville first honed their skills as land speculators, city planners, and state builders. There, an extraordinary group of men and women—families actually—built a life noted for its wealth, power, urbanity, and closely knit kinship groupings. Everybody who was anybody was related and interrelated to such magnate families as the Watkinses, Bibbs, Thompsons, Walkers, and Popes.

Historian-genealogist Ellis Merton Coulter, an authority on the Old South, brought his dual talents to bear in writing *Old Petersburg and the Broad River Valley of Georgia: Their Rise and*

Decline. From him we learn something of the intricacy of the interwoven family lines.

Huntsville to this day is home for Watkins' descendants, and what Coulter tells of the "Virginia family of Watkinses out of Prince Edward County" gives the reader a sense of the stuff of which Huntsville is made. The Petersburg Watkinses, we are told, "were prominent in business life of the town but they were also notable in their many marriage connections and in their migrations westward, principally to Alabama." James Watkins I, son of William, married Martha Thompson "of another prominent Virginia family...also to become outstanding in Petersburg." Their marriage produced nine children. Daughter Sarah Herndon married a first cousin, Capt. Robert Thompson. A successful Virginia merchant, Thompson, the grandson of a goldsmith and banker, was familiarly called "Old Blue" because he always carried some of his considerable wealth around with him in a blue pouch. Their first daughter, Sophia, married Dr. James Manning; their second daughter, Pamelia, married Thomas Bibb; and their third daughter, Elizabeth, married Dr. Waddy Tate.

To thicken the blood plot, Samuel, another son of James Watkins I, married Old Blue's sister, Eleanor Thompson, the epitome of the "aristocratic lady." Coulter writes:

> *Another son of James Watkins, I, was Robert Herndon Watkins, who married Jane Thompson, a niece of Dionysius Oliver's, being the daughter of Eleanor Oliver, who married Drury Thompson.*
>
> *The second son of pioneer James Watkins, I, in his family of nine children was named James, II, also. He married another Jane Thompson, also a niece of Dionysius Oliver by Isham Thompson (a brother of Drury Thompson) having married Dionysius' sister Mary Ann. All of this means that two Oliver sisters had married two Thompson brothers, and that each couple had a daughter which they named Jane—this would mean that the two Janes were "double first cousins."*

The Watkinses also were connected to the Bibbs. William Bibb had moved from Virginia to Georgia in 1789 with his second wife, Sally Wyatt, who, according to Coulter, was "an amiable young lady, with a handsome fortune." All eight of their children married and "did well." William Wyatt Bibb was the firstborn. A physician and a United States senator from Georgia, he became the first governor of Alabama. His brother Thomas, "of great intellectual force and indomitable energy, and of marked distinction of bearing," followed him as the second governor.

Alabama's second governor, Thomas Bibb, built the stately Belmina (Belle Mina) in Limestone County. About 1835 he moved to La Fourche Parish, Louisiana, and offered the 3,190-acre plantation for sale. At that time it featured a sawmill, a cotton gin and press, and quarters for 150 to 200 slaves. Courtesy, Mrs. William Henson

In public life John Williams Walker was a premier statesman, serving as president of the 1819 constitutional convention and as a United States senator from Alabama. In private life he was a man of tremendous charm, wit, and intellect and was married to Matilda Pope, daughter of LeRoy Pope and Judith Sale Pope. Courtesy, Archives, Constitution Hall Park

Other brothers also carved out successful careers in Alabama.

The Bibb family and the Walker family were neighbors and close friends. John Williams Walker, son of Jeremiah, a Baptist preacher who became wealthy enough to own plantations, town lots, slaves, and even an island in the Savannah River, "revered" William Wyatt Bibb. Both men shared broad intellectual interests and manifested a keen desire to serve their fellow man. They both bore the imprint of Moses Waddel, the uncommonly large-headed, bushy-browed, and austere classical educator who also taught such Southern worthies as John C. Calhoun, A.B. Longstreet, and William Lowndes Yancey.

John Williams Walker married well, joining his lot with Matilda, the eldest daughter of LeRoy Pope. Little is written about Pope and even less is verifiable. Born in Virginia in 1764, the future father of Huntsville was, at the age of 16, an aide and courier to his idol and possible relative, Gen. George Washington, at the Battle of Yorktown. In 1790 he moved with his family to Elbert County, Georgia, from North Carolina. His sister Ruth Pope was married to Richard Watkins, the grandson of William Watkins. Thus Pope was linked to the Walkers and the Watkinses and hence through these bonds to the Thompsons and the Bibbs. In Petersburg Pope made himself the cynosure. If a deal was brewing or if a worthwhile project needed sponsoring, LeRoy Pope was at the center of it directing the way. Coulter referred to Pope and his family as "that Petersburg Nabob" and "the royal family." He was an empire-builder and a risk-taker, willing to put his money on the line. An astute judge of the possible, his banking interests and land speculations helped to build two towns and made of him a frontier Lorenzo d' Medici.

Unlike artists, historians are not blessed with the talent or granted the prerogative of molding wings from clay feet. Obviously these cavaliers were no angels. They were powerful, wealthy, and possibly lusty men, the kind that other men measure themselves by. Rumors were made for such as they. It would not be surprising then, that when Lucius Bierce, the uncle of Ambrose Bierce (the better-known author of *The Devil's Dictionary*) wrote about his peripatetic tour through north Georgia and Alabama in 1822 and 1823, he picked up one such rumor and passed it on later in *Travels in the Southland: 1822-1823:*

A wealthy respectable man of a family, notoriously kept a mulatto girl with whom he associated as freely as with his wife. His wife finding them in each others embraces made so much fuss about it that he sent the girl on to his plantation near Mooresville where he then spent more of his time than he did at home. His wife complaining of this neglect, and knowing the cause, would consent to nothing short of the girls being sent to New Orleans and sold, which was done, when a merchant of Mooresville sent to his agent in Orleans, purchased the girl, and brought her back to Mooresville for himself. This but a specimen of manners in that respect.

The "Spite House" on Lincoln Street attests to the power of LeRoy Pope to stir the strong emotion of envy. The house was built tall enough to obstruct the view from Pope's house on the hill. Courtesy, Old Huntsville Magazine *and Huntsville Madison County Public Library*

Metaphorically, these squires brought with them a new heart for Huntsville, transplanted from Petersburg, Georgia, having already developed its muscle from a Virginia nativity in an earlier frontier. Possessing tautness and resiliency, it had strength enough to pump the bluest blood through the veins of the most intrepid, red-blooded American. Historian Thomas Jones Taylor lists seven of these Georgians—Walker, Pope, James Manning, Robert Thompson, Peyton Cox, and Thomas and William Wyatt Bibb—as "buying what has been estimated as almost one-half of the Madison County lands sold at that time." In the courthouse an old, oblong Government Tract Book for Madison County tells the tale. There one sees the effects of the great Nashville land sale of Madison County land. A cursory glance brings to focus the above named plus Isham Watkins, Thomas Freeman, Benjamin S. Pope, and Obediah Jones.

Since LeRoy Pope, "the largest planter and the wealthiest capitalist in the county," gained control of Hunt's Spring and the acreage surrounding it, paying $23 an acre, he had been able through the help of his friends in the territorial legislature to have that site christened "Twickenham" and then selected as the county seat. Historian Albert B. Moore, noting that those first fathers were college-bred and cultured, called them "log-house aristocrats, men of wealth and culture and men of marked political and professional distinction."

In 1811 the territorial legislature changed the name of Twickenham to Huntsville. Symbolically at least, the name change meant that the transplant of the Petersburg heart had taken, that the squatters had made room for the squires and that together with other newcomers, such as Clement C. Clay, Charles Cabiness, David Moore, John Connally, Thomas and Robert Fearn, they would fashion a frontier metropolis. They would build to last, having among their number the Brandon brothers, Thomas and William, who almost single-handedly converted the humble village to a "city of stone and brick." Arriving in 1810, they were instantly up to their elbows in brick and mortar creating a town atop Hunt's Spring and around the public square.

II

The Ways of the World

In the late 1840s George Steele was credited with adding the portico to the Federal period home of LeRoy Pope. Although the massing of the porch is Greek, Steele lightened its effect with delicate Federal-style motifs to avoid overwhelming the house. Photo by Ralph Allen

That marriage feast in the morn of my life was beautiful; the low, spacious house of primitive architecture was white with hyacinths, and foliage decorated every available space. The legislature came in a body, solons of the State, and young aspirants for fame; the president and faculty of the state University, of which Mr. Clay was a favored son; and, in that glorious company of old Alabamians, my identity as Virginia Tunstall was merged forever with that of the rising young statesman, Clement C. Clay, Jr.

A week of festivity followed the ceremony, and then my husband took me to my future home, among his people, in the northern part of the State. There being no railroad connection between Tuscaloosa and Huntsville in those days (the early forties), we made the journey from the capital in a big four-wheeled stagecoach. . .Stone Mountain reached, we were obliged to descend and pick our way on foot, the roughness of the road making the passage of the coach a very dangerous one.

We arrived in Huntsville on the evening of the second day of our journey. Our driver, enthusiastically proud of his part in the home-bringing of the bride, touched up the spirited horses as we crossed the Public Square and blew a bugle blast as we wheeled round the corner; when, fairly dashing down Clinton Street, he pulled up in masterly style in front of "Clay Castle." It was wide and low and spacious, as were all the affluent homes of that day, and now was ablaze with candles to welcome the travellers. All along the streets friendly hands and kerchiefs had waved a welcome to us. Here, within, awaited a great gathering of family

The following specification of the fare of the principal Stage Routes, by which the traveller may reckon the cost of his tour, will not be superfluous.

		Miles.	
From Philadelphia to Pittsburgh,		300	$15 00
Philadelphia	Baltimore,	128	3 00
Baltimore	Wheeling,	271	12 00
Pittsburgh	Wheeling	59	4 00
Wheeling	Columbus,	140	8 00
Columbus	Cleaveland,	177	10 50
Columbus	Chillicothe,	45	2 00
Chillicothe	Cincinnati,	94	5 50
Columbus	Cincinnati, direct,	110	6 50
Indianapolis	Madison,	86	4 00
Cincinnati	Lexington,	76	4 50
Lexington	Louisville,	75	4 50
Louisville	St. Louis, via Vincennes,	267	15 50
Louisville	Nashville,	180	12 00
Richmond	Cincinnati, via Staunton, Lewisburg, Charleston on the Kanhaway and Guyandot, thence 155 miles by steamboat,	515	28 00
Richmond to Knoxville, via Lynchburgh, Abington, Kingsport, &c.,		444	28 50
Baltimore to Richmond, via Norfolk, by steamboat,		378	10 00
Knoxville to Nashville, via McMinville,		119	12 50
Nashville	Memphis,	224	15 00
Nashville	Florence,	110	8 25
Huntsville	Tuscaloosa,	155	10 00
Florence	Tuscaloosa,	146	9 00
Tuscaloosa	Montgomery,	119	8 00
Tuscaloosa	Mobile, by steamboat,	676	12 00
Augusta	Montgomery,	300	18 50
Montgomery	Mobile	180	12 00
Mobile	New Orleans,	160	12 00
St. Augustine to New Orleans,		600	35 00
Boston and New York to New Orleans, by packet, cabin passage, fare inclusive, from			$40 to 50 00

Travel guides, such as the Immigrant's Guide and Citizens Manual by I.W. Warner, were a popular form of 19th-century literature. The guides covered practically everything to facilitate migration.

and friends eager to see the chosen bride of a well-beloved son. This was my home-coming to Huntsville...
Virginia Clay-Clopton, A Belle of the Fifties, *1905*

Huntsville, the city of new beginnings, was, as the times would have it, a city of sore endings. Travel in those days was rough, even treacherous. A steady flow of immigrants into Huntsville from the northeast had trampled and cleared the roads from Winchester and Nashville. But the approaches from the west, south, or southeast were still perilous. Lucius Verus Bierce, who traveled from Gunter's Landing via Huntsville to Mooresville in the winter of 1822 and spring of 1823, described the route he walked. The Paint Rock was "a deep but narrow river," with a rich cane bottom where he was "half-leg deep in mud and cane roots." After nine miles of canebrake he crossed the Flint and came to Blevin's Gap, "an opening in an otherwise impassable mountain." From there, after "wading through creeks and mudholes," he arrived in Huntsville.

From its beginning, Huntsville was beset with transportation problems. The discomfort and inconvenience for passengers was only one aspect. The cost of transport caused prices of goods brought to the city to be higher.

One of the earlier water routes for goods was up the Alabama from Mobile, to the Tombigbee, to the falls of the Black Warrior, and then overland to the Tennessee River. In 1816 James O. Crump, a Huntsville merchant on the square, transported a cargo of Brown and Havana white sugars, coffee, rum, wine, oranges, and a few dry goods upriver from Mobile on a 35-foot boat with a draw of about two feet when loaded. The trip up to the falls of the Black Warrior took 20 days. At the falls his goods were loaded on two wagons and driven overland to Huntsville. Crump was especially delighted that "out of one thousand oranges not more than half a dozen spoiled." By the next year Samuel Haines, a gazeteer of the time, wrote that since navigation of the Muscle Shoals was so dangerous and New Orleans so remote, "considerable merchandise" had "already passed into Huntsville, by way of Mobile, and the falls of the Black Warrior, on much better terms than by the former routes."

This transportation hookup between Mobile and Madison County only became feasible with the Creek cessions of 1813. Its prospect undoubtedly influenced John Williams Walker to change his advice to his dear friend and old-time intimate Charles Tait, who between 1809 and 1819 was chairman of the Senate committee responsible for the question of admitting the Mississippi Territory as a state.

CENTRAL RAILROAD,

FROM SAVANNAH TO MACON, GA.,
190½ Miles.

Passenger Trains leave Savannah daily, at......8 00 A. M.
"   "   "   Macon daily at.........8 00 A. M.
"   "   arrive daily at Savannah at....6 15 P. M.
"   "   "   "   at Macon, at......6 45 P. M.

This Road in connection with the Macon and Western Road from Macon to Atlanta, and the Western and Atlantic Road from Atlanta to Dalton, now forms a continuous line of 391½ miles in length from Savannah to Dalton, Murray county, Ga., and with the Memphis Branch Rail Road, and stages, connect with the following places:

Tickets from Savannah to Jacksonville, Ala.,...........$20.00
"   "   "   Huntsville,)
"   "   "   Decatur,   } Ala., ... 22.00
"   "   "   Tuscumbia, Ala., ... 22.50
"   "   "   Columbus, Miss.,)
"   "   "   Holly Springs, } 28.00
"   "   "   Nashville, Tenn.,)
"   "   "   Murfreesboro' } 25.00
"   "   "   Memphis, Tenn., ... 30.00

An extra Passenger Train leaves Savannah on Saturdays, after the arrival of the steamships from New York, for Macon, and connects with the Macon and Western Rail Road ; and on Tuesdays, after the arrival of the Macon and Western cars, an extra Passenger Train leaves Macon to connect with the steamships for New York.

Stages for Tallahasse and intermediate places connect with the road at Macon on Mondays, Wednesdays, and Fridays, and with Milledgeville at Gordon daily.

Passengers for Montgomery, Mobile, and New Orleans, take stage for Opelika from Barnesville through Columbus, a distance of 97 miles, or from Griffin through West Point, a distance of 93 miles.

Goods consigned to Thos. S. Wayne, Forwarding Agent, Savannah, will be forwarded free of commission.

WM. M. WADLEY, Sup't.

Savannah, Ga., 1852.

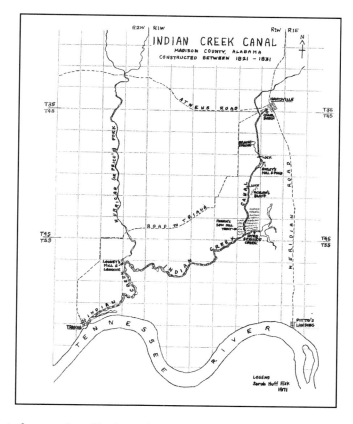

Above:
Quite frequently 19th-century travelers were forced to take the stagecoach or a steamboat to get from the terminus of one line to the start of another. While this 1852 broadside implies that the railroad linked Savannah and Huntsville, a passenger would have had to travel between Huntsville and Stevenson by stage, for the Memphis and Charleston tracks between the two cities were not completed until 1856.

Above right
After clearing and enlarging the streams from the Big Spring to Triana, Madison County planters could float their cotton to the Tennessee River on flatboats, which was easier than hauling it overland on wagons. Drawn by Sarah Huff Fisk

Walker had at first favored splitting the vast territory in half from east to west, assuming that north Alabama was most dependent on the Tennessee River to connect it with Knoxville, the Shoals, the Ohio River, and finally New Orleans. Later observers speculate that had Walker maintained his original position, North Alabama—or whatever it would have been called—would not have seceded from the Union in 1861. Be that as it may, Walker took a new assessment of conditions in 1817 and advised Tait: "Divide us, then, my dear Sir. . .by a N. and S. line."

First as a settlement, then as an important center of government and trade, Huntsville looked to the Tennessee River as its great highway. But in those early days it must have appeared as a rainbow—very real but out of reach. Ten miles separated Huntsville from the Tennessee, ten very costly miles. One of the first civic improvements attempted was formation of the Indian Creek Navigation Company, headed by Dr. Thomas Fearn and LeRoy Pope, with the purpose of building a canal from Hunt's Spring via Indian Creek to the Tennessee at Triana. This was the canal era, the Erie Canal leading the way in 1817, and enthusiasm ran high—at first. Chartered in February 1821, the canal was ready to ship cotton by February 1827. In April 1831 the announcement came that it was totally completed. By then called "Fearn's Canal"—in much the same spirit as "Clinton's Ditch" or "Fulton's Folly"—the citizens celebrated their long-awaited and much-scoffed-at canal. But what began with a bang ended after 1845 with a whimper. The race with time was lost to the Whitesburg Turnpike, which drew business from the canal and Triana, the canal town. Between 1832 and 1835 Alabama's first canal cleared $4,675.08 on tolls, and strollers enjoyed viewing the colorful boatmen and their cargoes. George Steele's magnificent bank built in 1836 on the bluff of Hunt's Spring owed its massive capitals, bases, and shafts to Fearn's Canal, which brought these architectural masterworks and the copper roof right up to town. These were to become proud memories of a bygone age.

Another water project inspired by Hunt's Spring was the public waterworks. Initially water was pumped up the 70-foot bluff to a reservoir on the public square level. This completed in 1823, the more arduous and novel task of laying pipes to individual streets and homes was commenced. Hunter Peel, the county surveyor who was a charmingly original English gentleman and a gift to any civilization, and Thomas Barclay, a Scots pump maker, drew up the plans for Huntsville's wilderness waterworks. The pipes—comprised of eight-foot-long sections of red and white cedar logs—were hollowed out. The waterworks required much timber. Hunter Peel was even arrested and brought to trial for having trespassed on government lands and felled trees without authorization.

County leaders also planned other improvements and created the Flint River Navigation Company. Their idea was to improve the Flint by clearing the trees lining the banks to remove any future hindrance. This they did, felling the trees in great numbers, anticipating that spring floods would float them into the Tennessee. Instead the trees all ran together, further clogging the Flint.

Better versed at business, many countians took advantage of

Cedar logs such as these first supplied Huntsville with water about 1827. After a rocky beginning, the water system was improved by Dr. Thomas Fearn and his brother George in the 1830s. The City purchased the waterworks in 1858 for $10,000. Courtesy, Huntsville Utilities

Bell Factory, the oldest textile mill in the state, was located about 10 miles northeast of Huntsville near Three Forks of Flint. The mill began in 1819, but in 1841 the original mill was destroyed by fire and replaced by these buildings, which housed textile operations until 1885 when production ceased. Courtesy, Huntsville-Madison County Public Library

the swift river and waterways to locate industry in the wilderness. The pesky waters of the Flint were especially appealing. North at the Barren Fork, Charles Cabiness started the the first cotton-spinning factory, and at the Three Forks of Flint—where William Haughton began a gristmill in 1812—Horatio Jones erected a yarn-producing and weaving operation in 1819. A mile downstream, Rudolph Boshart and William Derrick ran a grain mill on a particularly choice site that ended up being the home of the Bell Factory after Horatio Jones purchased it. Like the early cloth it wove, the Bell Factory's beginnings were rough and somewhat tangled. But under a series of leaders, most enduringly Patton, Donegan and Company, it became an industry aptly christened the "Early Pride of Huntsville."

The central point of Huntsville's transportation network was Ditto's Landing. Reputed to be the first settler in the county, James (often called John) Ditto came to the Great Bend of the Tennessee in 1802 and established a trading post in what was then called the Chickasaw Old Fields near Chickasaw Island (Hobb's Island). Intent upon Indian trade, Ditto, in 1807, built a ferry from a flatboat, a gunwale type propelled by sweep oars, and carried settlers across the Tennessee. Andrew Jackson used Ditto's ferry in 1813 to reach the Creeks on the Coosa. Ditto kept a boatyard, too, where he built flat litter-type boats for use over the shoals.

Between 1822 and 1825 Ditto's Landing became known as Whitesburg, named for James White who eventually owned most of the land on both sides of the river. Called "Salt" White, this

The stately Governor Thomas Bibb house is a noteworthy example of fine classical architecture. Owned by the Beirne family for many years, the home was purchased in 1927 by Bibb descendants, who retain possession today. Photo by Ralph Allen

Virginia entrepreneur built a Southern salt monopoly taking advantage of the Tennessee ports to control the supply of this necessary commodity. White easily undersold his competitors and controlled the price. He joined forces with John Read in Huntsville and John Hardie at Ditto's Landing to operate a mercantile house as well. White, like Ditto, looked to the river for profit, if not for the pleasures of river-folk camaraderie and the challenge of riverboating.

Profit, rather than romance, was also the concern of the cotton planters who anxiously awaited word that their factors in New Orleans had received shipments. Many months might pass before news of arrival. One Huntsville pilot, Richard W. Anderson, made it a point to hasten his return trips, and he consistently beat all others in the trek from New Orleans to Huntsville. But as slow as existing river and overland routes were, cotton still had to get to market. The life of the county and the business of the city counted on that. The fertility of Madison County soil, especially its ability to yield a consistent 1,000 pounds of cotton to the acre, convinced all who came to try their hand at cotton farming.

The cotton trade the South depended on also bolstered two systems of dependency that dominated Southern life and determined its course in history. Those two systems were plantation slavery and the credit system. Huntsville could no more escape this milieu than it could avoid seceding from the Union later on. Cotton, slaves, and credit were three sides of the Southern triangle that held all Southerners in its grasp.

In the algebra of the plantation production system, the

unknown factor was the price of cotton, set on the world market and determined by such variables as climate, war, supply, and demand. Alabama cotton prices had started high—the result of fresh, fertile land and inflation. From the 20- to 25-cent per pound high in 1818, the price of the average pound fell to about 9 cents in 1830. Then it shot up to around 14 cents again in 1835 in another inflationary spiral that catapulted the nation into the panic and depression of 1837, bringing cotton prices cascading down to around 6 cents in 1840 and touching bottom in 1845 at 5 cents. Rebounding with the Mexican War and the discovery of gold in California, cotton again rose to the profit side of the ledger in 1850 at 11 cents a pound. The 1850s saw a mid-decade dip to 8 cents followed by a strong recovery that lasted into the 1860s.

Slave prices did not fluctuate so radically. Starting low at $500 in 1820 for the average field hand, the price peaked at $800 in 1835, only to slump to $650 in 1845. But from then on, with the expansion of cotton production into the new Southwest, the demand for slave labor pushed the price up dramatically to $1,500 in 1860.

Land prices generally turned downward as new acres to the south and west were opened for sale and relief acts in 1820 and 1830 allowed settlers to purchase smaller allotments and exercise preemption rights. Town lots also illustrate the antebellum ups and downs. A study of the Thomas Bibb property on Williams Street is an example. LeRoy Pope sold the lot in 1817 to John M. Taylor for $445.50. Two years later, after Taylor built a dwelling on it, the property sold to John Read for $16,000. This tremendous increase was more a result of inflation than increased value. In 1821, after the panic of 1819, Bibb was able to purchase the same property for $8,000. Building the mansion for which the property is now famous, Bibb sold the land in 1836 for $5,000 to his son-in-law, James Bradley. The Bradleys were not able to enjoy it for long, however, as the panic and depression of 1837, which lasted into the 1840s, knocked Bradley and his commission house into receivership. The house was sold for $7,500 in 1844 to the Beirne family who held it throughout the Civil War. Tax assessments in 1856 valued the property at $11,000, reflecting a rising economy that boosted the confidence of short-memoried Alabamians as they entered the decade of the 1860s.

In addition, Huntsville was figuratively born into a sea of credit. Federal land sales until 1820 rested on credit, so that throughout its formative stage a man could buy now and pay later, he could use "Yazoo scrip," the federal government's solution to the lingering Yazoo claims. The banking system too

The Bibb house, constructed for Bibb's daughter, Adeline Bradley, and her husband James, was foreclosed when James could not satisfy debts totaling over $50,000. Family legend relates that Mrs. Bradley learned that her home had been sold when a gardener arrived to plant the new owner's favorite flower bulbs. Courtesy, Dr. Eleanor Hutchens

Top
Nicholas Davis, a delegate from Limestone County to the first state constitutional convention, was as well known in Huntsville as in his own county. An avid sportsman, he was a "patron of the turf." Courtesy, Archives, Constitution Hall Park

Above
Dr. John Watkins moved to the Alabama Territory from Virginia in 1813. In 1819 he was a delegate to the constitutional convention and enjoyed the comraderie of old friendships while visiting in Huntsville. Courtesy, Archives, Constitution Hall Park

was in flux, the first United States Bank having expired in 1811 and the Second Bank of the United States not chartered until 1816. Most of the capital coming into north Alabama was in the form of depreciated notes from United States, Georgia, and Tennessee banks. There was simply not enough specie in circulation. Yet there was wealth enough in Huntsville to capitalize a bank. With the frontier's ballooning demand for credit and for negotiable currency, Alabama's first bank, the Planters and Mechanic's Bank of Huntsville, opened in January 1817 ready to do a "land-office business." Chartered by the Mississippi Territory on December 11, 1816, the bank's name was changed later to Planters and Merchants by the Alabama territorial legislature.

The bank's board of directors varied over the stormy course of its short existence. Original trustees included such city leaders as Clement Comer Clay, John Williams Walker, David Moore, Benjamin Cox, Thomas Fearn, John M. Taylor, John P. Hickman, and Jesse Searcy. To these names were added John Brahan, John Read, Thomas G. Percy, James Manning, James Clemens, William Patton, and Willis Pope. Always at their head, by vote of the board, was LeRoy Pope, the bank's only president.

These bankers evidently had friends in high places. John Williams Walker and Clement Comer Clay pushed a usury law through the first legislative assembly of the Alabama Territory, which opened wide the floodgates of credit, allowing interest rates to seek their own level. Only bank loans were held to a rate of 6 percent. This meant that friends of the bank, or as Col. James B. Saunders, in his *Early Settlers of Alabama* put it, borrowers "in the family"—directors and stockholders—could get money at 6 percent and turn around and loan it out at from 5 to 20 percent *per month.* Ironically, even bank stock could be purchased on credit. It was feasible then, to purchase stock, "join the family," and, with money borrowed at the favored rate and loaned at the going rate, cover the original stock purchase.

There were other friends in even higher places. Longtime Georgia friend and United States Secretary of the Treasury William H. Crawford designated the Huntsville bank—the only bank in north Alabama—as a government depository for land office sales. Another old friend, Secretary of War John C. Calhoun, appointed LeRoy Pope as pensions agent for the District of Alabama. Like an arrogant admiral, buoyed by government specie and supported by friendly ties, Pope, ever imperious, steered his bank imperviously to the brink of financial disaster.

The year 1819 was a watershed. The panic of 1819 came like a thunderbolt. Huntsvillians were staggered. In 1818 cotton sold at

25 cents a pound, but in 1820 one was lucky to get 10 cents. Maybe it was because the citizens were preoccupied with state-building and constitution-making in that momentous year. Or perhaps the prosperity in the wake of the Great Migration and land sales of 1818 had turned the residents' vague hopes of individual fortune into banked-on expectations of the good life—land, slaves, and perhaps even 30-cent cotton. Even before the territory could become a state, Huntsvillians learned that their lives and fortunes were inextricably interwoven with the whole fabric of the nation. The 1819 panic had no respect for state lines. Alabama's star ascended just as her economic fortunes fell apart.

As early as April James Campbell, a recent arrival from Tennessee, wrote his brother:

I cannot but say that I am even gratified to see the sufferings of some individuals at that place in consequence of their voracious insatiable thirst for speculation. . . . They have got involved head over heels in debt; the price of cotton has fallen to a moderate price; they have no means of extricating themselves.

From top to bottom, aristocrats to artisans, Huntsville's citizens reeled in the shaky 1819 economy.

By August the bank's assets reflected capital of $164,000 having lent out up to $408,000, three times as much as it had on hand. Treasury Secretary William H. Crawford had written a confidential letter to Pope in July advising him that anything over 50 percent capitalization was foolhardy and that his bank had "during the last twelve months generally discounted to three times the capital actually paid in." Pope owed the treasury of the United States more than $100,000 in specie. In 1820 the bank would cease issuing specie. Meanwhile businesses all around were folding.

While a worried Pope was left pacing his bank vault, a gathering of brilliant men was down the street with John Williams Walker "cobbling up a Constitution." With Walker presiding and Clement Comer Clay chairing the Committee of Fifteen appointed to draft the new state's first constitution, the convention was certain to benefit from the urbanity of the former and the conscientiousness of the latter. Walker once described himself: "I drink buttermilk for the health of my body, wine for the exhilaration of my spirits & whiskey to prove & strengthen my republicanism: I sleep till 8 o'clock because I am lazy & smoke at all hours of the day & night because it is my good pleasure."

Alabama might have enjoyed this superb man's talents a few

The dour Hugh McVay was elected president of the Alabama Senate and upon the resignation of Governor Clay became the state's ninth chief executive. Apparently his personal life did not adversely affect his political career, for in 1828 his wife Sophia eloped with Samuel Shull, taking with her two slaves and two horses while leaving behind large debts. The McVays were divorced later that year. Courtesy, Madison County Commission

33

more years had he never smoked. Tuberculosis took him four years later at the early age of 40. Clay, on the other hand, was made of more solid stuff, and with Walker's notes he almost singlehandedly molded a constitution. To be sure, these two were not the only men of talent or liberal enlightenment. Rather, their social class, legal training, and sense of noblesse oblige bespoke that of the majority of delegates entrusted with state-making. Overwhelmingly, the so-called Georgia or "royal" element—the creme de la creme—had risen to the top.

Notable exceptions at the convention were Hugh McVay and Gabriel Moore, two frontier Democrats with a flair for the unusual. McVay, Madison County's perennial representative to the Mississippi territorial legislature between 1811 and 1818, and now a delegate from Lauderdale County, was cut from rougher cloth. Of limited education, his patriotism was as grass roots as the name of his second daughter, Atlantic Pacific, born in 1815. McVay was a simple, stern man whose first wife had died in 1817. His second wife left him shortly after the marriage. He was luckier in politics and filled Clement Comer Clay's unexpired term as Alabama's governor in 1837. "Crowd-pleasing" Gabriel Moore early became the squatter's favorite lawyer and representative. His opponents claimed that he "frequented every grog shop in the county and visited every old woman." A Jackson supporter, he was elected governor in 1829.

There were other diversions in 1819. President James Monroe's unexpected arrival created a flurry of activity. A banquet for "more than one hundred of the most respected citizens" was hastily put together, with LeRoy Pope, still the city's first father, acting as president of the affair. Clement Comer Clay and Henry Minor, two leading attorneys and soon-to-be delegates to the state constitutional convention, served as vice-presidents. A public testimonial dinner was also held for "the Hon. Charles Tait, long a distinguished member of the Senate of the U.S. from Georgia" and best man in the wedding of Alabama to the Union.

More everyday forms of entertainment also abounded. They ran the gamut from meetings of the Madison County Bible Society, of which LeRoy Pope was president, to concerts by the Huntsville Haydn Society, as well as plays by the Thespian Society, the Colt Sweepstakes at Connally's Green Bottom Turf, meetings of the Madison Jockey Club at the Huntsville Inn, and the arrival of "The Greatest Curiosity Now Exhibiting in America"—an elephant that would take commands, draw a cork from a bottle, and swill down its contents.

Drama came to Huntsville too that year, not only in the form of John Ludlow's acting troupe, but also in real life. Huntsville's newspaper, the *Republican,* announced the ever-changing cast of characters as it reported the area's runaway slaves in 1819. Jim, belonging to Robert Lankford; Harry to James McCartney; Bob to Jesse W. Garth; Matt, Davy, Vitus, and Milly to John J. Winston; Willis and Lazarus to Adison Benford; Jim to Job Key; Major to Nancy Graves; Lucy to Charles Whitson; Tom to Edwin Jones; Bob to Harrison Randolph; Charles, Jim, Levi, Jane, and Paul to Samuel H. Doxey; Moses and Stephen to Isaac Lane; Granville to William Thompson; Ephraim to Jonathan Grant; and Jack to William Whiteside.

These runaway attempts, whether they ended in success or failure, were filled with adventure and adversity. One advertisement had three fugitives going "down the Tennessee river in a small skiff. They had been last seen going through Muscle Shoals, and were presumed on their way to Ohio." Most runaways were trying to get back to where they came from, back to loved ones, family, and friends. The runaway slave was a frontiersman turned homeward or northward. Like other frontiersmen, the fugitives required courage and initiative. To be a free man took decision and action. Just as it takes money to make money; so too it takes freedom to make freedom. Huntsville's slaves were freer than most. In 1819 they could come and go pretty much at will and some did—for good.

Throughout the antebellum period, as the numbers of slaves in the city and county continually rose, another figure was increasing too: the number of free blacks, including mulattoes. The legislative session that met in Huntsville in 1819 authorized Thomas Johnson to free his slave, Martin, not yet 21; and Cesar Kennedy, "a free man of color," was allowed to free his wife Hannah and her seven children. Lemuel Mead, one of Madison County's delegates to the state constitutional convention, was granted the right to free his slave Richmond Richardson in 1820. While Mead served in the courthouse as county court clerk, his ex-slave, with his name changed to Richmond Terrell, ran a barbershop in the courthouse basement. In 1820 John N.S. Jones and Alexander P. Jones freed Elizabeth, a mulatto woman, and her three daughters, Evelina, Ann, and Shandy. The number of freed slaves grew throughout the 1820s, a trend that reversed in subsequent decades.

Not all manumissions were sanctioned directly by the legislature. Mary Ann Grayson allowed her Negro man, James Posten, to purchase himself for $900. Nancy Hunter and her children were manumitted in Georgia by Anderson Watkins, who wrote a certificate stating also that her husband, Lewis Hunter, had descended from free parents and both had "maintained a

Top
This old slave cabin was once located on Meridian where the Coca-Cola Bottling Company is presently located. Courtesy, Old Huntsville Magazine and Huntsville Madison County Public Library

Bottom
This photograph of a former slave was taken at the Quietdale Plantation off of Meridian in the early 20th century. Courtesy, Old Huntsville Magazine and Huntsville Madison County Public Library

reputation unimpeached."

Throughout the period, slaves were often liberated by will, Samuel Townsend freeing upon his death as many as 40. Several owners included provision in their wills for their mulatto children. Edmund, Samuel Townsend's bachelor brother, left real estate valued at $200,000 and 195 slaves to two mulatto girls whom he said he had every reason to believe were his children. George Steele asked the executor of his will to "make proper provision on the division of my estate for the care and comfort of any old and decrepit servants who may be alive at the time."

In many respects Madison County grew like a hungry adolescent. It practically attained its full size within its first 20 years. By 1820 the population had swelled to 17,481: 8,813 whites, and 8,668 blacks. Ten years later it reached its peak for the antebellum years at 27,990: 13,855 whites and 14,135 blacks. The county had filled out to over 800 square miles, or 512,000 acres. In its youth the only other Alabama town to compare it with was Mobile. But Mobile represented another era—the age of European discovery. Huntsville, on the other hand, represented the age of American settlement. From their beginnings, Mobile was cosmopolitan and Huntsville was urbane. Mobile was colorful and wild; Huntsville staid and mannerly. Not completely, though. City ordinances reflect the way things are as well as the way they are supposed to be. James G. Birney, an alderman and mayor in the late 1820s, pushed through the first Sunday Blue Laws, which were not popular but did reflect a growing evangelical fundamentalism.

Until the 1820s the citizens of Huntsville worshipped together as one body in the courthouse. Visiting ministers would perform the service and make themselves available to administer rites of marriage. The Baptists of the rural area had started their church, Enon, at the Briar Fork of the Flint in about 1808. Shortly afterwards slave William Harris founded the state's first black Baptist church in the area the slaves used as their graveyard and called Georgia. For the rest, an early visitor to Huntsville, Anne Royall, sums it up:

From what I have heard, it appears the methodists have braved every danger, and preached to the people gratis, in the settling of the country; and now that there is no danger, and the people have become wealthy, those sly fellows, the presbyterians, are creeping in to reap the harvest. But the methodists have a great advantage, in point of talent, many of them being the best orators in the country. But they all draw too many women after them, in my humble opinion.

Clement Comer Clay, chairman of the group that drafted the state's first constitution, was elected governor in 1835 by the largest majority polled to that date. During his illustrious career, he also served as a U.S. senator and chief justice of the state supreme court. Courtesy, Huntsville-Madison County Public Library and Constitution Hall Park

The Green Bottom Inn was said to be a favorite of General Andrew Jackson when he "raced his horses and fought his cocks." When the onetime tavern burned in 1931, it was serving as the president's home on the campus of Alabama A&M University. Courtesy, H. E. Monroe, Sr.

Early laws seemed intent upon legislating morality. Birney moved to shut down the tippling houses but could not get his motion seconded. Gambling, however, was outlawed: no faro, no bunk, no black and red tables, no dice, no cards, and no exceptions save chess. Notably missing from the prohibitions were the favorite sports of gentlemen and gamblers alike—horse racing and cock fighting. In 1833 billiard tables, chuckasuck, the thimbles or thin-ticket lottery, orange and noir, and rowley powley were added to the list of banned activities. Ten years later public opinion had softened on billiards. The game was allowed and taxes were collected from the popular activity. Betting, of course, enlivened every event, lending excitement to the commonplace;

sometimes the stakes went into the thousands.

Disorderly conduct for whites was punishable by a fine of up to $50, while slaves could receive a maximum of 39 lashes. As early as 1811 John and Louis Winston, Calvin and Luther Morgen, Alex Gilbreath, Dillon Blevins, Gabriel Moore, and others were charged

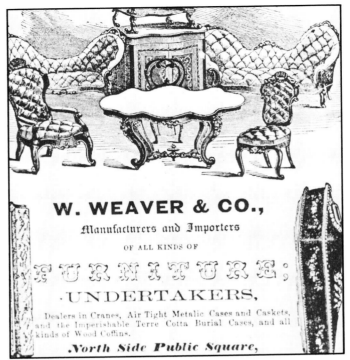

W. WEAVER & CO.,

Manufacturers and Importers

OF ALL KINDS OF

FURNITURE,

UNDERTAKERS,

Dealers in Cranes, Air Tight Metalic Cases and Caskets, and the Imperishable Terre Cotta Burial Cases, and all kinds of Wood Coffins.

North Side Public Square,

P. W. SPOTSWOOD,

WHOLESALE AND RETAIL

DRUGGIST AND APOTHECARY,

AND DEALER IN

Paints, Oil, Window Glass, Varnishes, Dye-Stuffs, &c.

Physicians' Prescriptions carefully compounded.

No. 16 COMMERCIAL ROW, HUNTSVILLE, ALA.

LARCOMBE'S

PHOTOGRAPHIC & AMBROTYPE GALLERY,

Franklin Hall, Franklin St., near Public Square,

HUNTSVILLE, ALABAMA.

WINGO'S

CELEBRATED RAT EXTERMINATOR,

WARRANTED TO KILL

Rats, Mice, Bed-bugs, Roaches,

AND

ALL INSECTS, WITHOUT POISON.

Unlike other Exterminators heretofore offered to the public, it contains a gas which swells the Insects and Vermin, which causes them to seek the open air, instead of creating a stench by dying under houses.

J. W. WINGO, Sole Agent,

North Cor. Public Square, Huntsville, Ala.

These advertisements from the 1859-1860 Huntsville Directory, City Guide, and Business Mirror illustrate the city's economic diversity. With a population of about 3,634, the town supported two female colleges, four male academies, five churches, and three newspapers. Public buildings included the courthouse, Northern Bank of Alabama, a jail, market house, and masonic hall. Courtesy, Strode Publishers

with assault and battery.

Clement Claiborne Clay, much remembered for his political courage and intractability, was another who could pack a pretty good punch and wasn't afraid to mix it up. The Clay boys used to fisticuff with the Pope-Percy-Walker clan. Clement Jr. explained such an encounter to his father: Willis Pope "jumped on me. . .& threw me down & bruised my face a little. . .As we went on home he was taunting & provoking me. . .when I went up to him & struck him & after bruising his face & being pulled off of him I went on home." This wasn't the end of it, though. The trustees of Green Academy would not brook such conduct in its gentlemen-scholars and meted out a two-week suspension for Willis, and one week for Clement. Warming to the justice of his action, young Clement concluded: "I commenced school this morning with the desire to keep out of all scrapes if possible but to fight when struck & to strike when my character is calumniated or my brothers imposed on. I think candidly that I have acted right & my breast is free from remorse of conscience."

It is amusing to note that the breast was considered the site of conscience. That could account for the notion that women were the conscience of the nation. But if women were the conscience, then men were the defenders of honor, and honor was the badge of conscience. On his way to and from Green Academy, Clay learned the lesson every Southern boy—rich or poor—learned by heart: There is no nobler life than one lived ever ready to defend honor; there is no greater death than that met in defense of honor.

Steele's courthouse, the second of four for Madison County, was completed in 1840. Although the building epitomized the Greek temple form, the dome was of Roman origin, frequently added to identify governmental structures. Courtesy, Huntsville-Madison County Public Library

Clay learned that lesson well. His own father had commenced his remarkable political career in a duel with Dr. Waddy Tate. Fortunately neither man was seriously wounded. Clay Jr.'s encounters lacked the dignity and discipline of dueling. They bespoke of the brawl, the sort of affray that laws were passed to discourage.

In 1843 Clay Jr. was at it again. This time his foe was Judge John C. Thompson. In a "street fight" he gave the judge a caning, "cutting his head badly." There were laws against disorderly conduct, but who was to enforce them if the lawmakers themselves broke them?

The ultimate breach of law came on July 23, 1827, when lawmaker James White McClung shot down feisty Scotsman and former Green Academy principal Andrew Wills. Green Academy had been chartered in 1812 and from its beginnings reflected the classical background of the scholarly squires and depended on them for financial backing. Having assumed his position in 1824, Wills was at first the darling of the Green Academy trustees, almost all of whom were associated with the Georgia "royal" or pro-bank party. Breaking with the school and "that obnoxious party," as he called it, Wills became editor of the antibank newspaper, the Huntsville *Democrat*. Wills was a fiendish publisher, zapping his opponents with his black ink and smearing their reputations.

Chief among Wills' targets were Dr. David Moore, a man of great wealth and accomplishment who was a perennial state representative, and Clement Comer Clay, the rising lawyer and legislator who was one of the Green Academy trustees (responsible for Wills' ouster as principal). Clay's law partner, James McClung, also drew fire, being accused of bribing the Alabama legislature to elect Clay to the United States Senate. The charge was specious and Clay was not elected. But there was no stopping the press war. As though caught up in a rendezvous with destiny, the two men inexorably marched to a deadly confrontation on a Huntsville street. At the trial that followed Wills' death, McClung was, in true frontier style, acquitted.

Bawdy houses or houses of "ill fame" were outlawed in 1834. The city fathers were all good family men and not sympathetic to the large single male population. Census figures state the case. In 1822 there were 308 white males to 180 white females over 21. In 1825 again 308 males were counted to 170 females. By 1828 there were 313 males to 165 females. At no time in the antebellum period did this disparity cease. The Civil War, of course, made short shrift of the imbalance.

Huntsville was no different than the rest of the South in 1831.

The elegance and fine proportions of Steele's bank confirm his mastery of Greek Revival architecture. This photograph dates from prior to 1900, when the side doors and second-floor windows were added across the facade. Courtesy, Huntsville-Madison County Public Library

Much of architect George Steele's understanding of the Greek Revival style resulted from a trip to Washington, D.C., in 1835. More than any other individual, Steele shaped the physical appearance of antebellum Huntsville through his numerous public and private commissions. Courtesy, Hoffman Shackleford, Jr.

Nat Turner's plotted uprising and grisly murders of women and children along with their men struck terror in the psyche of the owners of slaves. Huntsville responded with alacrity. A patrol law was passed, restricting the movement of blacks. The Alabama legislature echoed the pervasive alarm by barring immigration of free blacks into the state and by making it a criminal offense to teach a slave to read or write. Nat Turner had received his inspiration from the Bible, so even religious instruction, which had been esteemed as "civilizing," was henceforth suspect.

Just as things are not all black and white, Huntsville was far more than slaves and cotton. By 1860 town life had the ring not only of horses' hooves, wagon wheels, and market cries, but also the broken speech of foreigners and the familiar buzz of business activity. The heavy sounds of the Memphis and Charleston Railroad were becoming more familiar to ears originally tuned to the softer tones of bells and horns and the courthouse clock striking the hour. The rhythm of life around the square had picked up appreciably. There were four carriage makers, and one always had to be on the lookout for Lafayette Robinson, the young omnibus driver circling the square. And the smells: French bread baking at A.F. Yahr's bakery, dinner cooking at the Madison House, and the sweet scent of German and Swiss candies at Vogel's Confectioners. In the summer there were the smells of sweat and always there was the affront to the nostrils of horse manure that served as a reminder to watch one's step.

Stopping under the shade trees on the courthouse lawn, one could take measure of the town's progress. The courthouse had replaced the one built by John H. Hickman in 1817. This one was large and grand, a proud companion for the bank across the way, both reflecting the architectural genius of George Steele. Horses still hitched up to the square and an occasional dog ran loose, though there was an ordinance that permitted citizens to shoot loose dogs at will. As long as rabies was a threat, Huntsville's dogs were problems rather than pampered pets.

The writer of the *Huntsville Directory, City Guide, and Business Mirror* for 1859-1860 reminded its readers that the great fire of 1850, which took the "Splendid Caldwell House," an inn, and two and one-half square blocks of the downtown, was followed in 1855 by a blaze that razed the landmark Bell Tavern. But these fires were the sort that burnt themselves out or could be put out by the Huntsville fire company, of which the city was justly proud. A more subtle fire, long-smoldering as in cotton bales, was just beginning to catch the breeze of the southland, being wafted by the election of 1860. Huntsville saw signs of the inferno and tried to hold back the flames of secession and war.

III

We Have Met the Enemy and It Is Us

Norah Davis was born in Huntsville in the first year of the Civil War . . . Her family was one of the most prominent in both Madison and Limestone counties. Nicholas Davis, her grandfather, had been a delegate to the first Alabama constitutional convention in 1819. . .Three of his sons held public office. Nicholas Davis, Jr., was a delegate to the secession convention in 1861 and worked hard to keep the state from seceding. Zebulon Pike Davis, Norah Davis's father, served five terms as a Whig mayor of Huntsville before the war and three terms as a Republican mayor after Reconstruction. The Davises, with their roots in Virginia, were loyal Southerners and served the Confederacy, but they were strong and intelligent Americans, and if their counsels had been followed the South might not have been ruined nor the union blighted by the greatest blunder America has ever made, with the exception of permitting slavery in the first place.

    —"Norah Davis: 1861-1936" by Eleanor Newman Hutchens, delivered to the Huntsville-Madison County Historical Society, October 1982

The quaint southernism "Befo de Wa" carries with it much the same impact as the biblical "Before the Fall." As LeRoy Pope and his transplanted Petersburg planters would have had it, their city was at the heart of the "Southern Garden." It wasn't cotton alone that was picked in that garden. Nowhere were the apples plumper or prettier or eaten with greater relish than in Huntsville. Knowledge, as symbolized by the apple, was a shared

Top
Dr. Thomas Fearn settled in Huntsville about 1810 and amassed a fortune of almost $175,000, including 1,100 acres of land. His greatest renown came from his research on quinine, which he made from the bark of trees and used to successfully treat typhoid fever. Courtesy, Mrs. James McLeod

Above
Once a slave owned by Dr. Fearn, this woman raised his seven daughters after Mrs. Fearn's death. In addition, she tended their three daughters and a son, all of whom died in infancy. Courtesy, Mrs. James McLeod

value. Reminiscent of the 18th-century Enlightenment with its aspirations of building a heavenly city, the founders brought learning into the garden. But, as they used learning for ornamental purposes, to enhance the enjoyment of their faculties and their social usefulness, they did not cultivate their garden or their minds intensively or deeply. Nor did they get to the roots of the old problems of slavery or soil-depleting agriculture. Their brilliant display of intellect rested solidly on a callous prejudice that protected their innocence and kept them from coming to terms with themselves. But only in innocence—a profound innocence—could Southerners have perpetuated a social system that was so inherently evil as slavery.

One of the foremost among the city fathers, Dr. Thomas Fearn, who embodied the Jeffersonian idealism and Franklin pragmatism of the American Enlightenment, saw this. Writing to Clement Comer Clay from London on July 29, 1818, Fearn revealed his aspirations for his city. Aglow with national pride, Fearn shared his ruminations with Clay: "I am convinced that nature has bountifully contributed everything to render Huntsville the garden spot of the fairest country on earth & that enterprise is not wanting in its citizens, to elevate it to the proud destiny that nature has ordained." Among things needing doing, Fearn urged Clay to champion internal improvements especially as affected Muscle Shoals. Another improvement he was eagerly anticipating was the "establishment of a reading room" and "accumulation of a general library."

The thrust of Fearn's letter to Clay, however, was about his deepest concern, slavery, which he called "that foulest blot in our national character, that damning curse entailed on us by our forefathers, that glaring inconsistency between republican principles and despotic practice." That glaring inconsistency haunted him: "To plead equal rights of man & at the same time make the heavenly principle bend & yield to convenience or even necessity is too great an absurdity." Fearn based his attack on reason, not morality, on absurdity, not sin. He was a true son of the Enlightenment.

Never one to say "Why don't they?" Fearn said, "Why don't we?" emancipate our slaves according to a gradual plan providing that "every descendant of a slave born after a fixed period be free at the age of twenty or even a later age if this is thought too oppressive to the holders." Furthermore, he would charge the county court "to exact from those holding them in bondage an obligation to educate them to a certain extent (giving them the privileges of ordinary apprentices)." Having thought it through dispassionately, he shifted from analyst to advocate:

James G. Birney, a failed politician and planter, was bankrupted by gambling debts and land speculation, before succumbing to the religious revivals that swept the country in the 1820s. Converted like many others, he viewed abolition as a sacred vocation and culminated his political career in 1844 as the abolitionist Presidential candidate. Courtesy, Huntsville-Madison County Public Library

This subject is daily receiving greater attention & I must think the example of one Southern State, particularly a cotton state, would evince its practicability & open the brightest era that has occurred since the glorious achievement of our Independence, & oh how I should rejoice to see Alabama step forward & make this sacrifice if indeed it be even a temporary one...My dear friend I already see in anticipation posterity erecting monuments to the man who can boldly dare the prejudice of the day & transmit to them the blessings of unmixed, unadulterated freedom...

But Clay did not share Fearn's concern and the subject rested for 12 years until Fearn, James G. Birney, and Dr. John Allan formed the Madison County Colonization Society. Its purpose was to encourage colonization in Africa of emancipated slaves. Gradual emancipation, with an eye to returning those freed to their ancestral home, seemed the answer. It might have worked had reason maintained the upper hand.

In the ensuing years Thomas Fearn would own as many as 80 slaves. Presbyterian minister Dr. John Allan would raise a family of seven children, all but one of whom would choose as a young adult to move to Illinois and join the abolitionist movement. Only Euphemia, the mother of John Allan Wyeth, would remain true to her Southern nativity. James G. Birney, after serving in the Alabama legislature, as a trustee of the University of Alabama, and as alderman and mayor of Huntsville in the 1820s, would leave Huntsville in the 1830s to dedicate himself to abolition in the border states. He gained a national following when in 1840 and 1844 he was the Liberty Party candidate for president of the United States. His Huntsville years had kindled a hope that the political process would yield to reason.

Allan and Birney died before the Civil War. Thomas Fearn died of pneumonia contracted while being held by Federal forces under order of General Ormsby M. Mitchell. With ten other prominent residents and Episcopal Bishop Henry P. Lay, a past rector of the Church of the Nativity, Thomas Fearn bore a part of the burden of the South's involvement in a war he opposed, a secession he disapproved of, and a system of slavery he had learned to live with and, as it turned out, died for.

Dr. Allan's son, William T., became a pastor of the Presbyterian Church in Chatham, Illinois, where he wrote of his youth in Huntsville:

There was one plantation just opposite my father's house in the suburbs of Huntsville, belonging to Judge Smith, formerly a Senator in Congress from South Carolina, now of Huntsville. The

Top
Dr. John Allan Wyeth is pictured at left with local physicians Sam Lowry (right) and J.D. Humphrey. Courtesy, Huntsville-Madison County Public Library

Above
Like many of his fellow physicians, Dr. Francis H. Newman conducted research in other branches of science. His firm of Newman & Harrison dispensed drugs and other chemicals. Courtesy, Mrs. William Henson

name of his overseer was *Tune. I have often seen him flogging the slaves in the field, and have often heard their cries. Sometimes, too, I have met them with the tears streaming down their faces, and the marks of the whip on their bare necks and shoulders. Tune was so severe in his treatment, that his employer dismissed him after two or three years lest, it was said, he should kill off all the slaves. But he was immediately employed by another planter in the neighborhood. . .Tune became displeased with one of the women who was pregnant, he made her lay down over a log, with her face towards the ground, and beat her so unmercifully, that she was soon after delivered of a dead child. . .*

Facts might be gathered abundantly, to show that it is slavery itself, and not cruelties merely, that make slaves unhappy. Even those that are most kindly treated, are generally far from being happy. The slaves in my father's family are almost as kindly treated as slaves can be, yet they pant for liberty.

Dr. Allan's grandson, Euphemia's son, John Allan Wyeth, grew up in Marshall County and often visited Huntsville, which he referred to as the "Athens of the South." A product of the garden, Wyeth became one of the leading medical men in 19th-century America. Founder of the New York Polyclinic Medical School and Hospital, he served as president of the American Medical Association and authored medical texts as well as popular historical and biographical books. In *With Sabre and Scalpel,* Wyeth recollected the spirit that animated his grandparents' home and made it "a center of the refinement and culture of the community, a rallying-point of the remarkable group of men and women, many of whom as they grew to maturity found high places in the esteem of mankind and later wrote their names in history."

Wyeth had experienced antebellum Huntsville at full flower, when the sum of its parts—squatters and squires, newcomers and natives—blended brilliantly in the sunlight. But with the sunlight came shadows that, when cast in late afternoon, loomed larger than life. In the shadows of that luminous garden was slavery. Wyeth sought to reconcile the dichotomy in his own family and to explain to himself and his readers that had the Yankee serpent not come into the garden, had Huntsvillians and Southerners been left alone, they would have done the "right" thing sooner or later, as "they realized that the verdict of the higher civilization was against it."

In 1861 Huntsville found itself in the impossible position of opposing secession and frantically clinging to hopes of compromise. The idea of secession was as old as the Union and had been threatened by New England states as well as Southern. The issue had never been squarely met, however. The South had learned that if it put up enough of a holler, the United States would back down and come to terms. The grease of politics, after all, was compromise, but both sides were expected to use it. Tariff issues as well as slavery had been handled that way in each decade of the antebellum period. Why should the 1860s be different?

So in 1860 Huntsville and the South threw down the gauntlet: Abraham Lincoln, "the Black Republican," must not be elected. If he were, secession would follow. The burden of choice and guilt was to be the North's. The garden's gates would close. Only Yankee compliance could open them; Lincoln's election sealed them forever, and war lowered the garden into hell. William L. Yancey had said it for the South: "Ours is the peace to be destroyed. Ours is the honor at stake." Huntsville's Leroy Pope Walker, as the new Confederate states' secretary of war, ordered the firing on Fort Sumter, thus beginning the conflict that sundered the nation, destroying peace and union, leaving all to honor.

How did the South come to such a pass? Certainly it was not Yancey's rhetoric that shook Huntsville and other Southern cities. Abolitionist agitation and slave unrest had struck closer to home and often enough to upset. Theodore Weld, a leading abolitionist publicist and orator, visited the homes of Dr. John Allan and James G. Birney when he came to Huntsville in the early 1830s. They were struck by his eloquence and purity of motive. Most

The Confederate cabinet of President Jefferson Davis (seated third from right) featured Huntsvillian Leroy Pope Walker (standing at right). Walker served as Secretary of War, but resigned within a year to accept a commission of brigadier general. After the war he was chosen president of Alabama's second constitutional convention, a position his father, John Williams Walker, had held when the first constitution was written. Courtesy, Huntsville-Madison County Public Library

ATTENTION HUNTSVILLE GUARDS.

Thère will be a meeting of the Company at the Court House, on Thursday night next, at 7 1-2 o'clk. An election for officers of the Company will be held, and new members admitted. A full attendance is desired. W. M. GORMLY. Sec'y. March 20th, 1861.

Huntsvillians, however, viewed men such as Weld as the rankest kind of troublemaker and held them responsible for such murders as the one which occurred in July of 1835. The *Democrat* reported it. Willis Sandford, "an old and highly respected citizen" of the county, had been found in his bed, strangled. The immediate presumption was that slaves had committed the act. Two, Charles and Flora, were charged. The specter of midnight murders disquieted the sleep of slaveholders, and the *Democrat* called for more patrols "to keep this dangerous population in closer confinement."

In the 1850s the story was the same, only more horrifying. Only after he published *Recollections and Experiences of An Abolitionist: From 1855 to 1865,* did Huntsvillians learn that Dr. Alexander Milton Ross, a prominent Canadian physician and ornithologist, was also a field worker for the Underground Railroad who "remained four weeks in Huntsville" in the spring of 1858, "actively engaged in circulating information among the slaves."

Closer to home, other seeds were sown. The community gasped in horror that same year when the battered body of young Thomas Bibb, grandson of Governor Thomas Bibb and son of Peyton, was found, half eaten by animals, on the grounds at Belle Mina in Limestone County. Young Thomas had started out hunting when he was attacked by one of Peyton Bibb's slaves, who later confessed that he had killed the boy in order to get his gun with which he planned to kill the senior Bibb.

Abolitionist agitation was as real and almost as painful as that slave's blow to young Thomas' head, only the reverberations carried farther and persisted longer. But if hands turned clammy in cold sweat, the body politic remained calm. Perusal of city council minutes points up no sign of alarm until the end of 1859. Then an ordinance was passed that called for the removal of all free Negroes who had come into the city since 1832. When January 1, 1860, the enforcement date arrived, the council voted to delay removal until March first. As late as November a resolution to "arrest and bring before the mayor all free negroes who have come here since 1832" was withdrawn for lack of support.

But a complex of forces was at work in North Alabama to produce an overwhelming unionist sentiment against secession and war. In the outlying sand mountain and hilly stretches southwest of the Tennessee River, cotton and slaves did not polka-dot the landscape. The small farmers and "mountain whites" or "hillbillies" were a fiercely independent people who viewed slaves and slave-holders with equal hostility and wanted nothing to do with a government or a war.

Within Huntsville another phenomenon was at work. The city of new beginnings had in the antebellum period opened wide its doors to Yankees and foreigners. As the countryside became a homogenized blend of slave-owning Southerners, the city attracted a melange of skilled workers, artisans, and small merchants. These newcomers composed a kaleidoscope of political shades of opinion, but they all sought a government that would protect property, maintain order, and encourage free enterprise. Secession and civil war could spell economic disaster.

"We has met the enemy, and it is us," said Walt Kelly in *Pogo.* The questions of secession and war exposed Huntsvillians to the true enemy—themselves. This was so because they subscribed to two contradictory ideologies: reason as a method of problem-solving, and honor as the arbiter of human destiny. Reason is essentially a measured or tempered approach; honor is an all-or-nothing standard. In the case of a fratricidal war, reason was bound to lose. Yet such Huntsville Loyalists as Judge George W. Lane, Nicholas Davis, Judge David C. Humphreys, and Jeremith Clemens saw the liabilities and limitations of honor as a means to peace. Honor would require all-out war, as nothing else would vindicate it. Reason, on the other hand, could seek peace in the midst of war. Lives saved were a vindication, and not an indication of cowardice, as an advocate of honor would have one believe.

It should not be surprising then that Huntsville supplied some of the South's intellectual leadership of the anti-Secessionist

Shortly after Mitchell's occupation, a number of prominent secessionists were arrested; among them was Matthew W. Steele, an architect-builder. Only a few months later, Steele committed what a Union general called a "very grave offense and an insult to the U.S. Government." His crime was pulling a tailor's whiskers because he had been civil to a Federal officer. Courtesy, Matt W. Steele

forces; nor should it be surprising that Huntsville became a center of unionist and peace efforts during the war. Still, the county of Madison, including Huntsville, contributed mightily—and to the death—its men and material to the Southern cause. Heroes or traitors, they were for the most part simply fighting for what they believed in—honor or reason.

From the early morning Union takeover on April 11, 1862, when Gen. Ormsby M. Mitchell stealthily moved his troops into town, Huntsville had slept its last peaceful sleep. A malaise fell over the place. Thenceforth, citizens awakened to a new sense of impending doom that stayed with many long after the war ended. Huntsville was occupied or under passive siege unremittingly from that morning in April 1862, until the war's end—exactly three years and one month, minus the 10 months between August 1862 and July 1863.

One of the marvels of the war was the relatively light destruction of persons or property within the town proper. Fires started for warmth in the basements of the Methodist Church (January 6, 1864) and Green Academy (November 26, 1864) caused the careless destruction of two esteemed landmarks. During the winters of 1863 and 1864, almost every loose stick of wood, fencing, or unused structure was commandeered by Union soldiers seeking warmth and shelter. Yet the grand old forest oak on Adams Street, capable of warming hundreds of hearths and camp fires, was allowed to stand—testimony that the occupying Yankees respected the beauty, if not the politics, of the place.

One reason the city was spared while the countryside was scorched was that Huntsville was used as a communications center and a bedroom city for Union forces, especially the officer corps. The diaries and documents of the war reveal a partial but convincing list of dozens of generals and colonels who "slept" in the town. The highest ranking was Gen. William T. Sherman who occupied the Bibb-Beirne home on Williams.

War and occupation heightened the intensity of experience for all involved. A knock on the door or bell in the night struck dread in Huntsville hearts. Out in the country the danger was constant, from friend-turned-foe and marauding guerrilla warriors of all persuasions. Everyone was on edge, ready to react to almost anything. In its first encounter with the Union Army that daybreak of April 11, 1862, the city had been caught napping. Callow innocence and peaceful sleep gave way to recriminations and jitters. As the Cincinnati *Gazette* described it, "Never in the history of any military movement, was surprise so complete." Awaking to a nightmare, "men rushed into the streets almost naked, the women fainted, the children screamed, the darkies

Joseph Wheeler rose to the rank of lieutenant-general in the Confederate Army and brigadier-general in the U.S. Army during the Spanish-American War. During the Civil War he was engaged in about 500 skirmishes, commanded at 127 battles, and was appointed senior cavalry general of the Confederate forces. After the war he represented Lawrence County in Congress for a number of years. Courtesy, Huntsville-Madison County Public Library

laughed, and for a short time a scene of perfect terror reigned." Discounting editorial bias, the shock of the invasion of the garden was immediate and penetrating. The depot with its shops, 17 engines, numerous cars, several Huntsville-manufactured cannon and moulds were taken. A Confederate train carrying between 150 and 200 wounded and furloughed Confederates was chased and captured too.

Since the 1855 completion of the Memphis and Charleston Railroad through the city, Huntsvillians had enjoyed the growing importance of that more expeditious transportation medium to their economic well-being. The railroad spurred an economic boom and scores of young men from the North had been welcomed as employees of the road, its roundhouse, foundries, and ancillary businesses. Spanning the topside of the state and connecting with Memphis and Chattanooga, the railroad tied Huntsville more tightly than the wayward and temperamental Tennessee River had done, to the fortunes of Tennessee and the border states.

No other enterprise in Huntsville represented a Yankee presence as much as did the Memphis and Charleston. While its stockholders and subscribers, including the City of Huntsville to the extent of $50,000, were Southern, the skilled labor was

Union tents were pitched along East Side Square during the Federal occupation of Huntsville. The soldiers reportedly tore down dilapidated buildings to furnish lumber for their make-shift camps. A brick home, which was said to have cost $18,000, also was razed to provide brick for the soldiers' chimneys. Courtesy, Huntsville-Madison County Public Library

decidedly Yankee and immigrant in makeup. Once fighting began in the secession crisis, the pressure to take sides drove many of the workers to leave Huntsville. The Huntsville *Democrat* called it "Northern vamoosing."

When the Memphis and Charleston was captured, General Mitchel wired Secretary of War Edwin Stanton, "We have at length succeeded in cutting the great artery of railway intercommunication between the Southern States." George Edgar Turner's study, *Victory Rode the Rails: The Strategic Place of the Railroads in the Civil War*, pinpointed the road's importance:

In the four months after February 12, 1862, the Federals had driven the enemy from Kentucky, middle and western Tennessee and a strip along the northern borders of Alabama and Mississippi. The Union front roughly paralleled the Memphis & Charleston Railroad for nearly 300 miles between Memphis and Stevenson, Alabama. Behind that front lay a vast area of vital military and political importance to both sides. Within it were more than 1,300 miles of railroad. . .no less than a dozen railroad junctions, and over this rail network flowed munitions and supplies for nearly 200,000 soldiers and forage for their thousands of horses and mules. Not a single north-south line west of Virginia and north of Mississippi and Alabama remained in control of the Confederates.

The roundhouse at the Memphis and Charleston Depot is pictured about 1863. An adjacent engine house, a car shop, and a machine shop were constructed to handle repairs and to rebuild the rolling stock. In addition to the extant passenger and freight depots, the M & C built Venable's Hotel on the site of the former Dilworth Lumber Company. Courtesy, Huntsville Madison County Public Library

The photo above of the Huntsville Female College was probably taken in 1889. The photo below of the coeds on an outing is reportedly from the 1860s. Courtesy, Old Huntsville Magazine *and* Huntsville Madison County Public Library

Much of what is recorded about Huntsville's war years is found in the letters and diaries of the womenfolk. Like the Spartan women of a past civilization, they formed a stern and austere home guard. Keeping their dignity by meeting each indignity with a chilly reserve, they put off the most pompous Yankee officer, who, though trained to give and obey commands, could sense that the authority of these women's command went far deeper than his own.

Mrs. William D. Chadick's diary brings occupied Huntsville into focus. For through her intelligent eyes the reader catches glimpses of all who touched her life: the Federal troops in all their guises, the slaves emerging as free human beings, and the townspeople as they continued their daily lives. In the background, school and learning went on. Mrs. Sidney J. Mayhew kept lit the lamp of learning at the Female Seminary, which had been chartered in 1831 by the Presbyterian Church. Indeed, learning became the sacred trust of the young ladies of the town since the young men had traded their quill and ink for hard tack and musket ram. Learning did not go uninterrupted, however; both the college and Dr. J.G. Wilson's Female College served as hospitals during the Union occupation.

Also functioning, though in a more circumscribed manner, was the city government with Robert Coltart serving as mayor and Brittain Franks as constable. No sooner had General Mitchell occupied the city than he instructed the mayor to cater breakfast for 5,000 Federal troops or else see the food pillaged from private homes. This was a tall order for a mayor who in civilian life was an ice maker.

Business, too, carried on. But apparently only those who took an oath of loyalty to the Federal government were allowed to operate. Mrs. Chadick wrote that the new hotel could only open under those conditions: "An order has been given today," (June 25, 1862) she wrote, "that, if the stockholders of the new hotel do not take the oath of allegiance to the U.S. within three days, the hotel will be taken into the hands of the Federalists." The hotel, along with most other public buildings and large private residences, was taken over. After November 1, 1864, Mrs. Chadick later observed, no one could make a purchase over "$1 worth without a permit, for which they pay 25 cents, and if over $10, they must take the oath." By that time $10 was hard to come by, but even when they had it, the ladies preferred to spend it behind Confederate lines. The Union forces brought with them their own sutlers who sold goods for tokens issued to the troops. Huntsville had the distinction of having the only Southern-based Yankee sutler outlet, a firm called White and Swan.

Henry Figures, holding the bowie knife, posed with an unidentified friend about 1862. He fought at Yorktown, Fredericksburg, Manassas, Chickamauga, and Gettysburg, where he was cited for bravery. In an area of dense underbrush and scruffy trees aptly called the Wilderness, the 20-year old Figures was killed. Courtesy, Huntsville-Madison County Public Library

The immigrant Germans and established Jewish merchants in town apparently were less molested than native merchants. Margaret Anne Goldsmith Hanaw's study of her Jewish forebearers amplifies her contention that having been denied the right to own land or to exercise full rights of citizenship in their native Germany, Huntsville's antebellum Jewish settlers, including the Bernsteins and Hersteins, strove mightily and well to build strong businesses and contribute to community life. They let their business sense be their guide, often keeping commercial lines open to both sides.

Another German family with deep antebellum roots was the Francis Rebmans. Listed in the 1850 census as boot- and shoemakers, by 1860 the family had shifted to proprietorship of a bakery and confectionery shop. Mrs. Chadick reported to her diary that the family "got into a fuss" with the Yankees, but stood their ground well, Mrs. Rebman actually collaring one of the soldiers and her daughters pelting him with rocks. "The misses Redman [Rebman] cried, 'Havoc!' and let fly the rocks, with the most undaunted bravery. Every volley told on the enemy, about 25 strong." These skirmishes sometimes took on a more serious cast, as recalled by Margaret Henson to Sara McDaris in a recent radio broadcast: "Such as the time three soldiers from the 5th Ohio Cavalry went outside the Federal pickets to meet lady friends and were pounced on by Confederates who threw them into a well and covered them over with twelve feet of dirt."

Life often seemed reduced to such personal encounters. But in these small confrontations with the Federals, citizens came to grips with a fear and a horror too immense to approach full-face.

On the evening of the first day of Yankee intrusion, Mrs. W.D. Chadick, in concert with several "ladies from the college," called upon General Mitchell to secure permission to visit and tend the wounded in the railroad cars and the able-bodied in the depot. There was no wailing, wringing of hands, or clenching of teeth. These ladies knew what had to be done and efficiently went about doing it. The sick they removed to private homes or to hospitals. To prisoners cooped up in the upper floor of the Memphis-Charleston depot, idly passing the time by drawing graffiti on the walls, they brought food, blankets, and niceties such as flowers and wine. Besides capably running their own homes, Mrs. Chadick and her friends unofficially ran the town. The Confederate camp at Blue Spring was named Camp Bradford to honor Mrs. Joseph B. Bradford who had tirelessly nursed hundreds of sick soldiers.

At war's beginning there was the light-hearted gallantry of the young soldiers going forth to do battle with dragons, sensing in the excitement of the moment a heightened reason for being, but covering it over with banter. Henry S. Figures, seventeen-year-old son of William B. Figures, the editor of the Huntsville *Advocate*, keenly enjoyed the romantic prospect of war. He wrote to his sister on April 22, 1861:

I got a letter from Sandy White this morning. He said the college girls were going to give the Huntsville Guard a flag and Annie Brown & Sallie McGee were going to give it to them, I would like to be there very much & to have a little speech so as to respond to her [Annie Brown]. . .You must give her my love and kiss her for me, give my love to all the girls and boys. What did Liley Bibb want with my Ambrotype. . .P.S. Don't forget to tell Annie Browne what I said and to get her ambrotype for your brother.

Two years later, a much sobered and battle-worn nineteen-year-old Henry Figures wrote in July 1863:

Above
S.J. Mayhew, principal of the Huntsville Female Seminary, also taught at the school along with his wife. Courtesy, Huntsville-Madison County Public Library

Right
The Huntsville Female Seminary was chartered in 1831 under Presbyterian auspices. This George Steele building, however, dates from 1854. After Federal troops occupied the structure for 18 months, the school never regained its antebellum prominence. Courtesy, H.E. Monroe, Sr.

Gettisburg—where we had a great fight...Our regiment charged up the mountain for two miles, when it became so steep that we could not go any farther. We then fell back and charged it four successive times but could not take the heights. The enemy were upon the top of the mountain—the steepest place I ever saw in my life...killed and wounded in our regiment...Captain Leftwich, Tom Lanier, Jim Duff...Tell Mr. Leftwich that I have his son's sword and will send it to him as soon as I have an opportunity.

The following year, May 5, 1864, Henry Figures was slain in the Wilderness Campaign. He had left home a boy; he was returned a corpse.

Brought to Huntsville near the close of the war, Lilie Bibb and Miss Carrie Hentz, the governess in her uncle's family, were witnesses in a trial where her uncle was accused of being a

*Below
Captain Frank B. Gurley commanded a local cavalry unit under General Nathan Bedford Forrest. Captured by Federal troops, Gurley was charged with murdering a northern officer and sentenced to hang. He was freed only after Confederates threatened retaliation of a similar nature against Federal prisoners. Courtesy, Huntsville-Madison County Public Library.*

*Above
Brigadier-General Edward Dorr Tracy, a native of Macon, Georgia, moved to Huntsville in 1857 to practice law. Like many Southerners, he welcomed the prospect of war and the ensuing Confederate victory, reflecting in a letter that "God is manifestly on our side." During the defense of Vicksburg in 1863, Tracy was fatally struck by a minnie ball while he and his 1,500 men were positioned at Port Gibson, Mississippi. Courtesy, S. Rossetter Collins*

Confederate spy. Kept at the Rice home, which was then
Huntsville Union headquarters, she was marched to the courtroom
in the Calhoun building. Reduced in wardrobe but not in spirit, a
"ripple of amusement" stole over the somber faces of the judges
when they saw her.

The antebellum Calhoun House was built to last. It served as a federal courthouse during the occupation and also for the Frank James trial in 1884. Courtesy, Old Huntsville Magazine and Huntsville Madison Public County Library

*Being a tall, leggy girl, I was arrayed in my diminutive
grandmother's black silk gown. . .and full skirt. My puppy chewed
up one of my shoes and one of my grandmother's, so my feet
were shod in a kid boot and a cloth gaiter. On my head was a
Neapolitan skyscraper tied under my chin with a huge bow of
royal purple.*

Dignity came in all ages, shapes, and sizes. Another lady who
stood tall was Lilie Bibb's aunt, Mrs. Mills. Toward the end of
the war, when the Yankees came looking for firearms and
valuables, she "stuffed all the knives, forks and spoons in her
bosom; being a portly lady they projected at all angles." Arms
akimbo, silently daring her interrogators to search her,
notwithstanding the ready "evidence," Mrs. Mills swore to the
Yankees that there "were no firearms and not even a silver spoon
in the house."

Inexorably the United States crushed the Confederacy so that
after 1864 continued resistance was futile. Yet proud Southerners
refused to yield. Some still talked of probable, or at least possible,
foreign intervention to save King Cotton, and they stubbornly
looked forward to eventual victory and vindication of their rights.

As late as March 26, 1865, after three years of Federal sway
over their lives, Mrs. Chadick wrote in her diary: "We do not
believe that our cause is hopeless; [we] believe that it is a just
cause and put our trust in the God of Battles." Again on April 4,
five days before Gen. Robert E. Lee's surrender to Gen. Ulysses
S. Grant at Appomattox, she wrote:

*Heard that Richmond and Petersburg were evacuated and in
possession of the Feds! Can it be that so much precious blood has
been split to hold our Capitol, and that Gen Lee has been obliged
at last to abandon it?*

*The Yankees are perfectly jubilant. . .For ourselves, we are
not whipped yet, nor do we believe the Southern Confederacy
is either.*

The fighting and the hoping stopped for Huntsville with the
surrender on May 11, 1865, of Major Miles E. Johnston of the
Twenty-fifth Alabama Battalion and some 150 Confederates. The

Due largely to the efforts of his wife, Virginia Tunstall Clay, Clement Claiborne Clay was released from Fortress Monroe where he had been incarcerated for having "incited and concerted the assassination of Mr. Lincoln and the attempt on Mr. Seward." Mrs. Clay is shown here celebrating her 90th birthday. Courtesy, Mrs. James L. Jordan

actual surrender to Colonel William Given, accompanied by "national and patriotic airs" played by the bands of the 18th Michigan and the 102nd Ohio Volunteer Infantry, took place on Monte Sano at "Trough Spring on the Mountain" (Cold Spring). As though to wash away the sins of the world, it rained that day. Amid speeches by both commanding officers and the stacking of arms, the Federals passed around five gallons of brandy. W.T. Bennett, a Confederate involved in the surrender, later recalled, "They all drank the brandy in a drenching rain that fell that day." Because mud made treacherous the wagon transport of weapons, the Confederates were reissued their arms and marched down the mountain into Huntsville and then released. There was no sunshine all day.

When it was finally over there was left the pervasive numbness of a people stunned by defeat. Like a child's game of "freeze" or "statues," the war had set them twirling in the madness of the moment and then halted them dead in their tracks, eyes still ablaze with excitement, jaws set with determination. Their once-dashing grey uniforms, now stripped of brass buttons and gold braid, lay at their feet like crumpled dreams.

The end of the war did not bring peace to Huntsville. Occupation continued. For many, things got worse. In war there had been hope; now there was despair.

In 1866 Clement Claiborne Clay turned 50 years old. The antebellum embodiment of Southern pride had staked his fortune on the state's right to secede and his honor to uphold that right. During the war his aging father, the former governor, was subjected to arrest and harassment in Huntsville while the son was in Richmond serving in the Confederate senate and then in Canada as a commissioner for the Confederacy. At war's end, he was accused of being implicated in the assassination of Abraham Lincoln and a warrant was issued for his arrest. Always a man of honor, he turned himself in, fully expecting to be able to clear his name and secure release. Instead, he, along with President Jefferson Davis, spent the next year a prisoner of the U.S. government at Fort Monroe. Freed on April 18, 1866, Clay came home a shaken shadow of his former self. On his birthday he wrote:

Douglas Taylor became one of Huntsville's finest lawyers and dedicated public servants. His father was the city's pioneer historian, Judge Thomas Jones Taylor.

I have lived ½ a 100 yrs. in vain. . .For life has lost its chiefest joys with me, & I do not even hope to recover them. If I could only [settle my accounts] in this world, & leave property I hold, without incumbrance, to my wife, I should be content to go away from it at once. Debt is my heaviest cross & I long to lay it down.

Throughout the tense days of Huntsville occupation, the Thomas White home had been a catacomb of activity; as Confederates hid in the basement, Union officers sometimes took over the ground floor, and the White family was lucky to claim the upstairs. Son Sandy had joined the Madison Rifles in the first enthusiastic wave of volunteers mustered into the war as part of the soon-heralded Alabama Fourth Infantry. In 1862 when a Union officer asked Mrs. White where her two older sons were, she spunkily replied, "They are in the Confederate army in Virginia, and I wish I had 36 more there." Fifteen years later, in 1877, Susan Bradley White had lost that early fire. The war had devastated the financial empire of Thomas White, leaving the family "land poor." To her diary, Mrs. White confided her inability to accept intellectually or emotionally war's brutal destruction of her way of life:

July 4. It does not seem the same world it did when I was a child and the glorious 4th was celebrated. Then people were rich and seemed to be happy. Well sometimes I can hardly realize that this is the same body. It may be the same body—but the soul, the heart, or the inner life, call it by what name you choose, is not the same. It is all changed.

Like Southerners in general, Huntsvillians found defeat galling and Reconstruction repulsive. Peacemakers such as Jeremith Clemens, George W. Lane, Nicholas Davis, David C. Humphreys, Joseph C. Bradley, William B. Figures, Benjamin Jolly, their wives, and numerous others had tried to soften the transition from war to peace. But unlike other wars, efforts to secure peace were called treason. If only the "t" had been dropped, things might have been different. Instead these local men were obliged to pick up the pieces of their beloved city in an atmosphere of loss, anguish, and hate.

The pain of it all lent to thoughts of a happier past a greater comfort than they perhaps warranted. Within a year, nostalgia had taken the form of mass hypnosis. The major social event of 1866 was a jousting spectacle called "The Grove Spring Tournament," promoted by the Huntsville Tournament Association and scheduled for July 26th. Loss on the field of battle could be sublimated on a contrived field of honor, as with the knights of old. The newspaper announcement of the "Passage at Arms" makes explicit the psychological games these people played:

Do we not live in an heroic age, an era of wars and rumors of war, wherein we have learned, as well as any knight of old, the practice of martial arms, and the management of martial steeds, and the exercise of martial virtues? Truly our own country for the last few years, may be said to have exhibited to the world, the mighty image of a continental tournament in all the varied currents of a heady fight...
The time forsooth abounds with knightly deeds and chivalrous characters...Even now we call to mind, a thousand wild incidents of camp and march, bivouac and battle...Some mightier Tennyson will invoke the recent past and strike a grander lyre to the more glorious Idyls of the South. Riding down the shadowy lists of time, with phantom s'eed and "magic sword excalibur," the august form and stately mien of Robert E. Lee will outrival...the

Planter Thomas White, a native of Virginia, emigrated to Alabama in the late 1830s. On the eve of the Civil War, his real estate and personal property were worth about $160,000; but by 1870 their value had plummeted to only $11,000. Courtesy, Dr. Eleanor Hutchens

good old chief of the Round Table. . .The sainted Stonewall knight, companioned still with Lee, assumes the transfigured likeness of the brave Lancelot. . .

Like the kudzu plant, this romanticization of the past was to spread rapidly, smothering out fresh air, light, and new growth, wrapping the South in a protective mantle of folklore. But even this mantle with its seductive comfort was to give way to the spirit of a new age, the demands of a past that couldn't stay hidden, and a future that beckoned of new beginnings.

Clement Claiborne Clay (on right) has been compared with William Yancey as the leader of Alabama's secession movement. A strong states-rights advocate, Clay resigned his seat in the U.S. Senate when Alabama seceded and was elected to the Confederate Senate. Courtesy, Huntsville-Madison County Public Library

CHAPTER IV

All Out for Huntsville

There is one delightful shout that emanates from the throat of every conductor of every train that reaches our depot. It is full of significance and deep meaning. That shout is "all out for Huntsville," and in five minutes from fifty to one hundred strangers are on our streets taking in our glorious sunshine, beautiful scenery, sparkling water, and beholding with delight the great resources of our surroundings. There is no other city like Huntsville, for this is the fairest lily of the grandest agricultural and mineral valley that God's sun in its great rounds shines upon.
 —Weekly Mercury, *January 27, 1892*

Built upon Huntsville's mountain face to welcome its visitors and health and home-seekers, the majestic 200-room, Queen Anne-style Monte Sano Hotel signaled an auspicious new beginning for the city below. Combining the efforts of local leaders with outside capital, the erection of the hotel represented the triumph of the New South in the Old South hamlet of Huntsville. By June 1887 when the hotel opened with pomp and pageantry, Huntsville was in the mood to look up and build tall.

Hewn from timbers native to the area and rising some five stories above its high mountain foundation, the Monte Sano Hotel served as a beacon to the aspirations of the people looking up from below. In later years they would build a cross and put it on their mountain. For now they were still bearing a cross composed of broken dreams and fortunes. Indeed, the progress of the people in the 35 years following the war could be measured in the steps taken to reascend the mountain they had surrendered in the

The Madison Rifles, some members of which are pictured here about 1898, were organized in 1855 as a militia and became part of the Seventh Alabama Infantry during the Civil War. The regiment continued to the Spanish-American War days when this group posed at the southwestern corner of the Public Square. Courtesy, Huntsville-Madison County Public Library

spring of 1865.

In sad witness to the passing of the old, and making way for the new was the funeral of Mrs. Ellen Donegan. Mrs. Donegan was of that premier family whose name was so intimately associated with Huntsville's antebellum fortunes in the Bell Factory, Patton and Donegan Commission Merchants, and the Donegan Block. Writing in her diary, Susan Bradley White wryly commented that the funeral of her old friend, occurring on the hotel's opening date, was "so arranged that the gay crowd for the Monte Sano Ball would not come in contact. Oh me how life is made up of Sunshine and Shadow." The mountain remains; but the grandest hotel in the Tennessee Valley's history, like a child's Fourth of July sparkler, shone brilliantly in the night sky, flickered, and then died, leaving the mountain dark except for the lone scattered lights from the summer places of Huntsvillians.

After 1865, cotton was no longer the autonomous "king" of Dixie, as the South increasingly yielded its sovereignty to the Americanization of industrial enterprise. In the developing national network, cotton became the weak but sustaining heart of Dixie. The same soft stuff that had cushioned the lives of the planter-merchant aristocracy of antebellum days was tightly woven into the fabric of postwar society, holding white and black, rich and poor, young and old in its grip. For a whole society mired in debt and without capital, cotton became the only currency that people could get their hands on to pay the bills.

Vast plantation acres were turned over to the freedmen and anyone else who would farm as tenant or sharecropper. Before a crop could be made, credit had to be extended to landowners for the year's supplies and from the landowners to the workers to tide them over. All became beholden to the merchants who became beholden to the bankers. This whole system of interdependency became legally sanctioned by a series of state lien laws.

Between 1865 and 1900, in their struggle to make ends meet, these once-proud people became bent over, their backs to the sun. The image of slave cotton pickers still bearing their cotton crosses comes to mind. Only now the faces weren't all black, but white too. And the burn of the sun on those white backs made "rednecks" of many of them. Then too, many of them were not bent over the boll but over the spindle. And there were children among them, in field and factory, doing a man's work for a child's pay. The children's and women's faces bore the same furrows, the same glazed look and sullen signs of strain as the men's, only their sallow complexions could not be

An early morning in late autumn is pictured here. It was a time when the cotton was full for the picking. Courtesy, I. Schiffman & Co.

hidden behind ill-kept beards and whiskers. Hands rough and feet bare, the women and children became the mainstay of the mill villages, their smaller hands being quicker and their voices less strident against meager wages and harsh working conditions.

A popular immigrant's guide published in 1878, Berney's *Hand-Book of Alabama,* reflects the thinking of the day on the subject of women and child labor:

It is a sight to gratify any philanthropist, to see eighty or a hundred comfortably dressed, well fed, cheerful young people of both sexes engaged in their daily duties, bright, cheerful, good tempered, orderly, obedient young folks, as they pass rapidly among their exquisite machines, sometimes singing in concert, and content—the very people who have had all their lives long nothing to do!

The Alabama leader of the Knights of Labor, Nicholas Byrne Stack, surveyed working conditions in 1887 and found that "boys between six and thirteen years of age were working in the Huntsville Cotton Factory for eight cents a day." He further reported in the Alabama *Sentinel* that women and children were working there "from eleven and a half to thirteen

Loom workers at Dallas Mills are pictured around 1900. In 1892-1893 these men were paid an average daily wage of 68 cents for working an average 10.65 hour day. Courtesy, Huntsville-Madison County Public Library

hours a day." The Huntsville *Independent* that same year observed that the factory "employs one hundred boys and girls who would otherwise be out of employment."

In that day, among people who had not known the relaxation of earned leisure but rather the sloth of despondency, childhood was not a time of play, but rather of work. Youngsters accepted their work roles as automatically as today's youth accept their student roles. Indeed, the acquisition of skills and the building of community among a poor white people long deprived of education and advancement opened to young workers possibilities yet undreamed. For them Monte Sano with its magnificent hotel, as though encased in the morning fog, was just beginning to break through the mist. Its heights, though dimly seen, could be reached.

New industries were breathing life into the county's prostrate postwar economy. The coming of the Nashville, Chattanooga, and St. Louis Railway in 1887 was important, but until well into the 20th century progress was marked by a series of ups and downs. National monetary policy—the repudiation of the Confederate debt, resumption of inflationary greenbacks on a par with gold, tamperings with the monetization, and demonetization of silver—brought on a pervasive deflation worsened by the panics and depressions of 1873 and 1893.

Poor whites from the outlying hills and blacks from the surrounding fields flocked to Huntsville in search of work. As private businesses got on their feet, the whites were absorbed into the work force. Blacks looked to the United States government and to the Republican party for help.

With its Federal military encampment, its Freedmen's Bureau

Mill villages were generally self-contained entities with the workers' housing built and maintained by the mill owners. In West Huntsville the Merrimack Manufacturing Company also provided a playground for children. Courtesy, H.E. Monroe, Sr.

and school, plus its Freedmen's Savings Bank, Huntsville was attractive to freedmen and to black troops mustered out of Union service in the 1860s and 1870s. This massing of unemployed and uprooted population was viewed as a threat to the stability of the community. When the Pittsburgh Freedmen's Aid Society tried to build a black normal school in the city, Willis Winston Garth wrote to Governor Robert M. Patton in August of 1866 pointing out that Huntsville's population was already half black and that the proposed normal school would bring in thousands more blacks, spoiling the city's "high character" and resulting in "pandemonium."

In 1868 the area's Ku Klux Klan, in an effort to quell Radical Republican rabble-rousing among the city's freedmen, gathered just outside of the town 150 strong—mounted, clad in masks and sheets, and fully armed. Silently they paraded into town with backs straight and eyes fearlessly set and surrounded the square where a Republican rally was taking place. Panic ensued, blood was shed, and Athens Judge Silas Thurlow, referred to by "scalawag" Nicholas Davis as a "carpetbagger," was mortally wounded by a stray bullet. The Klansmen never raised a hand, but stood silent sentinel to the "pandemonium." Cause and effect blurred together, as blacks and whites vied for the balance of power in the city. Concentrated in ghettos such as "Georgia" and "Jonesville," blacks without employment were pushed back into peonage on the land.

In an effort to come to grips with their plight, black and white farm laborers were encouraged to recognize their common need and to organize. In 1874 the former slave of David C. Humphreys and Republican party spokesman William Hooper Councill, assisted by the silver-tongued "scalawag" attorney Nicholas Davis, started the Madison County branch of the Labor Union of the State of Alabama. The union sought to secure lower land rents, individual or cooperative land purchase, higher wages, prompt payment of wages, and a better bargaining position for workers whose alternative was emigration to another state such as Mississippi. The executive committee was composed of Councill and Davis along with Augustus W. McCullough, a schoolteaching carpetbagger with staying power who made the transition from bagger to community builder; William Gaston, a black educator and minister who served as assistant pastor of Saint Bartley Primitive Baptist Church for 35 years; and Sandy Bynum, a black livery driver and popular but controversial Radical Republican who was shot down by a white radical at a political rally in 1882. Neither the union nor the executive committee could be held together, as political and racial passions overrode economic interest.

Since deflation and low prices for cotton continued to hamper farmers, they rallied in 1878 to elect to Congress William M. Lowe, maverick Democrat-turned-Independent-turned-Greenbacker who was more sympathetic to black and farmer needs than Willis Winston Garth, the Conservative Democrat. Lowe's election, unique in the state, loosened the grip of the Huntsville Democrats on the electorate and sent them courting black votes in 1880, offering a marriage that lasted for over 20 years. The city's third and fourth ward became the electoral bailiwick of the city's black Republicans. Fusion politics brought greater opportunity for blacks, and a small but solid middle class emerged to provide leadership.

Chief among the leaders of the black community were three brothers-in-law, Daniel Shadrack Brandon, Henry Claxton Binford, and Charles Hendley, Jr. The three were teachers and Republican spokesmen. Hendley edited the influential Republican newspaper, the Huntsville *Gazette,* and played a mean game of chess with a circle of white friends. Binford, who often passed as white, was a steady contributor to the paper, writing under the pseudonym of "Jack Daw." Brandon served as the principal of Rust Normal Institute and then of the city's "colored" school. In a class all by himself was the town's only black physician, Dr. Burgess E. Scruggs, a skilled and highly successful practitioner loved by both the black and white communities. Samuel R. Lowery was probably the most eccentric and widely-traveled of the group. A prize-winning silkworm culturist, Lowery was among the first black attorneys in American history to be admitted to practice before the United States Supreme Court. Then there was William Hooper Councill, principal of the State Normal School, who was also an attorney, Methodist minister, classicist, author, orator, and the editor of the Democratic *Herald.* Black aldermen included Thomas W. Townsend, Nelson Hendley, Burgess E. Scruggs, William H. Gaston, Charles Ware, Lucien Jones, Daniel S. Brandon, and Henry Claxton Binford.

The *Gazette* summed up the status of the black middle class:

The state of Alabama is ten years behind Madison county...Cultured Madison is trying to let justice and fair play regulate the Negro question...peaceful and friendly relations exist...In Madison the Negro is accorded representation in the jury box, while in its county seat, Huntsville, he is found on the police force, in the city council, largely makes up the city employees and is generally treated by capitalists, merchants, business men, officials, with consideration and respect.

Dr. Burgess Scruggs was born a slave shortly before the Civil War. He received his early education in Huntsville and attended medical school in Nashville. After graduation he returned to his hometown to practice medicine and served a number of years on the board of aldermen. Courtesy, E.C. Smartt

When Daniel Brandon
(shown here) and Thomas
Townsend were elected
aldermen in 1880, they
became the first blacks to
serve on that board. Blacks
were well represented in
municipal affairs until 1901,
when a new state
constitution disenfranchised
many of them. Courtesy,
E.C. Smartt

The paper gave ample evidence of the richness and variety of black culture in Huntsville. Masonic and fraternal lodges flourished, as did religious and social organizations. A thorough study of the newspaper and the black community in the 1880-1900 period was done by Marguerite Dobbins Lacey in 1963. She leaves no doubt that from the volunteer firemen to the presidentially appointed "receivers of public moneys," blacks were in the thick of things during this era.

Ironically out of tune with his fellow blacks by 1878, William Hooper Councill had made some compromises in the politically tumultuous 1870s that were to cost him the support of many in his own black community. Having been the popular though unsuccessful Republican candidate for the legislature in 1874, the year the Democrats swept back into power, Councill, largely self-educated though an experienced schoolteacher, was selected by the Democrat-controlled board of trustees to be principal of the Huntsville State Normal School for Negroes. A normal school had been originally mandated by a Republican legislature in 1871, and was run by the Northern Methodist Freedmen's Aid Society, which had built Rust School on Franklin Street in 1869. The Democratic board did not acknowledge Rust as the State Normal since the act of 1874 repealed the 1871 legislation.

After his appointment as principal, Councill continued to speak up for Republican causes, seemingly unaware of the political sensitivity of his position. This did not sit well with his Democratic board and he was passed over in 1876, when a white local ex-Confederate hero, James McClung Robinson, received the

Henry Claxton Binford, a
late 19th century black
leader in Huntsville, posed
in the 1890s with his
handsome family. Courtesy,
Mr. and Mrs. Elmer C.
Binford

The North Alabama Improvement Company built the Monte Sano Hotel to attract to Huntsville wealthy men who would then invest in local businesses or move their families there. Beset with financial problems, the hotel was abandoned about 1900 and became a private residence until it was razed in the 1940s. Today only a portion of its chimney stands. Courtesy, Huntsville-Madison County Public Library

appointment in his place. To save his school and his position as principal, Councill in 1877 voted Democratic and won reappointment. By 1880, when the Greenback threat made local Democrats more conciliatory toward black Republicans, Councill was already marching to a different tune. From 1878 until he died Councill considered himself a Democrat, becoming one of the South's leading black party spokesmen. He was especially instrumental in the campaigns of Gen. Joseph E. Wheeler, who replaced William Lowe in the United States Congress in 1882.

As Democrats or Republicans, the black middle class, composed of former house servants or free blacks, modeled its society after that of the former slaveholders, whose names and fortunes they sometimes shared. For them Monte Sano and its grand hotel was within reach. But for the mass of blacks, the mountain represented an isolated, snake-infested, and ghost-stalked no-man's-land, where whites went to avoid summer's heat and diseases and blacks were brought along to do the work.

Cliche though it be, a city is often judged by its buildings. In the case of Huntsville there are few better ways to glean the values and motivations of so complex a community. Throughout its history no other buildings constructed with private capital have been able to compare in importance with Huntsville's inns and hotels. The Monte Sano was the most brilliant, but there were other fine hotels. At every stage of the town's growth, its citizens saw to it that visitors were welcome and provided for handsomely.

This graciousness to strangers, especially Yankees, was sorely tested by the Civil War. The animosities and losses of war aggravated by subsequent issues of race and grinding postwar poverty created in many Southerners, including inhabitants of Madison County, a paranoid style best expressed by the shibboleth of another hemisphere and era: "Yankee Go Home!" In 1865 a stunned group of citizens met and proclaimed to the world that Huntsville was off-limits to Yankees. But by the next year, the local press and public-spirited citizens tried to open the doors of their city, even if they could not pry open the arms of its citizens. As time went by and pride gave way to necessity, the struggle for survival forced open those clenched fists. Once-tightened arms were opened wide in welcome to Northerners— if they came bearing talents or gifts. Those arriving empty-handed or armed with Bibles, books, or political broadsides were called carpetbaggers and were given a decidedly cold shoulder.

Local author Norah Davis chose to write her first novel about an outsider in her scathing book, *The Northerner,* published in 1905. Using Adairville, a thinly disguised Huntsville as its setting, she explores the ramifications of the central character's treatment at the hands of the local gentry and the town roughs. His social equals and business associates conspire against him, and the town roughs are out to get him and his "nigger" because he fired an incompetent white man as driver for his newly acquired electric streetcar line and replaced him with a black man. The stereotypical representation of the old order is Mrs. Eldridge-Jones, a caricature of Virginia Clay-Clopton and her outspoken social leadership. Unlike the real Mrs. Clay-Clopton, Mrs. Eldridge-Jones is hollow sounding and pompously tedious, as the following conversation with Hugh Watson verifies:

"An electric light man! Waltzing here—with Jack Adair's daughter? What—what are we coming to!"...

"Why, even befo' the wah men were associated in business with others of quite a different stamp...But this 'new element,' as it calls itself! Never...will my doors open to one of them!"

"Are we never to grow any, Mrs. Jones? Never learn to forget?"

"Never!"...The question with me is how does the admission of these people constitute growth? To me it seems dissolution— disintegration! We do not really assimilate them; and the result is conflict—friction; where if we merely decline to admit them—go our way—let them go theirs!"

"The men are bad enough, but the women!...No, no Hugh, no introductions for me!"

The long-standing issue of Southern hospitality versus hostility

Born in North Carolina in 1848, William H. Councill was brought to Alabama by slave traders in 1857. Largely self-taught, he was instrumental in the establishment of Alabama A & M University. Before his death in 1909, Dr. Councill traveled to Europe and met with British Prime Minister Gladstone and King Leopold of Belgium. Courtesy, E.C. Smartt

The grandchildren of Henry Claxton Binford at tea, circa 1900. Courtesy, Huntsville Madison County Public Library

As newly elected president of the Huntsville Female College, Dr. Amos B. Jones arrived in Huntsville in 1880 with only $60 in assets and $200 in debt. He did so well, however, that in seven years he was able to purchase the college. After the school burned, he established Jones College for Women near Gadsden. Courtesy, Huntsville-Madison County Public Library

received congressional attention, as a subcommittee investigated alleged Ku Klux Klan outrages in Huntsville in October 1871. The testimony of Milton Moss, who with his wife Jessie M. Moss and Mr. William Fletcher Heikes established Madison County's first and for some time largest nursery business, Huntsville Nurseries, supports Norah Davis' interpretation of her hometown:

Q. Do you find yourself in any way slighted by the native population of Alabama on account of being a northern man?

A. They did slight us a good deal; I didn't feel it so much, because I was around all the while; but the women folks did. The first settlement we settled in was not a good neighborhood. We have got into a very good neighborhood now, and I don't know but that we are used as well as anybody.

Q. What did the women complain of?

A. Nobody would come to see them; nobody at all.

Q. Because they were from the North?

A. Yes, sir.

Q. That social proscription has passed away, you think?

A. Yes, sir...These people here had lived here so long together, and not had any emigration, that when a stranger came among them it was to them like going to the circus. When I first came here I drove my own team. I thought I could drive it as well as any negro, and sometimes I would have two or three negroes in the wagon behind but I should have been on a horse riding before or beside and had the negroes in the wagon behind; that would have been the style. So when I would drive my team in this way, the people would turn around as they passed and gawk at me like I was circus. Now they are all driving their own teams themselves.

Some visitors to Huntsville ended up wishing they had not come, as was the case with a widely sought forgery ring. Having operated "from the Pacific coast across the country to New York and Boston, down through Virginia and Tennessee," in December of 1892 two members arrived in Huntsville. Checking into the Huntsville Hotel, the city sister of the Monte Sano Hotel, the two men aroused the suspicions of an alert hotel manager who notified Police Chief Zebulon P. Davis. Davis then informed the local banks to be on the lookout and within hours, the erstwhile visitors were arrested across the street at the Farmers and Merchants National Bank after having attempted to cash a draft on a Tacoma, Washington, bank for $235. Thanks to swift telegraphy, other members of the gang were apprehended after they had fled from New Orleans to Mobile.

While it was decidedly unhealthy for the forgery gang to visit Huntsville, the city gained a wide reputation as a health resort, thanks to Monte Sano. The United States Army listed it as the second healthiest installation to West Point and placed troops in summer encampments up on the mountain in the 1890s. During the Spanish-American War, as many as 14,000 troops were stationed in and scattered all around Huntsville. The effort by members of the Chamber of Commerce to secure a permanent military post to augment the growing use of the city for summer encampments was defeated. William S. Wells, the chamber's representative, had the rug pulled out from beneath him when the War Department informed him of receipt of "a petition signed by a number of Huntsville citizens begging that no more troops be sent here."

What at first glance was taken as a residual reluctance to accept the soldiers was more likely the offshoot of three seemingly unrelated movements: fundamentalism, temperance, and public health. Military populations with their attendant social peculiarities pitted the wages of sin and Uncle Sam against a

Construction began on the four-story section of the Huntsville Hotel in 1857. The North Alabama Improvement Company modernized the hotel and added the three-story section in 1887. It burned in 1910; the following year the remainder of the block also was destroyed by fire. Courtesy, Huntsville Madison County Public Library

The Huntsville Female College, organized as a Methodist school, was designed by George Steele and erected on the north side of Randolph Street in the early 1850s. The imposing structure was destroyed by fire in 1895 and never rebuilt. Courtesy, Huntsville-Madison County Public Library

home mix of Victorian and fundamentalist morality. It was at long last being discovered that some men had been putting women up on pedestals just as much to take a peek at their ankles as to sing their praises, and that the deep swoon of the Southern lady in the late afternoon's sunset was in some cases the natural result of an opium overdose brought on by naive consumption of socially permissible patent medicines and remedies.

In Huntsville, as elsewhere, the cures for drug and alcohol addiction, like those for common illnesses, were often more deadly than the diseases themselves. The *Weekly Mercury* praised the local Hagey Hospital incorporated in 1892 to treat addictions. Its heralded cure was bichloride of gold. The local press applauded the cure, but the Madison County Medical Association suspended the practicing physician, Dr. Pierre Lawrence Brouillette, for "unprofessional practice."

The Madison County Medical Association and two Huntsville visitors at widely separate times packed a three-pronged punch against sin, addiction, and disease. In 1885 the fiery Sam Jones, evangelist extraordinaire, drew the following press comment: "On Wednesday night the most remarkable event that ever occurred in the history of Huntsville took place at the Methodist Church: From one thousand to twelve hundred men bending their knees before the altar of God." In 1902 fiesty, hatchet-swinging Carrie

Nation came to town and rekindled the prohibitionist enthusiasm of residents and members of the Women's Christian Temperance Union. And, thanks to the extended efforts of contractor and builder James M. Hutchens and his sons, William and Charles, the upgraded sewage and water systems enhanced the health of the city and made water a more acceptable substitute for tonics and spirits.

In the 1880s and 1890s a growing number of citizens had leisure and could afford the better things in life. For them the Monte Sano Hotel was a sign that Huntsville was prospering. Wealth and display always tastefully manifested would again be highlighted by bold investment and architecture. The city that the Brandons and the Steeles had fashioned was to be further enhanced by the Victorian cottages and public buildings of architects Herbert Cowell, Edgar Lee Love, and H.D. Breeding, as well as by John Rea, the hotel's designer.

Harkening back to its antebellum beginnings the city raised itself up holding fast to cotton, commerce, banking, and textiles, the cornerstones of the community's economy. The center of business activity was still the courthouse square. On Saturdays, especially in cotton season, it was jam-packed with bales, buggies, and bystanders. A favorite sport of the young boys was to bale hop as far as possible around the square without touching the ground.

The electric street railway, replacing its horse-drawn predecessor, was built in tandem with the Merrimack Mill in 1899, although the first streetcar did not appear until 1901. It promised to upset the ecology of the old square. The iron fence

Tracy W. Pratt provided the capital to construct Huntsville's streetcar system in 1899. Because the streetcar enabled workers to live farther distances from their places of employment, huge tracts of land were opened up for residential development, and the suburb as we know it today came into being. Courtesy, Huntsville-Madison County Public Library

Lewis Brockway, a Monrovia farmer, was also a Watkins salesman, selling his home remedies and seasonings door-to-door to county residents. For those some distance from a store, the availability of mail order and the presence of traveling salesmen were invaluable. Courtesy, Mrs. Gorden Darnell

around the courtyard had been used for years as a hitching post, providing the modern equivalent of easy access parking. People were torn between the excitement of the trolley and the comfort of their old horse or mule. Fortunately for the health of the city the iron horse carried the day. Far less refuse than had been seeping down into the spring water flowing beneath the square would find its way there again.

Those trolley tracks did not come easily for Huntsville. They marked the end of a long trail forged by statesmen, entrepreneurs, industrialists, financiers, and hard-working businessmen. Norah Davis' character Hugh Watson, the Southerner in *The Northerner,* advised Mrs. Eldridge-Jones:

Tut, Mrs. Jones, bury your old squirrel gun! "Weep no more, my lady, weep no more!" Accept the inevitable with the courage with which you accepted the war. Retaliate upon the past by the conquest of the future. We are coming out ahead in this new war of capital!

Judge Adair, the town's most mature voice of reason who lived in a home much like the Pope home and after whom the fictional town was named, bore a strong resemblance to Pope's grandson, Leroy Pope Walker. Walker embodied the continuity of responsible statesmanship when he chaired the state constitutional convention of 1875 much as his father, John Williams Walker, had chaired the state's first such convention in Huntsville in 1819.

Walker knew that only bold leadership in and out of politics was going to pull his valley out of the doldrums of defeat and the depression of 1873. His speech to the citizens, delivered at Madison, Alabama, on June 27, 1878, deserves a place in New South literature beside the writings of Henry W. Grady.

Walker compared the seven southern states with seven northern states in terms of population, square miles, patents granted, factories, laborers, capital invested, annual wages, and the annual value of products. The statistics were unevenly balanced in favor of the North. Walker argued that the statistics were so uneven because the South had always depended on "corn and cotton—cotton and corn." Claiming the right to speak up frankly because Alabama was his "native land," Walker urged his fellow countians to:

Give to the mechanic arts their due place in the roll-call of honorable pursuits. Make all labor respectable by honoring the true worker in every vocation...No people yet were truly great who had but one industry, for it is the cultivation of but a single faculty...Our plodding pursuit of agriculture has reduced it to an established system of never corrected blunders. The ways of our fathers are the ways of their children.

...We delve and dig, and plow and hoe...when all the inventive forces lie obedient to our command, much as our fore-fathers delved and dug, and plowed and hoed a century ago.

Of all the States of the Union, Alabama is the richest in manufacturing capabilities...But they are dead agencies until human hands put them in motion...The man who manufactures cotton is the friend and not the foe of the man who raises it...It is in this way, and not otherwise, that our people can recover

The Clay family posed in front of their Eustis Street residence. J. Withers Clay (not pictured) edited the Huntsville Democrat for about 30 years until a severe cerebral hemorrhage forced his retirement. His daughters Susannah and Virginia (on steps left and right) assumed the editorship for 35 years until the newspaper's demise. Courtesy, Huntsville-Madison County Public Library

their lost prosperity.

The textile manufacturing potential of Huntsville received steady boosting from Southern nationalist and white supremist J. Withers Clay, editor of the *Democrat.* Writing in early 1875, Clay complained that he had "tried, for twenty or more years, to induce our people to build cotton and other factories, and our efforts have proved futile." In 1881 Clay took editorial lead in fostering the labors of Mississippian D.L. Love to organize the city's first cotton mill, called Huntsville Cotton Mill. Traveling throughout the East, Love aroused interest in Huntsville, found subscribers for capital stock, and most importantly secured the services of Joshua Coons whose expertise was crucial to the success of the town's maiden mill. With Love beating the bushes and Coons in command, Mayor Thomas W. White and the city aldermen passed a 10-year tax exemption that set a precedent followed by other city councils. The factory represented a citizen effort to industrialize, and it served the primary need of the area, providing a market for cotton.

While the fortunes of the factory continued to prosper, such was not the case for its organizing genius. Apparently in his gallivanting about the country, Love fell in love with the young Ada E. Johnson of Huntsville. But following the demands of a busy travel schedule, Love did not press his suit in time. The *Democrat* on September 21, 1881, announced the marriage of Miss Ada E. Johnson, daughter of Mrs. E.K. Johnson, to Mr. John F. Lanier of Madison County. The paper further commented: "The Huntsville public were greatly surprised that Miss Ada, whose heart and hand had been sought by so many suitors, had, at last been bestowed on Mr. Lanier." None was more surprised than Mr. Love who, when he heard of the marriage, lost all sense of proportion or propriety and sought to revenge his loss by besmirching her character. So foul were his accusations that the young husband did what honorable young men of breeding were expected to do in such cases. He went to Greenville, Mississippi, and killed D.L. Love.

Defended by Huntsville's superb attorney Capt. Milton Humes, young Lanier was completely exonerated. The judge in the case announced from the bench: "It is. . .my opinion that he did just what I or any other man of honor would do, and I, therefore, discharge the prisoner, and bid him go hence without delay."

Love's labours were not lost, however, as the efforts of two other outsiders, the O'Shaughnessy brothers, mobilized citizens into action. When Michael and James F. came to town, Huntsville had at last found men and money to match her glorious

Michael O'Shaughnessy posed at his estate, now called Kildare, off Meridian Street. Like many entrepreneurs of the 19th century, O'Shaughnessy grew restless with Huntsville and moved away, but it was his vision and savoir faire that transformed the city into a successful textile center. Courtesy, James F. Reeves

mountain. Their Irish gusto could no more be constrained by a businessman's caution than their dreams could be limited to one place. Theirs was not a rags-to-riches Horatio Alger story so popular then, as their father had acquired a fortune before them in America and their proud Celtic heritage had been long rooted in Ireland's landed gentry. Using their father's Cincinnati commission house as a base, the brothers expanded their entrepreneurial skills during the Civil War and made Nashville an early center for a postwar commission business. Though they had served the Union, they were never called carpetbaggers. There wasn't a carpetbag made that could hold all of their deeds and securities.

In Nashville the brothers built one of the South's first cottonseed oil factories. They came to Huntsville in 1881 to build another, and they came often enough to help build a town. From the lowly cottonseed the brothers forged a mighty cottonseed oil kingdom, including a trust combining the operations of the Alabama Oil Mill at Montgomery, the Central Oil Mill at Selma, the Demopolis Oil Mill, Gulf City Oil Mills at Mobile, the Montgomery Oil Works, the Eufaula Oil Mill, the Mitchells Oil Mill at Mitchell Station, and Union Springs Oil Mill with the Huntsville Oil Mill. Michael managed these while his brother, James, oversaw a cotton refinery in Brooklyn and arranged shipments of cottonseed oil products to European markets.

It was not simply Huntsville's business potential that had caught their eye, but also the beauty of the place and the quality of the people. There was still a coterie that maintained the cultural level of the brilliant antebellum days. When Michael built "Kildare," he had his prize-winning foxhounds and his fine stable of horses brought in so that he could more fully enjoy the sport and the company of the chase—a tradition kept alive by Harry M. Rhett and members of the Moreland Hunt. Together the brothers took the lead in forming the North Alabama Improvement Company, a community-based corporation organized to develop the real estate, mineral, and transportation resources of the area. The company served many of the same functions of promotion and advertising that a later Board of Trade (1892) and Chamber of Commerce (1894) would do.

Among the notable achievements of the company was bringing the Dallas Mills to the plain below and the Monte Sano Hotel to the mountain beyond. Principal stockholders of the mills were Trevanion B. Dallas and Godfrey M. Fogg, both of Nashville. The Millikins of New York were also major stockholders. Land around the mill was developed by another stockholder, Oscar Goldsmith. Called Lawrence, the development consisted of double houses and

ANNIVERSARY
OF THE
CHAMBER OF COMMERCE!
TO-NIGHT!

The Chamber of Commerce is one year old to-night. Since its organization, one thousand people have been added to our city. During the next year we want to add two thousand more, and establish a canning factory, a wagon factory, a cheese factory, another cotton factory, an electric street car line and five hundred more thrifty farmers to our county.

Come to the Court House

TO-NIGHT!

at 7:30, and hear some reports of the progress made. If you want to hear the report of the committee on AMENDED CITY CHARTER, come early for the rooms will be crowded. The humble and the honored are alike invited.

"Let him that heareth, say come."

R. E. PETTUS, Pres.

A broadside such as this one, dating from 1895, typifies the effusive spirit that seized Huntsville once Northern dollars began to boost the sagging Southern economy. Courtesy, Huntsville Madison County Public Library

79

The Dallas Mills was chartered "to manufacture cotton and woolen goods and fabrics from raw materials preparing the same for market by dying (and) bleaching." Its principal product, however, appears to have been cotton sheeting, which was actually processed elsewhere. Courtesy, Linda Allen

lots for business or residence. It was primarily a residential area intended for mill workers.

The North Alabama Improvement Company counted on the great wealth of the O'Shaughnessys and on James F.'s vast business connections from his New York City home base to keep the company going. The expenses of building the Monte Sano Hotel, and performing a costly renovation on the Huntsville Hotel, plus giving land for the Dallas Mills and a lot on Monte Sano to T.B. Dallas, in addition to maintaining company operations, were greater than expected. Local stock subscriptions did not produce sufficient capital, and the company looked increasingly to O'Shaughnessy to either foot the bills or better yet find some capitalists who could.

James O'Shaughnessy was an empire builder, a man of extraordinary vision, nerve, and bad luck. He sank a fortune into creating a trade empire that all hinged on the digging of a Nicaraguan canal. Besides inducing the government of Nicaragua to sell him the franchise to build the canal, he also invested heavily in developing two seaport towns, Pensacola, Florida, and Brunswick, Georgia, through which goods would be transported by his railroad lines to Saint Louis and Cincinnati via Huntsville. A costly Camelot, the canal company alone was capitalized at $60 million. By 1891 more than $6 million had been spent on the canal and the end was nowhere in sight. An appeal to Congress for $100 million was thwarted despite the efforts of Alabama Senator John Tyler Morgan. Work on the canal stopped. James O'Shaughnessy's Irish green had turned to red, as his dreams of empire faded.

One can only speculate what might have been the future had O'Shaughnessy's Nicaraguan canal materialized or had the North West Land Association not been standing in the wings to bail out

ALL OUT FOR HUNTSVILLE

O'Shaughnessy and the North Alabama Improvement Company and keep Huntsville on the road to recovery. In what was hailed as a $6 million transaction, the North Western Land Association upped its capitalization to reflect its new worth, and the following land changed hands:

> *Five lots in Viduta, on Monte Sano; also the following schedule of properties: Five and a half acres of land near Dallas factory, the William R. Patton tract on Meridianville pike; the old Garth place of 138 acres on Athens pike; ten acres of land in section 20; sixty-eight acres in T3,RIW; the Isham Watkins place on Athens pike; Alum Spring and three and a half acres of land surrounding, on Monte Sano; the Huntsville Opera House; the Huntsville Hotel and block; 285 acres in East Huntsville; eleven and a half acres—the Sarah Scruggs place on Pulaski pike; the J.W. Scruggs place on Athens pike; thirty acres in Sec. 28,T3,R1E; the John Robinson place, containing ninety acres, on Meridianville pike; the J.B. White tract of land between Elora depot and Pulaski road and twenty-one and a half acres on Monte Sano. M.J. and J.F. O'Shaughnessy and wives to the northwestern Land Association, land in city near Elora Tennessee depot, $20,000.*

The courthouse was forced to hire an extra hand to keep up with all the copywork. On the day of the North Western Land Association's takeover, as though marking the transfer of the balance of power from old times to newcomers, the *Mercury* wrote, "Huntsville is no longer the city of the past, but a city that lives in the future."

There would be legal skirmishes and court battles and the beautiful hotel on the mountain would go into receivership and not open for two seasons. But somehow that didn't matter as much any more. Men could move mountains. An amiable capitalist coup had taken place: no blood or bullets, only bloated indebtedness, breakup, and the promised rescue had occurred. Huntsville, the Camelot of the O'Shaughnessy brothers, became the fiefdom of Huntsville's new barons of business Tracy W. Pratt, William S. Wells, William I. Wellman, and James A. Ward, with further infusions of capital from the Mayo brothers and T. Coleman du Pont of the du Pont dynasty.

Local historian Patricia Ryan in her aptly titled monograph, "Northern Dollars for Huntsville Spindles," keenly observes "not only did these men seek economic opportunities in Huntsville, but Wells, Wellman, and Pratt made this their permanent place of residence." It was "this troika, notably Pratt," she maintains, "who primarily set Huntsville's course for the next fifty years."

Tracy Wilder Pratt, a transplanted South Dakotan, moved to Huntsville in the 1890s. His 1928 obituary describes his influence: "It is generally agreed that he was responsible for more of the major industries locating in Huntsville than any other man who ever resided here, and he was often called 'Huntsville's First Citizen.' He was a member of and identified with practically every civic, social, fraternal, patriotic, and business organization in Huntsville." Courtesy, Mrs. John H. Wallace III

CHAPTER V

"Great Is The Power of Cash"

The city of Huntsville is one of the most progressive cities in the South. Her commercial enterprises, the foundation of any city's life, are large and varied. The educational advantages are well abreast of the commercial and industrial activities, and the religious and social life of the beautiful old town are all that the most fastidious could possibly desire.

Huntsville is the seat of Madison County, and is in the heart of the famous and beautiful Tennessee Valley, surrounded by a large and fertile agricultural, cotton, fruit and stock raising country, making it the most important commercial center of the entire valley territory. As a cotton manufacturing point Huntsville is today without a rival in the South.
—Chamber of Commerce brochure, 1919.

South Side Square was called Commercial Row in the 19th century due to the number of small retail shops that comprised the block. Like much of the downtown, the shops have now been replaced with professional offices.
Courtesy, Huntsville-Madison County Public Library

Until Memorial Parkway was completed in 1955, Huntsville's courthouse square was the center of town and served as the stage for a large part of Huntsville's happenings. The four sides composing the square provided the backdrop for scenes played in the continuing drama of small-town life. Over the years the courthouse has been changed three times. With the exception of Regions Bank, the blocks facing the courthouse have changed many more times. Standing on the courthouse steps and looking south at Commercial Row, one can see the layering of history on the building facade across the street. Harrison's Hardware catches the eye and carries one back to the turn of the century. Closer scrutiny reveals a burned out section down from Harrison's barely seen behind the free-standing face. It is a stark reminder of historic Huntsville's greatest menace—fire. Yet

through fire and water and several changes of face, that particular composite of bricks still stands. High above the modern street-level law offices tastefully dressed in their rich browns and Brooks Brothers decors, a faded-out collage-like sign obviously painted a long time ago in bold letters still can be seen spread across those old bricks. It proclaims "Great Is the Power of Cash." Old-timers may swear that they can see it all, so seared into their psyche has it become. Visitors may not notice it at all. Yet one who makes Huntsville home will come to perceive it, all or in part.

The industrial/technological revolution that swept America via the rails of the late 19th century and the roads of the early 20th century introduced the South to a plethora of new products and gadgets, not to mention labor-saving devices. But that same

The Historic Huntsville Foundation's purchase of Harrison Hardware, the famed hardware store on the square, assures Huntsvillians that nostalgia for the "good ole days" can be sustained. Courtesy, Malcolm Tarkington

The burning of the Huntsville Hotel in 1910 left Huntsville with a serious shortage of tourist accommodations. A few years later, the Twickenham Hotel opened and advertised itself as being fireproof, perhaps to allay ever-present fears concerning fires. Courtesy, Huntsville-Madison County Public Library

revolution did not solve the South's money problem. It was tied to an old-fashioned system of credit dictated by the seasonal and always arbitrary demands of a single-crop economy.

T.T. Terry's sign "Great is the Power of Cash" overlooking the square was a sermon, a voice in the Southern wilderness that called men to live within their means and to spend the money in their pockets, not the credit they banked on throughout the year. With the ushering in of the mill-village, textile-manufacturing era, the local dependency on a single-crop economy grew greater. Cotton was no longer a king but a tyrant. Factory doors,

warehouse ramps, gins and compresses all opened and shut, expanded or contracted their business according to the price of cotton per pound. Economic diversification and the growth of trades and services usually associated with industrialization did not occur in Huntsville. If tenant farmers and sharecroppers didn't have money to spend on a Saturday, neither did the mill workers. The cash workers received was said to be just enough for a worker to spend in town on Saturday and be hard pressed enough to show up for work again on Monday.

The lesson of Henry Ford—that workers had to be paid a decent enough wage to pay the bills and "afford a Ford"—never spread to the Southern textile industry. When he first went into textiles in 1892, a progressive businessman from South Dakota, Tracy Pratt, gave the workers in his West Huntsville cotton mill

an unsolicited raise in order to increase morale and production. It
worked. But he was a David trying to slay a Goliath. The push
to bring New England manufacturers South made so much sense
that few people analyzed it. Southern boosters reasoned that
home-grown cotton manufactured in home-owned factories was
bound to be cheaper to produce since the transportation costs
were eliminated or reduced substantially. And everyone knew that
Southern labor was considerably lower-paid. So cheaper cloth
could be produced more cheaply in the South. But since wages
were kept low and dividends were paid to growing numbers of
Yankee stockholders, the host economy did not substantially
benefit from the wealth created.

A Capt. T. Wilkes, who came to Huntsville in 1904 for an
extended visit, wrote a series of letters back to his hometown

The employees of Merrimack Mills are shown at a picnic during the 1920s. At times the company chartered railroad cars for an outing at Bell Factory or Three Forks of Flint. Courtesy, Huntsville-Madison County Public Library

newspaper, the *Republican* of Shelbyville, Indiana. Not all of his comments were flattering, but most seem close to the mark. "There is lots of the old yearly credit and advance system here, eight per cent interest," he wrote, "and the man who gets the credit or advance is practically a slave." Getting to the heart of the matter, he added, "the farmer as well as the laboring man comes in competition with the cheap negro, who lives on cornbread and bacon." He added, however, that they "all meet on a common level around the old court-house and sell what they raise." "The greatest trouble," he wryly commented, "is too many producers and not enough consumers." He was not altogether complimentary about the mill villages either, as he considered some of the housing as substandard, and he felt that "the employees work for low wages so they cannot buy much." He observed that unskilled laborers in one mill were paid 60 cents per day, and this did not include housing or other benefits.

A survey of cotton prices per pound over the decades in which the county became the state's cotton mill center as well as the leading cotton producer goes like this: between 1890 and 1910 the lowest price received was 4 cents in 1894 and the highest was 13 cents in 1910. The bottom fell out in 1914 when the price fell back to 7 cents, but the First World War lifted prices to new highs, 27 cents in 1916 shooting up to 35 cents in 1919. Then came the postwar slump down to 15 cents in 1920. In the 1920s the price bounced up and down beginning with 17 cents in 1921, then went up to 28 cents before falling down again to 12 cents in

A gala 21st birthday celebration was held in 1906 for Robert D. Lowenthal at the residence of H.J. Lowenthal at Franklin and Williams streets. Among the party goers were (clockwise): Harry J. Weil, Leo Damson, Leo P. Cohen, Ike Shiffman, Fred Wright, Aaron Metzger, Henry J. Lowenthal, Robert Lowenthal, Joe Landauer, L.B. Goldsmith, Sam Weil, Mortimer W. Weil, and George Heyman. Courtesy, Mr. and Mrs. Lawrence Goldsmith, Jr.

1926. A rebound in 1927 brought the price up to 20 cents, but in 1929 prices were on their way down again. In 1930 they fell to 9 cents, then to a low of 5 cents in 1931. New Deal programs were able to jack the price up to 12 cents in 1936, but when the Agricultural Adjustment Act (AAA) was ruled unconstitutional, the prices fell to 8 cents in 1937 and had only recovered to 9 cents by 1940.

Mill wages did not fluctuate with cotton prices; they stayed consistently low. The lower wages paid to women and children had a depressing effect on all wages. In the 1890s when the work week could occupy as many as 50 hours, the week's pay might amount to $8.50. In the period before World War I, wages stayed around $10.50. In the 1920s wages ranged from about $20 to $25, but during the Depression they declined.

Making ends meet was not simply a problem for farmers and laborers. Virtually all Southerners from Reconstruction through the Depression of the 1930s were poorer than their northern and western neighbors. The traditionally well-to-do may have owned hundreds of acres in the county and an antebellum home on Williams or Adams street, yet they had to struggle to pay the taxes and utilities. William P. Newman, whose father, Francis Newman, was a practicing physician and man of means in antebellum and Civil War Huntsville, had to scramble in order to maintain his family in a reduced yet still comfortable manner in postwar days. A substantial property owner, Newman worked at so many vocations that he may have broken some sort of record had such been kept. Among others he was a claims agent, a mail contractor, a postmaster, a stockbroker, a newspaper publisher,

The courtship of Annie Schiffman and Lawrence Bernstein Goldsmith was greatly facilitated by his handsome rig. Their marriage in 1908 united four of Huntsville's most prominent families: the Goldsmiths and Bernsteins with the Schiffmans and Hersteins. Courtesy, Huntsville-Madison County Public Library

the county superintendent of education, a real estate broker, and an insurance agent. As a member of the board of directors of the North Alabama Improvement Company, he had a hand in most business and political transactions in the county. His son William Wyeth Newman also ventured into an assortment of money-making activities, including managing the Opera House, coaching a semiprofessional baseball club, prospecting for silver in northern Canada, and cotton brokering on the square—the last two successfully.

As in the past, Huntsvillians hoped to attract more money to the area by building the biggest and the best hotels. In 1914 the city rallied for the biggest groundbreaking it had witnessed.

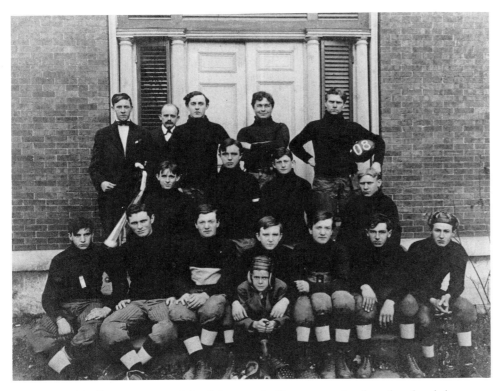

Above
For many years the Hotel Russel Erskine was the scene of Huntsville's prominent social functions. The decline of downtown businesses in the 1960s forced the hotel to close and an attempt to reopen in the 1970s failed. Today the building has been converted to housing for the elderly and handicapped. Courtesy, Huntsville-Madison County Public Library

Above left
In 1908 the Butler School football team posed for their portrait. The school, located at the corner of Eustis and White, had S.R. Butler as its principal. Courtesy, Huntsville-Madison County Public Library

William F. Struve, an old citizen of German stock who had long been a town booster, teamed with hotel man Quincy B. Love to build a hotel on the site of the old city hall. Struve's niece, Bess Hay, christened the hotel "Twickenham."

When it opened in 1915, with a seated dinner for 200, the newspapers heralded it as the "Dawning of a new Era," and the "beginning of a new and more prosperous chapter in the history of Huntsville." The toasts that evening rang euphoric, with Tracy Pratt still performing as Huntsville's "matchmaker" seeking to bring about more marriages between Yankee capital and Madison County "hopefuls." Stockholder Lawrence Cooper proclaimed that New York may have its "Astor-bilts and Vanderbilts," but Huntsville had her "Struve-bilt. . .the man who made all this progress possible for Huntsville."

Huntsville's skyscraper scamper in the late 1920s saw the construction of two highrises in the downtown area, climaxed by the last-minute scramble of the Huntsville *Weekly Times'* colorful editor J. Emory Pierce to add a 12th floor onto the Times Building so it could claim the title as tallest. The other contender was the Russel Erskine Hotel which opened in 1930. The hotel survived the Depression, but Russel Erskine, the man for whom it was named, did not. Ironically, Lawrence Goldsmith and Morton M. Hutchens, the hotel's major stockholders and directors, had intended to name the hotel the "Joe Wheeler," but

The Times Building, with its terra cotta eagles above the main entrances, was Huntsville's second skyscraper. Legend persists that Times editor Emory Pierce was determined to construct the tallest building in town, and, fearful that the Hotel Russel Erskine would be taller, he hastily added another floor. Since elevator service had only been planned for 11 floors, visitors to the top story faced one flight of steps. Courtesy, City of Huntsville Planning Department. Photo detail by Linda Bayer

they decided to name it the Russel Erskine instead, on the understanding that Mr. Erskine was going to become a major shareholder. Although he visited the hotel and was given the royal treatment, his stock purchases were minimal. Most folks did not know that though. As president of the Studebaker Corporation, one of the nation's leading auto producers, Erskine watched the auto company go into receivership in 1933 and killed himself in despair.

Southerners are often reminded that "the more things change, the more they are the same." The period between 1900 and 1940 in Huntsville and Madison County substantiates that assessment. It's not that things didn't happen; they did. Yet for all that, they stayed much the same.

The Chamber of Commerce called Huntsville the "Biggest Town on Earth for its Size." It acquired (and deserved) this title simply by not expanding its city limits the way most towns did in their efforts to become big cities. Rather than use its expanding population to appear larger in each decimal census, Huntsville had actually reduced its limits in 1876 from four square miles to three and one-half, which it maintained until 1925, when 100 acres of East Huntsville was annexed. Noted for its compactness, busy square, rich antebellum homes and lush lawns, gardens, and trees, the central city was almost surrounded by mill villages that were in turn surrounded by expansive cotton fields punctuated by waterways, roads, and hamlets. All this was barricaded by tall timbers growing freely on the neighboring mountains.

An occasional query in the newspapers sought to make sense of the city that refused to grow. Was it a ploy to attract industries to tax-free areas that were provided with peripheral police protection, free water, and in many cases free land? Or was it, as a Birmingham paper suggested, a reluctance on the part of its citizens to open the city gates to blacks, mill workers, or any persons who did not share the same historical and cultural past? Editor J. Emory Pierce touched on another plausible reason in a 1917 editorial comment:

A prominent citizen who lives outside the city limits said he didn't want any part of Huntsville until it lowered its debt. He didn't want to pay taxes for a debt he didn't incur.

The only way to get corporate limits extended is to get rid of the enormous debt.

Whatever the reason for containment, the result was racial and cultural homogeneity. At no time in its history before or since has

From Huntsville's streets as a child to London's fabled courts of royalty, Grace Hinds, the daughter of a U.S. marshal during Huntsville's Reconstruction period, is pictured here with her second husband, Lord Curzon. Courtesy, Trice Hinds

Huntsville been so homogenized. A study of the Alabama census indicates that in the whole state less than five percent of the population was foreign born. The hefty influx of German and Irish in the early mid-19th century was no longer statistically or culturally significant in Madison County. People were categorized as either townfolks, mill workers, or farmers, blacks or whites, but they were most of all Southerners.

A study of the city and county's population statistics, not including the mill villages to the north and west, indicates that the city numbered 8,068 in 1900, rolled backward in 1910 to 7,611, climbed to 8,018 in 1920, rose to 11,554 in 1930, and rested at 13,150 in 1940. Police jurisdiction was extended in 1910 to include the mill villages, and that area increased the size of greater Huntsville. Starting at 15,176 in 1910, the population increased to 16,275 in 1920, to 23,671 in 1930, and to 25,788 in 1940. The county's population did not backslide as the city's did. It began the century with 43,702, made it to 47,041 in 1910, eased up to 51,268 in 1920, and then shot up to 64,623 in 1930, coasting for the decade to 66,317 in 1940. Compared to urban population growth of northern and western states in the same period, these figures reflect a much slower rate of increase. Indeed, this sleepy little cotton town was even losing its position relative to other cities within Alabama. One factor contributing to Madison County's slow increase in population throughout the period was the outmigration of blacks. In 1900 the county included 19,875 blacks, in 1910 the number declined to 18,894 and then fell further to 17,483 in 1920. An upward surge took place in 1930 with 19,272 counted, but then the tide subsided to 18,385 in 1940.

The black exodus from Madison County represented a small part of a gigantic migration of the South's dispossessed, disenfranchised, and disgusted working-class citizens. The dawn of the new century had brought not hope but despair as white Alabamians carefully devised a new constitution in 1901 that effectively robbed blacks of political participation at the polls. The "solid South" no longer looked to fusion politics to achieve harmony, but rather to de jure segregation and terrorist tactics to maintain white hegemony.

Still, many of Huntsville's blacks clung tenaciously to their property and self-respect. Out in the county 295 still owned their own farms in 1925, but 71 percent were tenants. In 1896 the Seventh-Day Adventists had founded Oakwood College. Unlike Alabama A & M, the older state institution on the north side of town, which had been made the state's black land-grant institution by the Morrill Land Grant Act of 1890, Oakwood was a part of a worldwide religious organization that looked with pride and encouragement on its black institution. The presence of two schools with secondary and college level courses provided ambitious blacks in the area a chance to improve their economic and cultural conditions. The colleges also attracted to them talented and dedicated faculty. One of the most gifted and certainly the most famous professor to come to town and teach, if only for a few years, was William C. Handy, the Father of the Blues. In his autobiography, Handy recounts his teaching days at Alabama A & M College in 1900 and how he once pulled the wool over William Hooper Councill's ears just long enough to give a solemn Sunday evening chapel service a new beat:

With my band I rendered a program one evening in the chapel. But I had a secret plan to include a stirring ragtime number, "My Ragtime Baby.". . .I rewrote this high stepper and programmed it "Greetings to Toussaint L'Overture" so the manuscript sheets would create the impression of classical music without changing a note of the original. It did the trick. The students couldn't sit still, nor could the teachers. The president himself patted his feet.

A son of the Old South who led the way toward Huntsville's New South position, William H. Echols served as a civil engineer for the Memphis and Charleston Railroad, then ran the Bell Factory Cotton Mills from 1874 to 1884. As president of the First National Bank of Huntsville, he continued to lead until his death in 1909. Courtesy, Huntsville-Madison County Public Library

Although the Blues were nurtured in Huntsville, they would make St. Louis and Memphis their home—not that Huntsville's blacks didn't have cause to sing the blues. Lynching, the violent taking of the law into the hands of a mob bent on swift retribution, usually in the form of hangings, happened once in 1900 and again in 1904.

There was nothing new about lynching, but the new century seemed to usher in a more virulent nationwide epidemic. Huntsville had been spared the horror back in 1885 when Charles Townsend had been found guilty of murdering Madison merchant Nathan M. Freeman. The angry mob that had gathered to claim its victim was turned away by Capt. McGehee, the Madison County sheriff. Huntsville's *New South,* a Republican newspaper, cited him for doing "his duty at the risk of his life." Bucking the bloodthirsty tide was such a singular event that the Selma *Times* called his brave action "palliation for the inefficiency of numerous brethren in Alabama counties who have either failed in such emergencies or called on the Governor for troops."

The 1900 lynching of Elijah Clark fit the classic pattern. Clark had been charged with the rape of a young mill village girl. He was being held for trial in the county jail. Tempers in the Dallas Mills village raised with the temperature that hot July and on the night of the 23rd over 1,500 stormed the jail, dynamited their way to Clark, overpowered Sheriff Fulgham, and carried Clark away to

Horace Maples was seized from jail, taken to the southeast corner of the Courthouse Square and hanged before a large crowd. Later no eyewitnesses could be found to testify. Courtesy, Old Huntsville Magazine and Huntsville Madison County Public Library

Huntsvillians have always loved a parade. Here they are waiting for a victory parade in 1918. Courtesy, Old Huntsville Magazine and Huntsville Madison County Public Library

the home of his alleged victim where he was identified. All that was left was the ritual. Clark was tarred, feathered, and dragged to Moore's Grove for his hanging. The 1904 lynching of Horace Maples, who had been indicted for the senseless slaying of an elderly Confederate veteran, peddler E.D. Waldrop, was equally sensational. The mob again came after its victim with fire, and Maples jumped out of a window into the swarming crowd below. County historian James Record describes what happened next: "Maples was dragged before the crowd where Jack Waldrop, son of the victim, spoke and Maples blurted out a confession of the murder. . .the mob first hung and then shot Maples."

White supremacy in the 19th century had been maintained by corruption in politics and election tampering. In the 20th century, corruption continued as white cliques struggled for electoral supremacy and political privilege. So pervasive was election fraud that there is no way of determining if a particular election was honestly won or lost.

The pervasive belief that "everyone was doing it"—stuffing ballot boxes, tampering with absentee votes, purchasing votes, and paying other people's poll taxes—lifted dirty politics to the politics of acceptability. And in Huntsville acceptability became confused with respectability. Many of the most important people and the least important became one in a mutual corruptibility.

In 1911 Huntsville made what may have been considered at the time a progressive move; it changed its government from a council of aldermen headed by a mayor to a three-man city commission form. This turned out to be a mistake, or so it would appear from a reading of later city council minutes. The January 16, 1917, minutes noted that "certain" city employees had under the commission been receiving free water. The city clerk was authorized to hire additional help to "get the office work caught up." Delinquent street improvement assessments and delinquent water accounts had to be dealt with. Maybe the downward turn of the economy would have spelled trouble for any government. Whatever the cause, the citizens voted on August 21, 1916, to return to a mayor/aldermanic council form of government.

Undoubtedly the murder of probate judge William T. Lawler on June 14, 1916 contributed to the change in government. James Record called the murder "perhaps the greatest scandal in local government in the nation's history." Record summarizes:

Murder, mayhem, blackmail, shootouts, bootlegging, election contest, and suicides were all part of the most damning period in Madison County history, and before the turmoil settled, almost all the county officials, Huntsville city officials and judges were stained by it.

The facts are few. The probate judge's body was found near the Aldridge Creek bridge, weighted down with railroad iron, clothes pockets stuffed with iron bolts. There were two bullet wounds in the chest and repeated blows to the head. Earlier that year Lawler had narrowly won re-election in an overheated campaign against David D. Overton, one-time Huntsville police chief who had resigned his current position as circuit court clerk to challenge Lawler for the probate judgeship. Overton was later convicted of the murder after stating he had commited the act in self defense. On March 20, 1917 he escaped from the Jefferson County jail with six other prisoners and was gunned down shortly afterwards. In the course of events from Lawler's murder to Overton's death, Shelby Pleasants, prominent and esteemed attorney and former state legislator, and Sheriff Bob Phillips committed suicide, and Huntsville chief of police A.D. Kirby and patrolman George Blanton resigned.

Like the bull's eye on a target, the Lawler murder was at the center of a whole series of activities that encircled it. Events occurring long before and long after would have the murder as their pivotal point, as though all the dirty water that flowed in the county from 1900 to 1940 swirled around and around and eventually was sucked into the Aldridge Creek Slough along with the body of Probate Judge Lawler. A decided stench of bootleg booze remained.

The prohibition movement had been gaining momentum throughout the state since 1900. Prohibition and its antithesis, bootlegging, created centrifugal forces working against one another. In 1907 the antisaloon forces led by the 1,800-strong Woman's Auxiliary won a victory when the city was authorized to sell alcoholic beverages through a dispensary only. Alabama Governor B.B. Comer appointed David D. Overton dispenser. On January 5, 1909, the dispensary was closed and Huntsville was "dry" for the first time. The bootleggers, always busy, were inundated with orders.

Given a chance, Madison County usually voted "wet." When Governor Emmett O'Neal was elected on a county local option platform, the city cheered. In August 1911 the county voted for a dispensary. Other "wet" counties voted to open saloons instead. In 1914 the dispensary cleared $168,000. This money was shared by the city and county governments. It must have been a blow to those treasuries the next year, when on July 1, 1915, statewide prohibition took effect. Except for fines, the city and county had lost a valuable source of revenue. Liquor flowed freely throughout the "dry" spell, and undoubtedly big money and big names were involved. Although the Eighteenth Amendment was repealed at the end of 1933, the county did not go "wet" until March of 1937. Corruption had settled in by then in many socially acceptable ways.

If loose women (the *Times* called them "Fowl Birds" and their houses, "Cuckoo's Nests") and bathtub gin came to epitomize the post-World War I delirious delusion called the Roaring Twenties, Huntsville had its fill of them before and after as well as during that fling into national madness. The June 5, 1917, minutes of the city council read:

The following representatives of the Ministerial Association were present, viz: Rev. Tappy, Baker, Stoves, Gamble, Wier and Rickey, and each of them addressed the council urging strict enforcement of laws governing Prostitutes, Prohibition; and particular stress being laid on the necessity of a more strict enforcement of the laws against Bawdy Houses being allowed to operate in the city.

Apparently the city government was suffering severe corrosion by 1936, as the following communication signed by six of the aldermen was added to the council minutes.

Gentlemen of the City Board:

We want to bring to your attention the fact that we, as a Board of Aldermen of the City of Huntsville, are being criticized by many of our best citizens in the lax manner in which our laws are being enforced, especially in reference to the numerous gambling halls, bootlegging joints, and the steady increase of common street walkers.

We as a Board, are frequently accused of receiving from these violators money for protection. We are also told that our police force receive money from the bootleggers for protection.

These criticisms come from some of our best citizens and taxpayers, and they often ask just why we permit such conditions to exist. . .

Respectfully Submitted,

G.R. Maples	*Chas. O. Rolfe*
Herbert Johnson	*S.L. Terry*
H.C. Pollard	*H.C. Blake*

The minutes then concluded with a statement by President of the Council Frank Ford stating that he and Alderman Wells A. Stanley had recently met with Mayor Alex W. McAllister and

In 1899, at the Huntsville Hotel Bar, gentlemen took their drinks standing. Courtesy, The Monroe Collection, Old Huntsville Magazine and Huntsville Madison County Public Library

Chief Blakemore to discuss the charges of corruption. Obviously there was more than pool being played in River City.

The Depression did not strike Madison County all at once. Farmers felt it first, but by 1934 all were feeling the effects. Franklin D. Roosevelt's New Deal programs, especially the Agricultural Adjustment Act, reinforced by Alabama Senator John H. Bankhead's Cotton Control Act (CCC), helped raise and stabilize cotton prices while at the same time encouraging conservation and diversification.

Textile workers, reckoned to be 4,000 to 5,000 strong, did not fare so well. Roosevelt's National Industrial Recovery Act (NRA) depended upon voluntary compliance to codes regulating hours and wages. The textile code included acceptance of the 40-hour week, two work shifts, a minimum weekly wage of $12 ($13 in New England), elimination of child labor defined as employment of persons under 16, curtailment of plant expansion, and the controversial Section 7 (a), allowing for collective bargaining. In his comprehensive study *The Emergence of the New South: 1913-1945*, George B. Tindall describes in great detail the dilemmas of both management and labor as they sought what they perceived to be their best interests. The problem for both management and labor in the South was that the textile codes proved more beneficial to New England. Factories that had not been able to compete with cheaper Southern labor now could. Tindall notes:

Immediately prior to the code, average hourly wages in the North were 38.5 per cent above those in the South, a difference reduced to 15.9 per cent in August, 1933. The 80-hour limit on operations curtailed activity in the South while New England mills expanded their production... Before the end of 1933 many leaders of the industry were seeking to limit machines temporarily to sixty hours a week and workers to thirty. The code authority effected this during December, but the threat of another curtailment in the spring of 1934 set off a wave of labor unrest that generated a major textile strike.

By 1934 Southern textile workers, including Huntsville's, had a growing list of complaints. Workers' hours had been cut back so drastically that they could not live on the small wages. Many argued that the $12 minimum wage should be guaranteed for a 30-hour week since workers had no control over the number of hours they were hired to work. Others called for abolition of the one dollar differential that had been added to the codes as a sop to Southern boosters who insisted that cheap labor be protected

Shown hand in hand about 1930 are Bess Pratt (Wallace), the daughter of Tracy W. Pratt, Huntsville's turn-of-the-century industrial matchmaker, and Jack Hay, grandson of Huntsville's turn-of-the-century music maker, John L. Hay. Courtesy, Mr. and Mrs. Jack Hay

The Merrimack Mill provided a tremendous boost to Huntsville's economy when it was built in 1899. This 1948 photograph illustrates the monotony of mill architecture with its rows of identical housing. Courtesy, Huntsville-Madison County Public Library

as an inducement for industry to locate in the South. Another complaint was against the "stretch-out," so called because workers were expected to stretch out and operate more than one machine. This meant that they had to work faster and harder without let-up or increase in pay. This too meant that fewer workers were needed—or fewer work hours.

These problems and the growing psychological isolation of cotton mill workers became the rallying point for unionization. The United Textile Workers of America grew from a 40,000 membership in 1933 to 270,000 in August 1934. Increasing numbers of Huntsville's textile workers were finding a greater sense of community and mutual support in their locals than at the village church or YMCA.

As spring came to the valley in 1934, labor unrest grew. The Huntsville Trades and Labor Council moved into new quarters over the "reemployment" office across from the courthouse on the corner of Franklin and Eustis. Henceforth, Huntsville's labor headquarters would be on this southwest corner of the square.

On July 17, 1934, after two months of intense agitation and efforts at national mediation, Huntsville's textile workers announced a strike. The Huntsville *Times* estimated that 1,750 workers from Lincoln, 1,300 from Merrimack, 800 from Dallas,

240 from Erwin, 175 from Fletcher, and 40 from Admiral Braid walked out or did not show up for work.

United Textile Workers organizer John Dean coordinated the strike. Some workers grumbled that he was more interested in unionizing than striking. He was assisted by Mollie Dowd, a union representative from Birmingham who had grown up in Huntsville. Though the union representatives were Southerners, they were referred to by management and members of the Chamber of Commerce as "outsiders." The Chamber ran full-page advertisements in the *Times* urging workers not to rush into a union or a strike.

As state law prohibited boycotting and local laws forbade loitering, strikers and police clashed frequently. Strikers enjoyed parading around town and riding in carfulls from mill to mill. Some evenings the city took on the appearance of an armed camp, both sides carrying sticks or weapons.

On a Saturday night in August, sometime around midnight, strike organizer John Dean was abducted at gunpoint from his hotel room by some men who drove him to Fayetteville, Tennessee. Although they struck him over the back of the head with the butt of a gun, he wasn't seriously injured. His abductors registered him in the Pope Hotel and drove back to Huntsville. Dean immediately called Huntsville and got help. In a matter of hours a caravan of about a dozen cars full of armed and angry men arrived in Fayetteville. They brought Dean back and took him to the Merrimack village home of striking mill worker George Davis.

The story later unraveled that elsewhere that evening, the Newman-Hutchens home on Williams had been aglow with a party that included the town's leaders. Prohibition or no, whiskey flowed freely. There had been talk of little else besides the strike, and a few of the men came up with an idea to kidnap John Dean, the strike organizer, "just to scare him." The hosts knew nothing of the prank.

Later that night, long after midnight, Mr. and Mrs. Reuben Chapman, at home from the party and in bed, awakened with a start to the sound of feet treading their way up Maysville Road. Angry mill workers, having heard rumors that Chapman had been involved in the kidnapping, marched to the Chapman house. From the window Mrs. Chapman could see hundreds of torches making their way up the road. As quickly as he could, Reuben Chapman, grandson of Alabama's 13th governor, fled out the back. Mrs. Chapman, with one child in her arms and another at her feet, answered the threats at the front door. No, her husband was not home. No, she did not know where he was or when he would be

John L. Hay directed the Merrimack Manufacturing Company Band for many years. Merrimack was one of several local mills that sponsored a band. One of the first was Pratt's Military Band around 1900, named after Tracy W. Pratt, owner of the West Huntsville Cotton Mills. The Dallas Mills band also performed at many celebrations. Courtesy, Mr. and Mrs. John C. Hay, Jr.

back. The crowd was angry but strangely polite. They knew this woman to be kindly and generous. They turned and left. As they scuffled away, she heard one of them murmur, "We should have burned the place down."

The strikes of 1934 marked the beginning of the end for Huntsville as the textile center of Alabama. Walkouts, shutouts, and shutdowns characterized the last half of the 1930s. As workers swelled the unemployment ranks, the federal government's New Deal programs of relief and rehabilitation gave thousands of North Alabamians new jobs, new skills, and fresh hope. They were still short of cash, but in the crucible of Depression, old habits had finally been broken and a new faith was being forged.

Huntsville *Times* editor Reese T. Amis, as early as January 24, 1935, perceived the change. Concerning the President's social security program, he wrote that had such a proposal been made before 1933 it would have "aroused a great deal of protest."

It would have been called dangerous experimentation, and its attempts to provide protection for the victims of economic distress would have been dubbed an un-American form of coddling, designed to sap our national self-reliance...

But now the plan is offered—and the objection most commonly heard is that it isn't strong enough; that it does not provide enough security...

We have had a revolution in this country, after all, and it has taken place in our minds.

Our point of view has shifted. We don't look at things with the same eyes that we used half a dozen years ago.

Yesterday's dangerous radicalism is the height of today's conservatism—in this one field, at any rate.

This means that we have found out some things about our country and about ourselves.

We have found out that a country in which great masses of the people never earn more than $15 or $20 a week, and is subject to spells of complete unemployment at varying intervals, is not a country in which every man attains any measure of independence and security by his own efforts.

We have found out, simultaneously, that we as individuals cannot stand it to have that state of affairs continue indefinitely.

We are willing to subject ourselves to a complicated and expensive program to end it.

Despite labor and economic problems, the quiet life of the old town persisted throughout the 1930s. Dr. Eleanor Hutchens

At the exclusive Byrd Spring Rod and Gun Club, only decendants can be members. The Preserve is one of Huntsville's most prized, pristine ecological systems. Courtesy, Old Huntsville Magazine and Huntsville Madison County Public Library

recalls the Huntsville of her youth:

Members of the Huntsville Golf and Country Club competed at tennis and bridge and poker as well as golf. Members of the Byrd Spring Rod and Gun Club rose in the dark on winter mornings for the privilege of standing in icy water to entice mallard and teal with their duck calls; in summer they fished from flat-bottomed boats or long wooden walks, supported on piles, that extended from a bank or small bridge into the tupelo trees. Families with summer places on Monte Sano still moved up there for the hot months, occasionally inviting friends from town for parties. House servants were highly skilled and proud of staying with the same families for generations.

Actress Tallulah Bankhead was born January 30, 1902, in Huntsville on the second floor of the Schiffman Building on East Side Square. Stories abound concerning her flamboyant behavior, and she once commented, "A day without Tallulah is like a week in the country." Courtesy, Huntsville-Madison County Public Library

She remembers too, the excitement of seeing off the passenger trains, two a day, that went from Huntsville to New York. "When it came time to go to Chicago for the 1933 World's Fair, one had to motor to Decatur or Athens and board the train there. This irksome fact was attributed to the shortsightedness of some Huntsvillians in the 19th century who had kept the north-south lines out of town as they felt the roads would have been sources of dirt and noise."

The city was small and manageable. Dr. Hutchens evokes fond memories: "The old grocery stores and meat markets that took orders by telephone and delivered promptly kept much of their business despite the opening of the first self-service, cash-and-carry chain rivals." While some retail firms failed in the 1930s and 1940s, others rose and prospered. "Fowler's and Dunnavant's department stores flourished," but so did smaller businesses. "A widow opened a dress shop and built a solid business by buying for the known tastes of individual customers. Chain 10-cent stores and locally owned drugstores survived. Beauty parlors and barber shops held their own. Ambitious boys on bicycles delivered newspapers, not only the Huntsville *Times,* but the Memphis *Commercial Appeal,* the Chattanooga *Times,* and the Birmingham *Age-Herald.*" Depression or no, "school dances and plays went on, as did plays given by adult clubs." Dr. Hutchens vividly recalls the social scene: "High school girls or their mothers gave luncheons at the Russel Erskine. At Christmas, fraternities and civic clubs gave big dances practically every night at the Russel Erskine or the Twickenham, with long dresses and corsages de rigueur." Many would share Eleanor Hutchens' assessment of those times: "Huntsville did not seem like a sleepy little cotton town to the people who were shaping their lives here."

CHAPTER VI

We Have Lift-Off

Every Christmas, Olin King throws open the doors of his antebellum mansion and invites 300 of this Southern town's finest citizens to a party. Dressed formally in black tie, the partygoers eat exotic foods served by uniformed servants while they stroll past the French Empire furniture and the 15th century, silver-threaded Spanish embroidery in King's impressive 1819 home with its former slave quarters out back.

But among "Olin's 300," as some here call his glittering Christmas gathering, there are none of the wealthy cotton planters such as founded Huntsville and built its distinctive plantation-style houses. In fact, cotton and textiles are overshadowed in the area's economy now.

The wealthy cream of Huntsville society truly consists mainly of. . .engineers who once worked in the missile and space programs and have now become pioneers in burgeoning high-technology fields. . .

—Huntsville Times, *May 1, 1983*

Since its opening in 1970, the Alabama Space and Rocket Center has become a major tourist attraction. Today it features an extensive rocket park, the Spacedome Theatre, bus tours of NASA, a space camp for junior high students, and the monkeynaut Miss Baker. Courtesy, Alabama Space and Rocket Center

Perhaps it was the freshness of its mornings, even when the mist was slow to rise, that braced Huntsvillians for each new day. Some say it was the mountain spring water they drank and bathed in that bouyed them. Others, admitting the importance of air and water, would insist that it was memories of shared experiences that kept them going into their uncertain future.

To be sure some held so tightly to memories of a long distant past that both they and their memories atrophied. But there were more than the usual number who consciously or unconsciously used memory as momentum to carry them forward and over the rough spots much as a rope may be used to propel one over the abyss. Perhaps they did not analyze it but had they done so, they would have perceived that for them shared experiences or memories-in-the-making became passages to the future.

Celebration, the creation of joyous events and sharing of happy occasions, has played a vital role in the city's life since the Civil War. Defeat had created a great need for collective self-assurance, and the city's journalists became its biggest boosters. Since all newspapers are mirrors of community life, they held up to Huntsvillians reflections that helped shape their sense of self and community. Organizations such as the Chamber of Commerce pumped up the community's spirit at the same time it tried to sell Huntsville and Madison County to prospective investors and home seekers. Watercress from its cold springs was shipped all over the east, making Huntsville the "watercress capital of the world."

New leaders continued to arise reflecting the city's strengths, answering its needs, and projecting its fantasies. From the days of LeRoy Pope to the present, Huntsville has responded to the charisma of one man—a Lindbergh—who catches a people's imagination and pilots them safely if narrowly above the rooftops to new horizons.

In the 1930s it was young John Sparkman, teacher, lawyer, Chamber of Commerce leader who took a seat in Congress, first in the House and then in the Senate, but always kept his ties close to home. His legislative record showed that he was a working Congressman, a New Deal Democrat, and an upland Southern liberal. He championed progressive new programs for small businessmen and greater expenditure for housing, roads, schools, old-age pensions, public health, and farm subsidies. His appeal was so broad that blacks supported him even though he was a conservative on racial issues and conservatives supported him even though his liberalism threatened their pocketbooks.

When Adlai Stevenson selected Sparkman to serve as the vice-presidential nominee of the Democratic party in 1952, constituents gathered 60,000 strong to celebrate his homecoming. The occasion resembled a victory parade, which perhaps it was for Huntsville. Chattanooga's *News-Free Press* called it "the biggest celebration in Huntsville's history—the homecoming of its most famous citizen, Sen. John J. Sparkman."

John Sparkman was living proof that aristocracy of spirit and intellect could belong to a tenant farmer's son and that hard work, honesty, and genuine caring for people were characteristics equally valued by all strata of society. Once a newcomer, born in Morgan County on December 20, 1899, Sparkman moved to

The New Market watercress ponds of C.E. Denna were some of the world's best in the 1940s. Courtesy, Old Huntsville Magazine and Huntsville Madison County Public Library

Senator John Sparkman and Adlai Stevenson are pictured planning their 1952 Presidential race. Senator Sparkman, a veteran Congressman with 42 years service before retiring in 1978, has been credited with almost single-handedly securing Redstone Arsenal's location in Huntsville. Courtesy, Mrs. John Sparkman

Huntsville after graduation from the University of Alabama Law School in 1923. He helped Huntsville out of its worst economic and spiritual slump and opened its doors to other newcomers.

Industrialist Milton Cummings, Sparkman's staunch supporter, also exemplified in his citizenship role the quality of human being that set Huntsville above the ordinary town. Cummings rose from a background of poverty to become a captain of industry. Growing up in the Lincoln Mill village, he worked for Shelby Fletcher's cotton company after graduating from high school. He made a great deal of money on the cotton market, dealing in spot cotton and futures. But, he never forgot where he came from and worked to help others achieve.

It was in little-known ways that Cummings shone as a man. During World War II, for instance, Cummings, who had lost a limb as a child, played exhibition tennis at veterans hospitals. Being a top-seeded player, he usually won, but either way he would bound to the net in championship form. Only then would he lift his pants leg and reveal the handicap he had played with and learned to overcome.

When Meredith Willson's *The Music Man* opened on Broadway in 1957, no one predicted that it would take its place among the nation's favorite musicals. When it came as a movie to the Lyric Theater in the fall of 1962, Huntsvillians lined up to see it. "Schmaltzy" some called it; too small-townish with its unsophisticated hoopla said others. Not to mention the characters: a stereotypical traveling salesman, Professor Harold Hill, and a public librarian, Marian. The quick-witted, fast-talking con artist hit the town where it least expected it, in the imaginations of the people.

In the course of winning the town over to the need for a snappy brass band, the scheming salesman falls in love with the librarian, the town's cultural reservoir and custodian of its memories. He and River City experience conversion as a new synthesis of values, based on memory and underscored by an awakened confidence, carries them forward.

River City, Iowa. Huntsville, Alabama. The cast of thousands, accents varying from Midwestern to Yankee to German all blending into a new Southern accent, was led by such stars as Sparkman and Wernher von Braun. From the 1940s to the present, it was not 76 trombones, but the sound of another kind of brass that brought about Huntsville's metamorphosis. The deadly sounds of war and the threat of impending American involvement brought to the city a vital defense mission that was to rally the citizens and give them new purpose.

The Chamber of Commerce, with business leaders like Lawrence

Goldsmith and George Mahoney, had been working quietly behind the scenes for almost a year to land something big for Huntsville, but the news burst upon most with the suddenness of a tornado and its effects were to be about as uplifting.

Red fire trucks clanged their bells with abandon as they twisted through the neighborhood streets flooding the city with Huntsville *Times* extras. The headlines blared out the tidings: "Huntsville Gets Chemical War Plant; Cost Over $40,000,000." The date was Thursday, July 3, 1941. By Monday, July 7, over 500 men had applied for site preparation and construction jobs.

The next six months of 1941 were momentous. The chemical warfare plant quickly augmented by an ammunitions arsenal awaited men, muscle, and machines. There were jobs aplenty. In early September 1941 Nancy Dickson with husband Tom, a surveyor, packed their clothing, coffee table, record player, and several 78 r.p.m. records into their black 1939 secondhand Chevrolet and set out from Memphis for Huntsville. Tom already had a job lined up with Whitman, Requardt & Smith of Baltimore, Architects and Engineers. Nancy, after spending one day in the only room Tom could find them, approached job hunting with full vigor. Their room in a flimsy house on the outskirts of town was "bare of any signs of comfort, the bedding scant, the mattress thin, and springs non-existent. Linoleum, worn through in some places, covered the floor." With "no place to sit except on the bed, with no lamp to read by," Nancy Dickson, educated at Houston's esteemed Rice Institute and possessing well-honed secretarial skills, went job-seeking at the arsenal. She well remembers that cow pasture-turned-arsenal:

After a few false starts, I learned the route to the arsenal, where salaries for skilled office workers were of course higher than in local offices. By this time, the fall rains had begun, and the scene of desolation which the jobsite presented was almost enough to drive me back to the bedroom. Bulldozers had cleared the site of every tree and shrub and blade of grass. Red mud in deep troughs stretched in every direction to barbed wire fences, broken here and there by guard towers in which were stationed M.P.'s. A number of regulation Army barracks had been erected, interconnected by wooden walkways, some bearing names of organizations painted on signs at the corners, others bearing only a letter and a number. At the front gate, every visitor was interviewed by an M.P. and, if given permission to enter, handed a temporary badge without which the visitor would not be permitted to leave again. When I learned the amount of salary earned by a temporary Civil Service clerk-stenographer—$135 per *month, sixty-five percent more than the salary I had earned in Memphis, the mud and the rain and our dreadful room seemed more bearable.*

The 40,000 acres that changed the course of Huntsville's history at the time the government announced its plans in 1941 were owned by a cross-section of the community. Some of the larger spreads were rented; other plots were worked on shares. But there were many smaller cuts of land that had been in families for years, belonged to church congregations, or had been used for schoolhouses and playgrounds.

Former owners who were interviewed later remembered the hasty transactions attending government land purchases. Within six months families were to harvest their fall crop and find a new place to live. Hugh B. Gillespie, Jr., in charge of land procurement, faced multiple problems. Many tracts had no clear title. Some families could not be found to negotiate with at all. Many others had nowhere to move and little means for removal. The Alabama Relocation Corporation was organized to assist them.

To the urban eye the land may have seemed little used or valued, but it was dotted by small communities. Almost every inch of it had a name, too. There were Mullins Flat and Pond Beat and Cave Hill. Dock Jacobs was raised in Mullins Flat and his wife Zera grew up in Pond Beat. Only separated by a creek, they bridged that when they married in 1922. The area was populated with homeowners of both races. Mrs. Jacobs recalled that "they got along mighty well. Wasn't no integration, but they all understood each other." There were also Hickory Grove, with its gin, store, and schoolhouse; Horton's Ford, where Spring Branch crosses Patton Road; Bettle Slash, a swampy area; and Madkin Mountain to look up to.

The site was ideal for the government's intended use. It was cheap, sparsely populated, within the Tennessee Valley Authority's (TVA) power range, located in the protected valley of a great river with access to the gulf, and connected by rail to both the East and West coasts.

John McDaniel started work at the Huntsville Arsenal in February 1942. For a salary of $6.24 per day, he worked in a plant manufacturing mustard gas. There would be six of these in all, plus two chlorine-producing plants. "The output of the manufacturing plants," explained McDaniel, "was piped to the filling plants and loaded into 105-MM M60 shells, M70 bombs, M47A2 bombs, and the Navy bomb MK42." The work was hazardous. But there was a war on that had to be won. McDaniel

Cora Barley and Elmer Binford were among those building new lives when their farms were purchased by the U.S. Government in 1941 for conversion to the arsenal and chemical war plant. Cora Barley's family fields at Pond Beat were soon interlaced with army jeeps and heavy earth movers. Courtesy, Mr. and Mrs. Elmer C. Binford

Toward the end of World War II, Redstone Arsenal housed German prisoners of war. This photo was taken behind the Post Hospital in 1945. Courtesy, Old Huntsville Magazine and the Huntsville Madison County Library

describes the precautions taken:

To do this work, it would be necessary for me to wear clothes impregnated with a substance to prevent the mustard gas fumes from coming in contact with the skin. The long johns underwear were thick with the substance, as were the socks, coveralls, shoes and hat. I have scars today on my wrists where I was careless in joining the underwear sleeves and the gloves. A gas mask completed the uniform. Sensitive skin was not a particular advantage since the showers used kerosene to remove any mustard or vapor contamination from the body.

After three months of training, he was qualified to manufacture mustard gas and to supervise others in the operation.

When the newly arrived Dicksons learned that poison gases were to be the products of the plant, Nancy later recalled, "none of the outraged horror which seizes the innocents of today caused us to reconsider." Memories of German use of poison gas in World War I were still fresh. Nancy's favorite uncle had died of its effects. She wrote: "It was assumed that the Nazis would not scruple to use it and that the United States must be prepared to counter any such plan with equivalent weapons." There was a growing sense of urgency, too, as Hitler's Nazis swept across Europe. "Probably because of this unspoken sense of common danger," Nancy observed, "the Huntsville people gave the newcomers a kindly welcome." But soon there were no more welcome mats. The town's spare room had filled up overnight and there was no place for newcomers to rest their heads. Families slept in cars parked along roadsides. Courthouse benches and the cool grass of its lawn became sleeping quarters in the evenings. At Big Spring Park could be found more bodies and bedrolls, many using bunched up newspapers or rolled up clothes as pillows. The park in the night flickered with cigarettes as well as the usual lightning bugs. A hum of snores mixed with laughter, and singing blended with nature's choir of frogs and crickets.

The Dicksons were luckier than most and eventually found splendid accommodations:

Miss Susy Moorman, the lady kind enough and brave enough to rent a bedroom in her home to these two strangers, was the sort of Southerner who believed in Southern gentility, and my husband's Vicksburg connections may have had something to do with her decision. Other Southern gentlewomen were renting rooms to officers or company officials of WRS [Whitman, Requart, & Smith] and KBE, [Kershaw, Butler, Engineers, Ltd.] though they, no more than we, took meals with the family. These ladies were not operating boarding-houses, though there were some of these where many of the workmen found rooms and meals.

Mary Parker of New Market was the first female to serve as a Redstone Guard during the war. This photo is dated 1943. Courtesy, Old Huntsville Magazine and Huntsville Madison County Public Library

To help ease the housing shortage, the government brought in trailers and established trailer parks. Some arsenal employees had worked on construction jobs in other parts of the country and had grown adept at building instant communities in their trailer parks. Two of the parks, one on Holmes and another in the west Merrimack area, filled rapidly. A trailer was even set aside for a library. The "trailer wives" as they called themselves were among the first to volunteer for Red Cross work and then when war was declared to urge that women go to work to free the men for fighting. One trailer wife turned her home over for use as a day-care center for children.

Many of the thousands seeking employment in the area were unskilled and unable to hold their jobs. Men who showed up at the back doors of the well-to-do were not turned away or reported to the police. But if beggars were tolerated, burglars were not. The *Times* observed on September 17, "It has become unsafe for doors to remain unlocked, or houses to be left open in any way lest they be broken in." It was the end of small-town tranquility.

Other problems, like fleas on a dog, became noticeably more irksome. The *Times* reported "an increase in the number of lewd women coming into the city, in anticipation of the big crowds and the easy money that soon will be flowing." Public drunkenness interfered with business in the downtown area and upset the decorum so diligently upheld by clergy and women's groups. The compactness of the town meant that there were few places to hide, and misbehavior often became a public nuisance.

It was at this juncture in the fall of 1941 that the county voted whether to stay "wet" or to go "dry." The *Times* made a strong statement for reason and the controlled sale of alcohol, reminding citizens of the not-so-distant past when bootleggers had the county trapped under their heel. But religious leaders came down on the side of prohibition. It did not help either side that many Huntsvillians preferred to purchase from their bootleggers charcoal barrels filled with pure whiskey that could sit in their attics or basements mellowing with time. The dry victory did not stop the flow of alcohol, but it did cut into the flow of tax revenues. The county lost over $30,000 annually in taxes, not to mention salaries and profits from distribution and sales. The burden put on city resources by the arsenal and by the demands of war could have been considerably eased—along with the thirst of a lot of hard workers.

During World War II, Redstone needed workers and so did the textile mills that were producing uniforms and tents. Courtesy, Old Huntsville Magazine *and Huntsville Madison County Public Library*

As John McDaniel made his way up the management ladder at the Huntsville Arsenal, alcohol control became part of his supervisory duties:

The handling of intoxicated personnel while they were performing hazardous operations was a particularly challenging part of the job of the supervisor. Ethylene for use in making mustard gas was made from pure grain alcohol and each of the six plants had approximately 20,000 gallons in underground tanks adjacent to the building. Lewisite used pure grain alcohol as a coolant for the reactors and each of the six plants had approximately 100,000 in above ground tanks. The alcohol was delivered to the Arsenal in trainloads of tank cars. Since Huntsville and Madison County were "dry," it did not take the workers long to find out that the Arsenal had a large supply of 200 proof moonshine. A number of ingenious methods were devised by the workers for drawing the alcohol from the tanks; and before long, each worker had a coke bottle of alcohol in his locker. But this time I had some supervisors working for me and I gave it the usual book solution. I instructed my supervisors to have the workers remove the alcohol from their lockers, and stop drinking on the job. The problem did not go away when I found that the coke bottles of alcohol had been moved from the lockers of the workers to the lockers of the supervisors.

As usual, alcohol found its way to most parties. Nancy Dickson describes a get-together of her husband's fellow workers up at the Civilian Conservation Corps-built tavern on Monte Sano. "When we entered," she later recalled, "I could smell the aroma of the new boards." The jukebox was playing "Elmer's Tune," and later she would clap with the others when it played "Deep in the Heart of Texas." The climax of the evening came when the party was over and cars began descending the mountain. Nancy recalled:

It was a wild party. We realized that as we drove back down the mountain over a road completely hidden by thick fog. Here and there, partygoers, some very intoxicated, all unable to see the road through the fog, had driven into the ditches at the side, had climbed out of their cars, and were walking around them or leaning dangerously to leeward, depending on their sobriety, as they tried to find a way to extricate themselves.

But if people drank hard, they also worked hard and they played hard. There was an intensity about Huntsville High's football fortunes that year. Perhaps those boys and their parents knew they would be soon trading their footballs for hand grenades. When the team defeated Decatur by a narrow 7 to 6, having been cast as two-touchdown underdogs, school officials announced a half-day holiday for the following Monday.

Like most every other American who lived through the war years, Nancy Dickson has vivid memories of Sunday, December 7, 1941—and of Miss Susy's announcement: "Nancy, Nancy, come quick. Japan has bombed Pearl Harbor!"

Dreadful fear and outrage washed from my memory what I did that day after that; I have a dim recollection that Lt. Kaminer sent a staff car for me and I spent the rest of the day at the job, but I cannot really recall anything. On Monday no one was absent and no one suggested we stop work to send a radio to listen to the President. We knew he would declare war. All leaves, including Christmas, were cancelled. . . Anyone who did not report for work was subject to dismissal without recommendation. . . civilian personnel were subject to call seven days a week. Sometimes the work went on until nine or ten o'clock at night, with meals of sandwiches and coffee brought in on trays by enlisted men and eaten at the desk. If you were called and had no transportation, an olive-drab Ford was sent from the Motor Pool to fetch you. Bulletins from the Commanding General were circulated, warning workers against loose talk that would aid the enemies' spies.

Once war was declared by Congress, working men and women at the arsenal became soldiers in overalls, some even offering the government one workday free a week. Textile workers and management also came together in order to fulfill wartime orders. Unionization took a back seat to defense of the nation. Construction at the arsenal was a top national priority, but civilian housing construction was also ticketed by the federal government for priority in Madison and Limestone counties for houses costing $6,000 or less.

Huntsville mobilized for defense. Because there was fear that the community's water supply could be sabotaged, a heavy wooden cover was built closing off public access, and a guardhouse was erected above the spring which was still its source. Citizens were drilled in air raid procedures and there was a rush on the Red Cross to learn first aid and to roll bandages. Even children and the elderly were called upon to sign up as a part of volunteer civilian defense.

The war years were busy, prosperous ones for the area. By

Production of smoke shells was going full-blast for delivery overseas in 1944. Courtesy, Old Huntsville Magazine *and* Huntsville Madison County Public Library

A fence was put up around the Big Spring to help prevent sabotage of the city's water supply. Courtesy, Old Huntsville Magazine *and* Huntsville Madison County Public Library

The Redstone Ordnance Plant produced conventional artillery shells up to 155mm caliber, as well as rifle grenades and demolition blocks. Here, 81mm shells are being assembled. The sister plant, Huntsville Arsenal, manufactured incendiary material, smoke, and toxic agents, such as mustard gas, phosgene, lewisite, white phosphorus, and chlorine gas. Courtesy, U.S. Army Missile Command

1942, 15,000 people were gainfully employed in the county. By May 1944 manufacturing employment in Huntsville alone had risen to 17,000 and total jobs in the city had reached 30,000. A 1943 count of the mill villages and unincorporated areas put that population at 40,354. In 1945 Huntsville's three mills employed a total of 2,775 with 725 at Dallas, 850 at Merrimack, and 1,200 at Lincoln.

The main business of the area was the arsenal complex. Land and construction costs at Huntsville Arsenal and the Gulf Chemical Warfare Depot built on the Tennessee River totaled $70,000,000. The Redstone Arsenal's construction costs amounted to $11,500,000. At their peaks, the Huntsville Arsenal employed 6,707 civilians and the Redstone Arsenal 4,500.

A study, "Historical Highlights of the Redstone Arsenal Complex," by Cleo S. Cason and Winona Y. Stroup points out that as the war progressed, a shift took place in the work force. An increasing number of women were hired to fill fighting men's jobs. An outstanding example of women's willingness to serve was brought to the city's attention when the president of Atlanta University in Atlanta, Georgia, a predominently black university, strode into the office of the Huntsville Arsenal commanding officer and "offered the services of approximately one hundred young women in the graduating class." The offer was accepted and the young women did a job that "could hardly have been surpassed."

The same civic pride that carried Huntsvillians through the war was manifest at its conclusion. Two glorious events dovetailed to give the city cause for joyous celebration. The long, drawn out victory over Japan coincided with a mammoth local "heroes day" planned for Madison County's two Medal of Honor winners. The citizens delighted in the death-defying exploits of their native sons, Lt. Cecil H. "Bushy" Bolton and Sgt. Paul L. Bolden, who had earned the nation's highest honor.

The challenge of peacetime after an all-out war effort was to plan for sustained growth and development. Fitzgerald Hall, the president of the Nashville, Chattanooga and St. Louis Railway, knew that one must first lay track before firing up the engine. He also knew that once track had been laid, business would flourish around it. In the case of Huntsville, Hall had watched his road increase its freight handling by 600 percent during the war. At its peak in May 1945, traffic had increased an amazing 7,000 percent over the January 1941 figure. Understandably Hall did not want to lose this business. Yet he knew government cutbacks would follow victory. In the fall of 1944, Hall and his two directors organized a meeting with Huntsville business and community leaders to plan for future peacetime development.

From this meeting grew the Huntsville Industrial Expansion Committee. Its stated purposes were to collect data and make it available to prospective industries, to advertise, and to plan for rational expansion. One immediate objective was to involve local companies in the city's business future by calling upon each to contribute $250 to the organization. By the end of 1946, 248 businesses had joined. The first study the group conducted was historical in nature. They learned that because of the transition from agriculture to industry, the city could count on an expanding labor supply, and they knew that the economic health of the city depended upon matching people to jobs. To maintain full employment the city's economic base had to diversify. The data also suggested that small, locally owned businesses were of vital importance and should not be overlooked in the quest for big-name firms.

At war's end, much as a home movie is run backwards to the delight of its viewers, the frantic activity of loading 20 freight cars a day with munitions was slammed into screeching reverse. Instead of being loaded, each car was unloaded. Instead of being filled, shells and bombs were emptied. From all over the globe munitions were called home and brought to the arsenals for deactivation and storage. Thousands of wooden crates with incendiary bombs were returned. The bombs were burned and the

Declared surplus property, the Huntsville Arsenal, containing almost 35,000 acres and 900 buildings, was offered for sale by the Department of the Army. The sale never took place, and eventually Huntsville Arsenal consolidated with its sister arsenal to form the Redstone Arsenal, Guided Missile and Rocket Research Center. Courtesy, Huntsville-Madison County Public Library

General H.N. Toftoy was the man who was responsible for bringing the German rocket team to America and, later, to Huntsville. Courtesy, Huntsville-Madison County Public Library

wooden crates were sold for 25 cents each, finding their way into many a wall or floor of homes being built in the postwar rush for housing. Two local men, Jeff Smith and Tant Dowell, assisted by John McDaniel, were able to build a whole ice plant on Clinton Street using government salvage sold at the arsenal as an offshoot of the demilitarization process.

Except for the necessary yet bone-chilling destruction or burial of poisonous and toxic gases and residues that continued at Huntsville Arsenal until it closed down in June of 1949, the vast acreage and buildings of the military complex were standing under-utilized. At least three times "For Sale" signs were posted and Huntsvillians shuddered at the prospect that the government was going out of business in the area.

In retrospect, its citizens recognize that Huntsville entered the space age in steps, but always in hand with the United States government. First it was the New Deal agencies that brought Uncle Sam into the valley. Then it was Huntsville Arsenal and its sister ordnance plant, Redstone Arsenal. Most recently it was the merging of the two arsenals into Redstone Arsenal with its missile program and school, and finally the evolution into the Marshall Space Flight Center.

There is a heroic Lindbergh quality to the story behind the transition from "For Sale" signs to signs that read "Rocket City U.S.A." Or perhaps, like Professor Harold Hill in the fictional River City, one man captured the imagination of an entire community. In either case Col. Holger N. Toftoy's innovative program, to collect "intellectual reparations" in what Winston Churchill called the "Wizard War"—code named "Paper Clip"—possesses a whimsey all its own. It is not too fanciful to say that Huntsville's future hung on the twist of Toftoy's "Paper Clip" operation. Colonel Toftoy, who had been chief of the Army Technical Intelligence Teams in Europe in 1945, arranged for not only the gathering of all German V-2 parts for thorough study but also the gathering of the top German scientists who had put them together at Peeneumunde, the German rocket research center. The United States would save years of research and development, not to mention millions of dollars, if it accepted Toftoy's plan. Toftoy later explained:

A lot of these men had spent their entire adult professional career in rockets, and others who were brought in were highly specialized and renowned throughout Germany in other fields of science. The team was the most complete and competent that I had ever run into, and they had years of experience in working up to that particular point. So I felt they should come as a team—not as individuals.

Toftoy was limited in the number of scientists he could recruit, so he and Wernher von Braun sat down in a schoolhouse at Witzenhausen, Germany, and put together what many have considered the best team of technical experts the world has ever known. Toftoy's orders called for 100 German scientists, but team—or specialization—requirements dictated 127. Toftoy gambled his military future on America's missile future; no fuss was made over the additional 27. The team first was brought to El Paso, Texas, to Fort Bliss. White Sands Proving Grounds, New Mexico, was nearby. Finally, clearance was secured from Gen. Matthew B. Ridgway and Congress to designate Redstone Arsenal (including the defunct Huntsville Arsenal) as the Ordnance Guided Missile Center. With Redstone secured, Huntsville's future was secured—the foreseeable future that is. As Cleo Cason recalls, "it was largely at Toftoy's urging" that Redstone was chosen as the "rocket arsenal" where all rocket research and development could be carried out. The date was November 1949. The news made an exceptionally nice Christmas present to Huntsville from Uncle Sam.

A parade was held in 1945 to honor Madison County's two Congressional Medal of Honor recipients: Paul Bolden and Cecil Bolton. Here returning servicemen march along East Side Square. Courtesy, Huntsville-Madison County Public Library

Even after Colonel Toftoy succeeded in uniting the German scientists with their families, the Germans had felt like aliens in the southwestern American desert that for them represented a cultural as well as a physical void. Still referred to as "prisoners of peace" and constricted in their movements, they had signed a contract to work for the United States government for five years. In 1950 when their contracts expired, they were free to choose "between remaining in the United States by declaring their intention of becoming American citizens and accepting civil service status or seeking employment with private industry, or returning to their homeland." Only a few returned to Germany. Approximately 100 chose civil service in Huntsville at Redstone. As free men and women then, the German contingent came to Huntsville.

Wilson Smith, Jr., a successful Huntsville building contractor, recalls an experience that occurred in 1950 when he was a senior at Huntsville High School. One day when he returned home from school he found a large moving van and an old Nash car parked across the street from his house on Locust Street. Curious to see who was moving in, he wandered over and introduced himself. Only one thing struck him. The young husband, very blond and handsome in his trenchcoat, and his pretty wife were conversing in a foreign language, possibly German. When Wilson reported to his father that their new neighbors were German, the elder Wilson, reflecting the residual prejudices from the war, announced with a shake of his head, "Looks like this neighborhood is going to the dogs."

In April 1955 some 40 German scientists, their wives, and children became U.S. citizens at Huntsville High School. Dr. von Braun is visible in the second row at right. Courtesy, Huntsville-Madison County Public Library

Dr. Wernher von Braun left Huntsville in 1970 after serving 10 years as director of the Marshall Space Flight Center. Thousands of people bid farewell with banners reminding him, "Don't forget you're from the South." Courtesy, Huntsville-Madison County Public Library

The "dogs" in this case turned out to be the Wernher von Brauns. Wilson Smith's dad learned to enjoy eating his words. In the new wave of prosperity brought on by the missile program, the senior Smith gave up his teaching job and became a builder; when the Whitfield section was opened and Locust Street extended, he built homes for some of the German families who bought there. The burgeoning space program brought such an avalanche of people into the city that Smith couldn't build fast enough. His life and fortunes had been turned around by von Braun and his German rocket team.

The city, thanks to Uncle Sam, received a human contribution of incalculable dimensions. Huntsville became home to families whose husbands would send a man to the moon and whose wives and children would eagerly enter into town life. Although these families contributed significantly to Huntsville's "lift-off," or new beginning, it is often overlooked how vitally Huntsville contributed to *their* new beginning. It was here that their "new burst of freedom" occurred. The Germans' efforts at community building resounded with gusto, and the reverberations were heard and felt throughout the city.

Huntsville's rich musical tradition, its bands, its community chorus, its church choirs and liturgical music, and its music study clubs all had been built upon each other and were ready when the Germans, with their passion for Beethoven and Brahms, Mozart and Mahler, added their skills to the mix. The result was the assembling of a symphony orchestra without parallel for a city of its size. Like an increasing number of Huntsville's institutions, the orchestra was composed of a marvelous blend of nationalities.

All cultural and recreational aspects of the city's life received a boost from Huntsville's newest citizens. The Huntsville Museum, the Little Theater, the Arts Council whose task it was to coordinate a developing program in the arts, and the Huntsville Symphony Orchestra would find a permanent home in an exciting civic center structure begun in 1970 at the crest of the city's celebration of its space-age identity. In honor of the citizen whose genius, personality, and perseverance most closely represented the aspirations of its citizens, it bore the name von Braun. On a clear night, visitors winding their way toward downtown from the parkway on Williams experienced a thrill of future shock when they beheld the diffusely lit outlines of the civic center's multi-purpose arena.

In his timely thesis, "The Impact of The Von Braun Board Of Directors On The American Space Program," William Joseph Stubno, Jr., described Huntsville on the eve of the space program in 1950. With a population officially counted at 16,437 and

The Goddard House, circa 1960s, awaits important arsenal guests who will be impressed with the missile launcher parked out front. Courtesy, Old Huntsville Magazine and Huntsville Madison County Public Library

another 16,000 in the fringe areas, Huntsville was still a small town and a relatively poor one. In 1949, Stubno writes, "only 9 percent of the population earned over $6,000 per year." Citing a report of the newly organized Huntsville Planning Commission that "In 1949, the population of Huntsville was overwhelmingly grouped at the lower income levels, with perhaps only a quarter of the families being able to afford anything more than the minimum necessities," he pointed out that in 1950, "25 percent of the population of Huntsville had less than five years of education, although 19 percent did have a high school diploma." Stubno notes the quiet beginning in 1950 of the University of Alabama Center. With an original enrollment of 139 students, it was "established at the request of a number of substantial citizens who wanted an academic institution in the town." The seeds for solid growth as well as a space odyssey were being planted.

Shirley Thomas, one of Wernher von Braun's biographers begins her study by saying: "The story of Wernher von Braun is a true story. It has to be. It is too improbable to be accepted as fiction." What she has said of von Braun must also be said of Huntsville. In 1931 no one would have dreamed that ten years later Huntsville would be the site for a multimillion-dollar military chemical plant, depot, and munitions arsenal. In 1941 no one would have predicted that ten years later this chemical plant and arsenal would have been transformed into the combined Redstone Arsenal housing the nation's missile program and the superlative German rocket team led by Wernher von Braun. In 1951 no one would have imagined that ten years later the Huntsville team would have sent a space vehicle into earth orbit, launching the satellite Explorer with a mighty thrust from Jupiter-C into the heavens, no longer to be the domain of the Russians with their Sputnik, but to be America's new frontier. In 1961 when President John F. Kennedy announced that "this nation should commit itself to achieving the goal, before this decade is out, of landing a man on the moon and returning him safely to Earth," and designated von Braun's Marshall Space Flight Center as the group to get us there, few could have envisioned the glory of Neil Armstrong's 1969 lunar landing. In 1971 few would have foreseen the ten-year tailspin the space program and the Marshall Space Flight Center was to experience as younger American scientists replaced the Germans and the whole space effort was subjected to redefinition and retooling with American industry assuming a partnership role.

In Erik Bergaust's *Rocket City U.S.A.*, published in 1963, the story of Huntsville, Alabama, found national recognition. Bergaust wrote:

It may be a bitter deal for all Americans. But it remains a fact. The guys who really put this country back into the rocket race were a group of German Ph.D.'s and technologists. Furthermore, the important rocket work performed in this country for perfection of intermediate and long-range missiles and space vehicles of various kinds was not performed at Buffalo, Detroit, Los Angeles or New York. It was done in Huntsville, Alabama, often referred to by rocket people as Peeneumunde South.

Herein lay the seeds for the demise of the German rocket team. The early 1970s saw the redistribution of space responsibilities to other installations, the switch from in-house production to contract-management by vast corporations, and broadening of the entire space program. NASA—like the Redstone Arsenal's Army Ballistic Missile Agency, Army Missile Command, and the Army Ordnance Guided Missile School—was created by the federal government and could be transplanted or destroyed by the federal

President John F. Kennedy and Vice-President Lyndon B. Johnson visited Redstone Arsenal in September 1962. Others pictured include: General R.M. Hurst (in background, facing camera); Major General F.J. Morrow, Dr. Wernher voh Braun, James E. Webb, Lieutenant General Besson, and Dr. Eberhard Rees. Courtesy, U.S. Army Missile Command

Thousands gathered around the Courthouse Square as Dr. Wernher von Braun of Marshall Space Flight Center was carried to the speaker's platform during the Apollo 11 splashdown celebration on July 24, 1969. The spacecraft that planted an American flag on the moon was powered by a rocket developed at Marshall. Courtesy, Huntsville-Madison County Public Library

government. Civic leaders assessed Huntsville's vulnerability to governmental whim and political caprice and resolved that it had to be reduced to manageable, elastic proportions. If the city had learned anything from its textile past, it should have learned not to look to one basket for its eggs.

Some of the conservatism of old-time Huntsvillians was an almost visceral reaction to the fear of loss. It had happened all too many times. Embedded in the collective memory of its people was this lesson of the past. While it crippled some, it inspired others to continue seeking through such organizations as the Chamber of Commerce, the Huntsville Industrial Expansion Committee, and Cummings Research Park to build a more stable and prosperous community.

Erik Bergaust noted the reluctance of Huntsville to completely adopt the military and space mission. "The truth is," he explained, "that much of old Huntsville's power structure does not place its real and inner trust in either the NASA or the Army rocket programs." Snake-bit too many times, the older leaders knew instinctively what Bergaust did not recognize, that Uncle Sam could be as limiting and arbitrary a master as textiles.

Because of the wary and wise leadership of such forward-looking citizens as Milton Cummings, Reese Amis, John Sparkman, Harry Rhett, Leroy Simms, and Walt Wiesman, and

Huntsville mayors A.W. McAllister, R.B. Searcy, Glenn Hearn, and Joe Davis, the quest for economic prosperity and diversified but steady industrial growth was to continue in a logical, life-saving progression. From space exploration to space-age industry, computers and high technology, younger leaders made the city one of the nation's most dynamic high-tech centers.

The missile and space programs joined by high-tech did for Huntsville what the textile industry did not do. It attracted to the city people of extraordinary intellectual and cultural attainment. And it paid them well. Less flamboyant perhaps than the leadership of earlier entrepreneurs, these newcomers were more intent upon building community than they were upon building fortunes. These men and women from all over the country and every corner of the world came not to exploit but to add their seed to the beauty and bounty of this area aptly

Space Shuttle Enterprise with its "running mate," a modified Boeing 747, has the distinction of being the first space shuttle, although it never went into orbit. As a test vehicle, it came to Marshall in the late 1970s for vibration testing. Once the shuttle program got into orbit, Enterprise became a celebrity, appearing at the Paris Air Show in 1983, the New Orleans World's Fair in 1984, and making a return visit to Huntsville in 1985 on its way to lasting fame as a Smithsonian exhibit. Courtesy, NASA

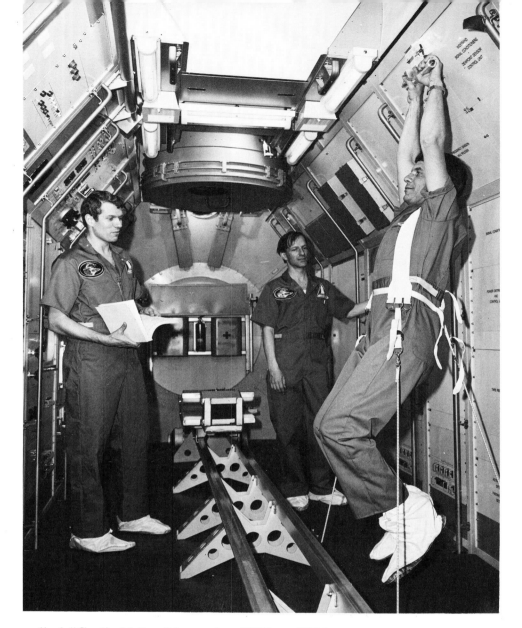

The crew of Spacelab conducted experiments in such areas as solar physics, astronomy, life sciences, and atmospheric physics. Here astronauts determine heart functioning under weightless conditions at Marshall's Spacelab simulator. Courtesy, NASA

called "God's Valley" by writer Willson Whitman.

A *Times* article in March 1965 called Huntsville progressive and vibrant because of its citizens' "keen public interest in local governmental affairs." The muscle and sinew of city government was its volunteer boards and agencies that carried out local programs. "The majority of the private citizens who help guide municipal affairs are comparative newcomers to the city," said Mayor Glenn Hearn. They are "well-educated and highly qualified" with an "overwhelming interest" in participating.

This enlightened approach to city government was bound to loosen the racial restraints and strict segregation patterns that had regulated race relations. In 1956 the Southern Depot removed its segregation signs; more barriers began to fall as the glare of national and world attention focused on other Alabama cities: Montgomery's 1955-1956 bus boycott, George Wallace's 1963 stand in the University of Alabama schoolhouse door in Tuscaloosa, Police Commissioner Eugene "Bull" Connor's hosing of black children in Birmingham, and the bombing of a Birmingham church. Huntsville reacted. Black and white leaders took each other's measure and went to work looking for peaceful solutions to their problems.

Huntsville's black population had often prided itself on, yet criticized itself, for its many middle-class assumptions. There was an old black Huntsville just as surely as there was an old white one. These citizens tended to be conservative on racial issues. They, like their white counterparts, had been more concerned with economic factors than with ideology. Among the more conservative was Lawrence B. Hundley, owner of Royal Funeral Home, who was also affiliated with the Huntsville Housing Authority. In an interview granted in 1973 to a student of the civil rights movement, Mr. Hundley spoke serenely: "I find that here in Huntsville we have been a little more fortunate than in other places. There has always been a good relationship in Huntsville between the Blacks and the whites. . . I have friends in both races."

Mr. Hundley favored the Huntsville Housing Authority's handling of urban renewal. Black poverty was not as great in Huntsville as in many other cities and towns. Huntsville's urban renewal plan, though designed primarily to create a metropolitan downtown center that would expand from "a nine-block 40-acre area to an 840-acre tract bounded by Memorial Parkway, Governors Drive, Pratt Avenue, and California Street," did

Marshall's huge Neutral Buoyancy Simulator approximates the zero-gravity of outer space and serves as a training ground for many of the astronauts. In this photograph the space-suited engineers are experimenting with a mobile work station. Courtesy, NASA

remove most pockets of black and white poverty in Huntsville. "To my knowledge," Mr. Hundley said, "urban renewal has been a blessing especially to the Black man in Huntsville, Alabama."

Without improved economic and political conditions for blacks, better housing would not have achieved positive results. Huntsville's black middle class of proprietors and professionals had filled the needs of a segregated black community. What was needed was affirmative action to bring blacks into the suburban work force located in research parks and to enable them to climb the same managerial ladders of the growing number of firms located in the city. Alabama A & M president Dr. R.D. Morrison in a *Times* interview in 1978 cited the role of industrial leadership in effecting meaningful change here: "It was men like Milton Cummings. . .who led the way." As president of Brown Engineering, the area's largest industrial employer hosting 1,922 workers at the end of 1962, Cummings founded the Association of Huntsville Area Contractors and led the way in the drive to give blacks equal job opportunities. To broaden those objectives and strengthen the community base, Cummings also founded the Huntsville-Madison County Community Action Committee, serving as its first chairman. It is no wonder that the city honored him as the "Man of the Year" in 1965.

The dollars and sense of integration found stubborn resistance when the community dealt with school integration. Yet Huntsville simply could not afford blatant defiance of federal law and constitutional rights of citizens if it was going to honor its commitments to the federal government. Billions of dollars, the future of Huntsville's missile command and space program, were stakes too high to jeopardize; and all sides knew it.

School integration took individual courage and conviction but most of all persistance. In 1962 a young sergeant and his wife, the Marvin Burnettes, stationed at Redstone Arsenal, sought admission for their daughter at Madison Pike School. The Associated Press picked up the story.

At Huntsville, Ala. city school officials rejected a Negro mother's efforts to enroll her fourth grade daughter in a white public school, saying she had been assigned to a Negro school. The child's father is an army sergeant stationed at Redstone Arsenal.

The wheels of change were set in motion. In January 1963 the justice department brought suit in federal court on behalf of the black children of the arsenal who were bused to all-black schools. The case was thrown out on a "technicality." But Huntsville

The Big Spring swimming pool was for "whites only" and was done away with in the 1960s. Courtesy, Old Huntsville Magazine and Huntsville Madison County Public Library

physician Sonnie Hereford III had greater success when he brought suit for his son, Sonnie IV, in March, seeking an end to segregation. The court finally issued an injunction shortly before the fall term ordering the school board to desist.

On September 6, 1963, four lonely, frightened, and brave black children walked the distance to their respective school doors and were turned away by state troopers sent by Governor Wallace to bar their admission. The next school day, however, citizen wishes overrode Wallace's tour de force and the racial walls came tumbling down. Veronica Pearson, John Brewton, David Piggee, and Sonnie Hereford IV entered all-white schools. The day after George Wallace took his last stand in the Tuscaloosa schoolhouse door, a young black engineer employed by the Marshall Space Flight Center quietly went about the businesss of enrolling at Huntsville's University of Alabama campus. According to a *Times* article of March 25, 1963, Dave M. McGlathery had been seeking admission since February of that year; the state school had found some "technicality" that stymied his admission.

At the same time blacks were seeking integrated schools in Huntsville, they were also seeking through sit-ins to dramatize discrimination in public accommodations. Lunch counters became symbolic battlegrounds for civil rights. Joan Carpenter Cashin, wife of dentist John Cashin, founder of Alabama's National Democratic Party, was in the forefront of the campaign to secure equal seating and service. When she, with her youngest child Cheryl in her arms, was arrested along with Mrs. Sonnie Hereford and taken to jail because they attempted to eat at the Walgreens Drug Store, the lunacy of resistance brought shame to Huntsville's leaders. With meteoric swiftness the city cast off its legal armour of segregation.

Overcoming racial hurdles added to the city's esprit de corp. But perhaps it was helping to put a man on the moon and being at the forefront of technological change that gave young Huntsvillians an almost unbounded faith in the future. Then too there are those families who have been in Huntsville from the beginning, maintaining their dignity even while losing fortunes, marrying one another and weaving close-knit ties of consanguinity and affection. Someone jokingly exclaimed that old Huntsvillians have more connections than a New York City switchboard, and indeed, a perusal of the numerous books of family history available in the Huntsville Public Library Heritage Room bears this out.

Alex Haley, the author of the bestseller *Roots,* spent his formative years in Madison County, at Normal, where his father was a professor of agriculture at Alabama A & M. Young Haley

After Walgreens Drug Store lunch counter was integrated, others like Anderson Drug's soda fountain followed suit. Courtesy, Old Huntsville Magazine *and Huntsville Madison County Public Library*

read every book he could get his hand on, but he spent even more time exploring the mountains and woods and gaining a spiritual attachment to this land. The author relates how, in each generation of his family, the newborn child was lifted up and held heavenward as it was given its name. It is this looking upward to the stars and backward to his roots that gives Haley his breadth as a writer and human being. It is this that he shares with so many Huntsvillians.

In addition, the thousands of newcomers to Huntsville, mostly young families eager to get on with living, created a new Huntsville that encircled the old, much as an artichoke's leaves encircle the heart. Lacking the attachment that deep roots provide, these newcomers mingled their youth and dreams of the future with the city's memories and landmarks of the past. It

While many historic buildings have been preserved, Huntsville needlessly lost many treasures to urban renewal under the guise of progress in the 1960s. Residential gems, like the Rison house pictured here, lined West Holmes and West Clinton and were razed for architecturally bland low-income housing. Courtesy, Smallwood family

was as though they were fulfilling some fundamental law: the farther one extends out into space the deeper grow the roots of attachment to this earth. Space gave to the new Huntsvillians a unique sense of time and place right here on earth.

It is this rich but new heritage of space technology that makes Huntsville's Alabama Space and Rocket Center, "earth's largest space museum," a unique experience. The nationally acclaimed space camp was only one of many innovations introduced by Edward O. Buckbee, one of Huntsville's dynamic new leaders. Another is the space flight library that has as its nucleus "over 200,000 papers, notes, books, and memorabilia" donated to the museum by the family of the late Dr. Wernher von Braun, plus thousands of items donated by other rocketry pioneers or ordinary citizens.

Huntsville's other history museums are equally special. Constitution Hall Park presents a re-creation of the city's 1819 role as a constitutional spearhead. The Huntsville Depot is a vital history center and museum that presents the story of Huntsville and Madison County in terms of their transportation systems, industry, and commerce. Occupying 167 acres atop Monte Sano, the Burritt Museum and Pioneer Village, besides offering visitors a spectacular view of the city and beyond, contains a variety of experiences that bring the city's past to life.

One of the reasons Huntsville has become such a popular place to visit is that young and old, space buff and antiquarian, will find solid nourishment for their minds, and imaginations. There is nothing superficial about the city. One sees some admittedly unattractive snatches along the Parkway and Governors Drive, but one can always look up to the mountains and find beauty. Or one can go downtown and find still vibrant remnants of the past. The city's architecture represents a layering of human experience that is both rich and diverse.

If anything brought old and new Huntsvillians together it has been the common goal to preserve the past. Historical preservation has become a way of life for the inhabitants of Huntsville's first historic district, Twickenham, containing within its bounds marvelously preserved homes of the city's original founders. Inhabitants of Old Town with its nucleus in the city's Victorian era have painted their wood cottages and patched their gingerbread, giving the area a colorful atmosphere accentuating the individualities of each home. The mill villages reflect another slice of Victorian life. Mill housing, much like modern apartments or housing projects, reflects mass-produced sameness, but in the yards and gardens, personality found expression.

For all of its bounty, Huntsville had not known the lever of large-scale philanthropy that can lift ordinary towns into extraordinary places in which to live in and to visit. The city has not until recently produced great wealth for its citizens, though there has been a substantial core of millionaires, old and new. A part-time resident in the early years of the century, Virginia McCormick, daughter of inventor Cyrus McCormick, stands head and shoulders above any other citizen in gift-giving to benefit the city. Miss McCormick's wealth was given upon recommendation of Grace Walker, her companion and business manager. Miss Walker was a kindly woman sensitive to the needs of the poor and of blacks, supporting YMCAs and health facilities for each group.

An editorial in the September 10, 1945, *Times* addressed the need for philanthropy. What was needed was a new library. "Shelves are overflowing and books are piled high in the basement." The appeal for "some Huntsvillian... to earn the lasting gratitude of his or her fellow citizens and of future generations" went unanswered for some time. When answered, it was not by the largesse of one but rather by the combined efforts of the many that a new library was secured. The Friends of the Library, formed in 1958, helped find the money for a new library.

Continuing in this tradition, every cultural, health, and recreational need of the city was met by volunteers who give as generously of their time as their money. Individual Huntsville citizens gave the money in 1959 to found Randolph School, 20 percent of whose seniors becoming National Merit finalists since it began awarding diplomas. Mrs. Chessie Harris and her husband George built a home for hundreds of disadvantaged youngsters. She started out with nothing but love and a good idea—to provide a home for children whose parents could not provide one. Shelby Fletcher took an interest in a crippled mill village kid and gave him an office job; when he died in 1936, Fletcher left the young man $5,000. With that legacy Milton Cummings was able to parlay a fortune. He continued the private sort of philanthropy Fletcher had introduced him to. Other prominent citizens supported their own private philanthropies. Dr. William H. Burritt's gifts to the city and its citizens go on in perpetuity enriching our landscape and our lives.

Since its beginnings, the marvel of Huntsville's history has been its citizens' ability to launch boldly into the future— while at the same time keeping their feet firmly planted on this piece of earth called home, extending their hands to one another in community. Huntsville had achieved lift-off. All systems were go.

One of Huntsvlle's leading Jewish families was that of Robert Herstein. Born in Darnstadt, Germany, Herstein settled in Huntsville in 1855 and married Rosa Blimline of Baltimore, Maryland in 1859. A dry goods merchant, he and Rosa had seven children. This painting of three of the Herstein children is attributed to William Frye. Courtesy, Mr. and Mrs. Lawrence Goldsmith, Jr.

Jones Valley, 2000 *by Ed Starnes. Tucked between the eastern mountain chain enveloping the city and Garth Road is Jones Valley and the Jones Farm. For generations, going back to Isaac Criner, family members have helped develop Madison County's resources, making large contributions to the city and state. Courtesy, Ed Starnes*

Oak Place, the George Steele home on Maysville Road, was the scene of one of Huntsville's most gala events, the inaugural celebration of President James K. Polk. A reported 2,000 persons feasted on turkey, duck, veal and mutton as well as 200 cakes. Special hickory canes were given as a keepsake. This water-color is by Albert Lane. Courtesy, Historic Huntsville Foundation

One of Huntsville's leading Jewish families was that of Robert Herstein. Born in Darnstadt, Germany, Herstein settled in Huntsville in 1855 and married Rosa Blimline of Baltimore, Maryland in 1859. A dry goods merchant, he and Rosa had seven children. This painting of three of the Herstein children is attributed to William Frye, Courtesy, Mr. and Mrs. Lawrence Goldsmith, Jr.

Facing page, bottom Huntsville water colorist, Ed Starnes brings history alive in such paintings as Bright New Morning, a 19th century pastoral scene at Constitution Village. Courtesy, Ed Starnes

This is the only known
self-portrait by poet/painter
Maria Howard Weeden
(1847-1905). Her dialect
poems and portraits
primarily depicting blacks
filled four slim
volumes—Shadows on the
Wall, Bandanna Ballads,
Songs of the Old South,
and Old Voices. Courtesy,
Burritt Museum and Park

As was frequently her
custom, Miss Weeden did
several studies of the same
person, this entitled
Dancing Jane Anna. While
some contend that she
patronized and caricatured
the blacks around her,
others believe hers was an
honest interpretation of late
19th century black culture.
Courtesy, Burritt Museum
and Park

In 1805 John Hunt settled in the area that would soon be named Huntsville, building a log cabin near a natural spring that flowed into the Tennessee River. The Big Spring, which long provided Huntsville with an abundant source of water, is depicted in this circa 1850 painting by Austrian artist William Frye. Frye had settled in Huntsville in the late 1840s. Courtesy, Harry M. Rhett, Jr.

Right
In the heart of downtown Huntsville history is relived each day at Alabama Constitution Village. Thousands of school children and adults visit each year. *Courtesy, Huntsville/Madison County Convention & Visitors Bureau*

Below
The arts and crafts of the early 1800s find a natural setting in Constitution Village. *Courtesy, Huntsville/Madison County Convention & Visitors Bureau*

At Early Works children learn that history is a story of the past that they can try to recapture through play and imagination. Courtesy, Huntsville/Madison County Convention & Visitors Bureau

Top
One of the Monte Sano cabins that was built in the late 1930s by the Civilian Conservation Corps encamped on Monte Sano. By 1940 there were 14 cabins that rented for $15.00 per week. Courtesy, Huntsville/Madison County Convention & Visitors Bureau

Bottom
Built in 1860, the Huntsville Depot housed Civil War prisoners who left graffiti on the walls. Strategic to Union victory, the station houses memories of all our wars, their leaves-taking and welcomes-home. Courtesy, Huntsville/Madison County Convention & Visitors Bureau

Like the man who designed it as his residence, it is one of a kind. Dr. William Henry Burritt applied his singular tastes to its construction and design. Shaped like a Maltese Cross, its walls are insulated with 2,200 bales of straw. Courtesy, Huntsville/Madison County Convention & Visitors Bureau

Top
Sharing Greek Revival architectural elements with its neighbors, this red brick home blends in with its antebellum neighbors, all a part of the Twickenham Historic District which was placed on the National Register of Historic Places in 1973. Courtesy, Huntsville/ Madison County Convention & Visitors Bureau

Bottom, left
A popular gathering spot in the 1990s, Bubba's patio could be reached by a stroll down the colorful alley back Bubba's and the Heritage Club. Courtesy, Huntsville/ Madison County Convention & Visitors Bureau

Facing page, bottom, right
Another gathering spot
atop the Big Spring offers a
vista of the Indian Creek
Canal and the area being
transformed by Jim and
Susie Hudson into Electric
Avenue. Courtesy, Hunts-
ville/Madison County
Convention & Visitors
Bureau

This panoramic captures
far more than the Big
Spring Jam Festival it
depicts. Looking to the
northeast, from above the
Monroe-Williams inter-
section, Huntsville's
skyline rises to meet the
mountains encasing the
city's eastern expanse.
Courtesy, Huntsville/
Madison County Con-
vention & Visitors Bureau

Top, left
Consecrated in 1860, the Church of the Nativity in the Twickenham Historic District was organized as early as December 1842 when a vestry was formed and the parish was named "Nativity" in recognition of the impending Christmas vigil. *Courtesy, Huntsville/Madison County Convention & Visitors Bureau*

Top, right
A somber winter scene of an angel in Maple Hill Cemetery reminds Huntsvillians that a burst of flowering pink and white dogwoods will usher in Spring and tours of this venerable place where time and eternity meet. *Photo by Daniel Little*

Bottom
Located in Huntsville's Old Town District, Temple B'Nai Sholom on Lincoln Street was built in 1898 by the local Jewish community. *Photo by Linda Allen*

*An African American
display at EarlyWorks
instills pride in young and
old alike. Courtesy,
Author's collection*

Huntsville's Botanical Gardens is one of the regions most pleasant surprises. Visitors drive from a busy street back into a beckoning garden wonderland. Every season has its delights. Courtesy, Huntsville/Madison County Convention & Visitors Bureau

Facing page, top, left Pumpkins are in colorful display at the Botanical Gardens. Photo by Daniel Little

Facing page, top, right Opened in 1999, the Butterfly House has attracted visitors from afar, especially families with young children. Photo by Daniel Little

Facing page, bottom This 100-year-old dogwood tree was saved from destruction when Madison Pike was widened and the tree had to be removed. Volunteers and school children campaigned to get the tree safely removed to a "Place of Honor" in the Botanical Garden. Photo by Daniel Little

At Cathedral Caverns visitors view fossils of sea life over 220 million years old. Stalagmites that have built up and tower over heads are reminders that space is not the only less-explored region in our cosmos. Courtesy, Huntsville/Madison County Convention & Visitors Bureau

Top
This awesome view from the shuttle encompasses the Space Station but can only catch a snatch of space as the shuttle circles the earth every 90 or so minutes. Courtesy, NASA

Bottom
Allowing a close-up view of the millions of parts and pieces that went into construction of the Apollo spacecraft, young and old become part of America's space adventure at the Space and Rocket Center. Courtesy, Huntsville/ Madison County Convention & Visitors Bureau

Inside and out, the Space and Rocket Center is a living history museum of the Space Age. Bus tours of adjoining Marshall Space Flight Center complement the flights of fancy and space activities the Center offers. Courtesy, Huntsville/Madison County Convention & Visitors Bureau

Facing page, top
Between September 12–20, 1992, the seven crew members sharing eight days of research in support of Spacelab pose for the traditional in-flight portrait in the science module. Left to right, back row, are Robert L. Gibson, mission commander, Jerome (Jay) Apt, mission specialist, Curtis L. Brown, pilot, and Mae C. Jemison, mission specialist. Front row, Jan Davis, mission specialist, Mark C. Lee, payload commander, and Mamoru Mohri, payload specialist representing Japan's National Space Development Agency. Courtesy, NASA

Facing page, bottom
Space Camp gives youngsters a dress rehearsal for future careers in space science and engineering. Young people and adults can train like fighter pilots using flight simulators and a 40-foot tower to parachute. Courtesy, Huntsville/Madison County Convention & Visitors Bureau

All roads lead to the Von Braun Center. Huntsville's convention center is also a civic center. To accommodate expansion Williams Avenue was taken up by the South Hall. Directly north is Memorial Parkway and to the upper right is the vital interstate connection I –565. Courtesy, Huntsville/Madison County Convention & Visitors Bureau

Top
The Von Braun Center North Hall, pictured here set up with booths, also makes into a beautiful banquet hall for gala events. Courtesy, Huntsville/Madison County Convention & Visitors Bureau

Bottom
Owned and operated by the Historic Huntsville Foundation, Harrison Brothers on the Square is manned by volunteers and retains the charm of yesteryear. The store is a museum in motion. Courtesy, Huntsville/ Madison County Convention & Visitors Bureau

*Japanese cherry blossoms
provide a tranquil place
for picnic lunches and
leisurely strolls. Courtesy,
Huntsville/Madison
County Convention &
Visitors Bureau*

In his watercolor, Morning in the Park, *Ed Starnes depicts the essence of Huntsville's recent past. Bridging Big Spring, the site of Huntsville's nativity, is the Red Bridge, symbol of the city's international role. The American flag flies betwixt flowering cherry blossoms and the whole scene is banked from left to right by the Von Braun Center, named for Huntsville's Space Age immortal, Wernher von Braun. Courtesy, Ed Starnes*

CHAPTER VII

Hitch Your Wagon to a Star: Space and Beyond

This day before dawn I ascended a hill and look'd at the crowded heaven, And I said to my spirit When we become the enfolders of these orbs, and the pleasure and knowledge of every thing in them, shall we be fill'd and satisfied then? And my spirit said No, we but level that lift to pass and continue beyond
  —Walt Whitman, *Leaves of Grass*

Hitch your wagon to a star.
  —Ralph Waldo Emerson, *Civilization*

The sky is not the limit.
  —Chamber of Commerce, Huntsville/Madison County

Every age has its memoirists. Homer H. Hickam, Jr. chronicles the Space Age. An autographed inscription in his acclaimed *Rocket Boys* states: "Aim High!" Hickam's quintessential coming of age memoir is of a time and place—rural West Virginia—much like Huntsville and other North Alabama towns. Hickam's mining folk lived and worked among mountains that let only a sliver of sky shine through. Not asking much from life, they had little time for dreams of space and adventure among the stars.

All that changed for Hickam and others of his generation who experienced Sputnik as a life-transforming event. He wrote:

Burritt Park, atop Monte Sano acquaints visitors with the region's pioneer past as well as its role in space. The park, with its sweeping vista, shares Monte Sano with star-gazers who visit the Von Braun Astronomical Society Observatory and Planetarium nearby. Courtesy, Huntsville/Madison County Convention and Visitors Bureau

I guess it's fair to say there were two distinct phases to my life in West Virginia: everything that happened before October 5, 1957 and everything that happened afterward.

Describing a boy's epiphany, he continued:

Then I saw the bright little ball, moving majestically across the narrow star field between the ridgelines. I stared at it with no less rapt attention than if it had been God Himself in a golden chariot riding overhead.

Much like the Three Kings of Biblical time following "yonder star," Homer Hickam resolved to follow his star to Huntsville, Alabama, by extension, the "Bethlehem" of America's space program:

I began to hear about one particular rocket scientist named Dr. Wernher von Braun....At night before I went to sleep, I thought about what Dr. von Braun might be doing at that very moment down at the Cape....I started to think about what an adventure it would be to work for him, helping him to build rockets and launching them into space....

Ray Garner, the editor of *Technology Valley*, credits von Braun's 1952 articles in *Collier's* magazine for inspiring production of "the newest star for our planet."

The sheer size and challenge of building the space station will ensure its inclusion in the annals of human events...a launching pad for ambitious space exploration missions.

Women learned that von Braun's dream could be theirs as well, and they rose to the challenge. Called NASA's "rocket girls," these women serve as role models for countless others. Among them is Susan

Turner, a Huntsville native who graduated from Huntsville High School in 1979. Named assistant director of Marshall's Propulsion Laboratory in 1998, she is project director for the X-37, Boeing's small, reusable, winged rocket that will "dramatically reduce the cost of space transportation." At Marshall since 1963, Dr. Ann Whitaker is director of the Materials and Processes Laboratory. Leslie Curtis is project manager for space transportation technologies. One of her projects is the electrodynamic tether "that will use the earth's magnetic field to generate thrust." Marshall Center deputy director, Carolyn Griner, was her role model and inspiration. Sherry Buschmann is project manager in the Advanced Space Transportation Program working on the International Space Station. Wendy Cruit, came to Marshall as a coop student in 1990, following in both parents' footsteps. Her mother is an engineer; so is Wendy. Her father, Steve Richards, came to Marshall in 1976 and in 1999 managed the International Space Station propulsion module.

In *Journey into Space: The First Thirty Years of Space Exploration,* Bruce Murray points out that space shuttle development focused on earth orbiting rather than unmanned planetary exploration, needlessly endangering lives.

America met its crucible that cold, awful day in January 1986 when its storybook shuttle blew up seconds after launch. In horror, disbeliev-

Used from 1969 to 1997, Marshall's huge Neutral Buoyancy Simulator approximated the zero-gravity of outer space and served as a training ground for many of the astronauts. Here space-suited engineers are experimenting with a mobile workstation. Courtesy, NASA

The "rocket girls," top row, left to right: Leslie Curtis, Sherry Buschmann and Dr. Ann Whitaker. Bottom row, left to right: Wendy Cruit and Susan Turner. Courtesy, NASA

In April 1986, the families of Challenger Seven *established the Challenger Center for Space Science Education with the "vision of continuing the crew's educational mission," stating that "education was the common love they all shared." Pictured are, in the back row, from left to right: Ellison S. Onizuka, mission specialist; S. Christa McAuliffe, teacher in space participant; Gregory B. Jarvis, payload specialist; and Judy A. Resnik, mission specialist. Front row, from left to right: Michael J. Smith, pilot; Francis R. (Dick) Scobee, commander; and Ronald E. McNair, mission specialist. Courtesy, NASA*

ing television viewers shared the agony of Christa McAuliffe's parents, whose expressions told the world in split-second intervals of their change from pride mixed with joy and apprehension to a stunned realization that what they were seeing was not what they were supposed to be seeing, that in fact the burst of flame and smoky trail were the fiery last words of their daughter and her six companions.

The nation mourned in a deep, personal way. Murray remarks:

The Challenger Seven could hardly have been a more representative group of American martyrs——three races, four religions, male and female, military and civilian, married and single, fathers, and a mother.

Huntsville reeled. Its scientists and engineers at Marshall Space Flight Center bore responsibility for what went wrong. A "faulty joint in the segmented booster that allowed hot exhaust to shoot through and ignite the external liquid fuel tank" was the "proximate cause." "Management isolation" at Marshall was a contributing factor. Creeping complacency and underlying bureaucratic glitches nagged Marshall's collective conscience.

President Reagan promised the nation, "The shuttle will fly again." Eleven months later, Huntsville *Times* science writer Martin Burkey labeled the year one of "tragedy, shock, controversy, and recovery." New Marshall Director, J. R. Thompson called the shuttle the workhorse "we're betting on." Resilient scientists and engineers at Marshall corrected errors and added other challenges—the Hubble Space Telescope and the International Space Station, both depending upon the shuttle to keep them supplied, repaired, refurbished, and in orbit.

The Hubble Space Telescope has introduced space exploration as an inactive learning experience for students and the scientific community the world over. The Telescope enables scientists to see back in time, as it searches the universe and assists mankind to comprehend the cosmos. Courtesy, NASA

As the civilian space program faced funding cuts and setbacks, city leaders joined with military leaders to keep their projects and the economy afloat. "StarWars," President Reagan's missile-defense shield was augmented after 1986 by advocates of the military and reinvigorated by President George W. Bush in 2001.

The region's economy soared as entrepreneurs acquired military contracts to provide the systems engineering, sensing, communications, thrust and myriad other components necessary to field and test the multi-faceted defense configuration. One commentator remarked, "Daddy Warbucks has replaced Buck Rogers."

Like baseball's field of dreams, since 1962, Cummings Research Park has been the sowing field for Huntsville's technology. The *Times* parallels "the research park's story" as "the story of the city during the past quarter century." In 2000, Cummings Research Park West counted 26,000 employees in 185 high-tech companies; in 2001 Alex Hardy, the director, called the Park "the Heart of High-Tech in Alabama." Housing 18 Fortune 500 companies, it is an international orchestra of the sciences and engineering bringing together in one place over 220 companies that join with the military and NASA to produce master works of our technological age.

Among space and defense companies, Teledyne Brown Engineering is legendary. The same leadership that brought together the core of defense and space research and development companies in Cummings Research Park, has, since 1971, had the key job of evaluating and monitoring the effectiveness of other contractors doing work for the Army Strategic Defense Command.

For 50 years, Huntsville pioneered the rise of the military industrial complex that underlies our national fabric and economic well-being. The insertion of American free enterprise into military and space programs, from the largest corporations to smallest home start-ups, has not only revolutionized the way the government and the military do business, but it has created a managerial and technological revolution few cities anywhere in the world have been more involved with more than Huntsville, Alabama.

John McDaniel, who established a "national reputation as a manager of massive and complex research and development programs," saw its beginnings, describing what took place at Redstone: "From the work of this group of people has come the greatest engineering and scientific feats known to civilization."

As Redstone Arsenal's defense and missile sphere expanded, contractors became the mainstay of the economy. Their success is tantamount to progress and prosperity for the region. Increasing numbers of start-up companies offer innovative products and services. City leaders scurried to secure the infrastructure, research and industrial parks, retail shopping centers, roads and financial packages including

From the 1950s to the present, lobbying businessmen go to Washington to promote the region's military and space programs. Courtesy, Old Huntsville Magazine *and Huntsville Madison County Public Library*

In 1961 the Army's missile family consisted of: Nike Hercules, Sergeant, Nike Zeus, Pershing and Nike Ajax. In the background is the Lacrosse; in the foreground is the Hawk. Soldiers in the foreground hold the M72 Rocket Grenade, the Redeye, and the Entac. Courtesy, U.S. Army Space & Missile Defense Command

tax abatements that spurred healthy development and population growth.

One hundred years ago, cotton fields and pastures led up to the city's gates; 50 years ago cotton mills and mill villages crowded its perimeter. The small town had no idea what was in store. In a speech before the Huntsville/Madison County Chamber of Commerce on the 20th anniversary of Explorer I, January 31, 1978, General Medaris recalled:

The first time I flew into Huntsville to begin the process of setting up the new agency in October 1955, I could hardly find the place. The green and white beacon of Huntsville Airport rotated in a sea of blackness. At 10 o'clock that night most of the lights in the then tiny area of Huntsville were already dim or out....The figures say Huntsville had 17,000 people but it did not seem to be that many! The city did not abut the arsenal and Jordan Lane was a rundown area, ready to be the honky tonk line for a growing military base.

Medaris helped the city extend to the arsenal, not a popular idea with many in West Huntsville who feared higher taxes. New Hope native Mack Vann, whose father Herman Vann was the state senator for Madison County, writes in his book *Creek Bottom Home,* that General Medaris insisted "the Army Missile Command would not relocate to Redstone Arsenal as long as sewage flowed from West Huntsville onto Redstone Arsenal property," which happened when heavy rains caused flooding. Vann's father "introduced legislation down at the state capital which in effect, made West Huntsville part of Huntsville proper without a vote by West Huntsville citizens." In addition, zoning was put in place that "kept the red lights away from the Arsenal." Herman Vann lost his Senate seat to a Mill Village lad, West Huntsville's native son, Dave Archer. Mack Vann argues that it was his father's swift action for annexation that lost him the election but saved the day for Huntsville and for Redstone Arsenal.

Huntsville became the vanguard of change. Its Arsenal, "the original birthplace of missile and rocket development programs in the USA," sent a man to the moon. Its rockets probe the universe, and its Hubble Telescope reveals its secrets. It is the home of NASA's thrust or propulsion center, the Army's weapon systems and lasers, industry's micro-chips and telecommunication systems which speed and direct cargo, men and messages forward.

Rapid change was accompanied by rapid growth in population and size. Huntsville's population numbered 16,437 in 1950. By 1970, it had risen to 139,282 and in 2000 it crested at 158,216. The suburb of Madison contained only 530 in 1950, crept up to 6,081 in 1980 and then zoomed to 14,904 in 1990 and 29,329 in 2000. The county population catapulted from 72,903 in 1950 to 276,700 in 2000.

So much has happened and Huntsvillians have had so much to do with making it happen, that only now at the turn of a new millennium are many able to take stock and gain perspective.

Deeply rooted in history, Eleanor Hutchens, whose family helped found the city and state nearly 200 years ago, reflects upon the sweep of events noting "not all change was for the better." In the '50s, the Chamber and the town boosters were talking up the town's "modern" aspects while short-sightedly tearing down such beautiful historic structures as the Greek Revival courthouse, the Elks Opera House, the Federal Building, and the little Carnegie Library that housed more aspirations and memories than it did books. Eleanor Hutchens laments: "The new courthouse was built at an unfortunate decade in public architecture and rose as a depressing dark blot in midtown."

Huntsville changed, but the state of Alabama lagged behind. There is a culture and perception-gap a mile wide. Until the constitution allows home-rule or a new one is written, the city is captive to the Alabama Legislature. Following von Braun and Senator John Sparkman's lead, Huntsville addressed the civil rights issues raised by blacks and women. It faced up to the pockmarked, poverty-ridden areas between downtown and the arsenal, hosting three urban renewal projects at once. Calling Huntsville "the town that space built," Mike Wright wrote in *Alabama Heritage Magazine*, 1998 that von Braun showed photographs to civic leaders of the deplorable housing visitors saw when they came to Huntsville and

The canal built in the late 1820s is still an important part of Huntsville's history, now as a tourist attraction, then as a means to convey cotton to market. Huntsville/Madison County Convention and Visitors Bureau

the Marshall Center, stating that "Millions in federal funds changed that image."

As long as Huntsville is in Alabama, it will share dual billing. Commentators refer to the state as the "A-word," a label that sticks like the letter "A" stuck to the condemned Hawthorne heroine. Arsenal workers are still sometime referred to as "rednecks in neckties." The Alabama image impedes tourism and recruitment of new business, industry, contracts and contractors, especially the talented pool of young 20s and 30s who have the pick of high-tech towns.

In 1994, four of Alabama's leading historians wrote *Alabama: The History Of A Deep South State*. Only referenced seven times in the index, the city was slighted because it did not fit the description of a Deep South city. "Although many Alabamians considered stock car racing, country music, and the annual Alabama-Auburn football game all the culture they needed," they admit, "well-educated scientists often looked for more." By the mid-1980s, "Huntsville's economy was considered one of the most technologically sophisticated in the country."

Huntsville is the exception. It no longer automatically uses race as a means to keep blacks and whites in separate spheres to ensure white supremacy. Dr. Sonnie Hereford's son, after graduating from Notre Dame and earning an M.A., has become a successful software engineer for Lockheed-Martin. Pittsburgh Steelers' pro-football great and Alabama A&M graduate John Stallworth, voted into the Pro Football Hall of Fame in 2002, has succeeded in establishing his own Madison Research Corporation. *Times* columnist Beth Thames addressed the dichotomy of being a progressive city in a state more noted for its backwardness and racial politics: "In spite of our negative image," she writes, "we don't make those rocket boosters by candlelight."

This 1991 Cartoon by Swann for the Huntsville Times *speaks for itself. Courtesy,* Huntsville Times

The Huntsville-Madison County Chamber of Commerce heralds Huntsville's success. In a foreword to the 1993, *Huntsville: Where Technology Meets Tradition,* Steve Monger, Chamber chairman stresses:

Since its incorporation in 1811, Huntsville has continually set the pace for other cities in the south as well as the nation. Those who visit our city come to realize quickly that it is not the typical southern city. With the surge of high-tech firms located in the area, Huntsville/ Madison County has become a global, multicultural community.

Huntsville/Madison County: To The Edge of The Universe, contains an evocative, personal essay by astronaut Jan Davis. Having traveled among the stars, she writes:

Without Huntsville, the space program would have taken a completely different and more difficult path, or perhaps would have been impossible altogether.

Down there were also the streets of my past, the places where my dreams of going into space had taken shape and had been nurtured in countless ways. Without Huntsville, my own personal path to the heavens would have been a lot more difficult.

As a nation, we owe much to this small, unpretentious community. It is here that people have dreamed large, and where confidence, community, and steadfast determination have made those dreams unfurl in magnificent triumphs for us all.

Toyota Motor Corporation President Fujio Cho proudly shows off a model of the V-8 Engine Toyota will build in Huntsville. Looking on are Mayor Loretta Spencer, Mike Gillespie, Chairman of the Madison County Commission, Clay Vandiver, Chair of the Chamber of Commerce, Governor Don Siegelman and State Senator Jeff Sessions. Courtesy, Chamber of Commerce of Huntsville/ Madison County

Jan Davis, the first Huntsville native to go into space, shattered the southern lady stereotype. She is not only attractive but extraordinarily bright and ambitious, serving as director of the Flight Projects Directorate at the Marshall Center. Furthermore, she went into space with her husband, another first. Her shuttle-mates reflect the city as well as NASA's intention to attract "the right stuff" from all backgrounds. Mae Jemison, who made neighboring Decatur her home, was the first black woman in space. Mamoru Mohri, from Japan, completed the diverse group of astronauts.

Huntsville has close ties with Japan. In 1965, Mikio Kimata headed the first Japanese contingency to attend the Redstone missile school. So impressed with the friendliness of the people and their kindness, especially the valuable assistance of T. Pickens Gates who founded the Huntsville-Madison County Council for International Visitors, he and his wife gave the city its beloved red bridge in Big Spring Park and also the mystical cherry-blossom trees that invite lovers of all ages to sit below them and enjoy the sounds of ducks and geese paddling by. In 1989, Kimata sent a $1,000 check for tornado relief. In his own country, he has acted as Huntsville-Madison

The Red Bridge in Big Spring International Park has become a symbol of friendship between nations and people. The Red Bridge in Spring, photo by Daniel R. Little

County's good-will ambassador, hosting civic and business leaders seeking closer ties and trade possibilities with the island nation. Those ties have grown stronger over the decades, abetted by the Saturday Japanese language schools sponsored by First Baptist Church and others.

In 2001 when Toyota chose to locate its Tundra Truck engine factory in north Huntsville Industrial Park, a move bringing millions of dollars into the economy and upgrading the schools and neighborhoods adjoining, many Huntsvillians thought of their friend Mikio Kimata. Toyota's President, Haruaki Hoshino, received a warm Alabama welcome from Governor Don Siegelman and all North Alabama.

Alabama's progressive governor takes every opportunity to put a positive spin on the state's high-tech role. So does Boeing whose welcome sign reads: "Welcome to Alabama, Home of the Space Station, Delta IV, National Missile Defense and Stuff You Haven't

Even Thought of Yet." When its rocket plant opened in Decatur, October 2000, Siegelman declared that "Alabama's place in the history of our nation's space program is firmly established."

As Alabama progresses and redresses its image, the oft-repeated expression that "Huntsville is the country's best kept secret" will be heard less often.

Huntsville's humanitarian programs have garnered national attention. Madison County District Attorney, Bud Cramer initiated a children's advocacy program. By taking the issue to Congress in 1990, he helped the nation face up to child abuse and address the necessity of providing safe havens, medical and mental health personnel, prosecutors and law enforcement protections for victimized children. His legislation made the Huntsville Children's Advocacy Center the national model for communities to copy. By 1998, more than 400 programs spread across the nation and abroad. Local philanthropists,

John Stallworth and his son are living proof that nurture and pride lead to success in this city. Photo by Joyce Jones

founder of WHNT-TV, Charles Grisham and his wife Betty, a nationally-acclaimed fabric artist, deeded their magnificent home on Monte Sano overlooking the city to be used to fund construction of what Cramer calls the "Mayo Clinic of Child Abuse."

Since 1980 city leaders have created unique events and special places that locals and tourists enjoy. Panoply, a showcase of the arts, is the annual family event in spring. Big Spring Jam in the fall brings teens and adults to the downtown park for rock, rhythm and blues. The Space and Rocket Center continues its role as a major tourist destination. Space Camp and Space Academy assure the nation as well as the region that America will have a future in space. The Von Braun Center has been expanded twice to accommodate increased demand. The Art Museum has moved into a handsome building designed by local architect, David Crow, majestically situated in Big Spring Park. Constitution Village has evolved from a single block of simulated circa 1819 structures to include the Humphrey-Rodgers House and the children-family-centered museum called EarlyWorks.

As soon as the Joe W. Davis Stadium was finished in 1985, professional baseball, with the Class AA Huntsville Stars, drew a crowd. The University of Alabama in Huntsville's nationally ranked Chargers with their winning ways, convinced promoters that professional ice hockey would win a following. The Huntsville Tornado of the Central Hockey League swung forth in the late 1990s to be followed by the Huntsville Flight basketball team and the Tennessee Valley Vipers arena football, all in the spectator comfort of the Von Braun Center. Cotton Row Run and the Rocket City Marathon challenge runners to test their endurance against the city's hills, the routes twisting through welcoming neighborhoods. Some stop and smell the roses.

Using the satellites his hometown helped put into space, John S. Hendricks, a graduate of Butler High and UAH, founded television's innovative Discovery Channel, "a window on the world."

Reflecting an affinity for nature and compelling realization that it must be preserved, two grass-roots organizations have sprung forth like bees swarming to protect their hives: the Huntsville Madison County Botanical Garden and the Land Trust of Huntsville & North Alabama.

The Botanical Garden illustrates the magical transformation a few acres can undergo when tended by dedicated and knowledgeable volunteers willing to put "sweat equity" into it. By Act of Congress the Army deeded the northeastern fringe of Redstone Arsenal to the Alabama Space Science Exhibit Commission from which the city under Mayor Joe Davis leased 250 acres. In 1983 the city turned over 110 acres for 18 months in which time the Botanical Garden Society was challenged to raise $200,000 which would be matched by the city if raised in the time allowed. They did it in 12 months.

The gardeners will tell you that raising rare orchids is easier and more fun than raising money. "The Bushwhackers" made the site presentable enough to convince the public the project would succeed. They were later cited by Mayor Steve Hettinger for their backbreaking, poison-ivy-laden, hard work clearing the brush and tangled undergrowth. The garden is "World-class."

Slope development in the 1970s on the western side of Monte Sano and surrounding mountains alerted citizens to the danger of permanently losing a vista carried in the hearts and minds of generations of Huntsvillians who look to the mountains for spiritual sustenance. As development concreted over green spaces and bulldozers leveled slopes, the terrain underwent permanent change. Flooding and erosion resulted. The beautiful mountain face was changing before their eyes. Heavy rains brought flooding to creeks below. Something had to be done.

The Land Trust, incorporated in November 1987, saved the western slope of Monte Sano, the city's natural backdrop, from imminent threat. Its long-term goal is to preserve an ever-growing treasure of field and forest, mountain and valley, waterways and wetlands, all deeded to the public trust. Rare species of plants and animals have a fighting chance of survival in protected preserves.

The city purchased, with a grant from the Federal Emergency Management Agency for $2.9 million, the houses and land on Atwood Drive in the southeast on Aldridge Creek in order to broaden the creek. The removed houses were given to nonprofit organizations. Even positive action by city government cannot fully compensate for what happens when our natural environment plays second fiddle to our man-made structures.

Rivers, wetlands, and the creatures that inhabit them are being protected by the Land Trust of Huntsville and North Alabama. Here witness a sundown on the Flint River. Photo by Daniel R. Little

One of the "Bushwhackers," Seth Mize was especially instrumental in the early stages of the Botanical Garden's development. He and his wife Lucy devoted their efforts to building a world-class herb garden. Courtesy, Lucy Mize

Three indices to growth potential are technology base, welcoming diversity and quality-of-life standards with emphasis on the arts, parks, entertainment venues for young adults, urban amenities and stimulus for creative activity.

The New Urbanism movement fostered by Mayor Loretta Purdy Spencer for a neighborhood development in westernmost Huntsville, called Providence, appeals to creative, community-oriented individuals. Streets are tree-lined, automobiles are afterthoughts, schools and shops are handy, offering a tranquil setting.

Eleanor Hutchens sees Huntsville's historic Five Points neighborhood as another prototype of urbanism that incorporates new concepts in settled surroundings:

The evolution of such a neighborhood, non-ethnic and without homogeneity of class, but somehow knit by certain preferences (walking distance to stores, unpretentious lifestyle, interest in coffee shops and antiques, a mild turn for the unusual, etc.), to me shows that Huntsville is making important progress as a multifaceted city.

An enterprising couple, Jim and Susie Hudson, have taken up the challenge that, to compete with Austin or Atlanta, Huntsville must provide lively entertainment, a variety of restaurants and bars, attractive living accommodations, a "swinging" atmosphere—all in a downtown that becomes a neighborhood with its own folk culture. They formed CityScapes and hired Ralph Gipson to be president. The three are fulfilling their mission "to bring an energy and vitality that we think we need to keep the young people in Huntsville and to recruit people from out-of-town."

Long popular with the military as a convenient and inexpensive place to live, the area abounds with retirees who provide an invalu-

Calling themselves "the longest running jazz jam in Alabama," musicians Devere Pride, bass, Eric Rogers, alto sax and Fred Lamour, keyboard, still hold forth at the House of Alpha every Sunday night. Courtesy, Shelley Williams

able consumer base, volunteer source, and seasoned leadership in community life. UAH's Academy for Lifelong Learning attracts hundreds of participants, as experts in various fields give classes to their fellow senior citizens.

Eleanor Hutchens calls the *Huntsville Times* "a continuing dynamic force for the broad cultural development of Huntsville."

It gives constant coverage to the schools and colleges and is unusually attentive to church life. The efforts of our thousands of volunteers are encouraged in a generous spirit that welcomes diversity. Scheduled events that, seen listed together, show the impressive variety of goings-on in Huntsville.

The *Times* tells citizens the bad news too. Sad memories will be jogged by allusion to the gasoline tanker-truck collision with a freight train near the Arsenal, killing seven in 1981. Then in July, 1984 "the worst boating accident in state inland waterway history," claimed the lives of 11 people, including four members of one family and three of another who drowned when the SCItanic, a refurbished paddle wheeler owned by SCI Systems, Inc., overturned in sudden 75 miles-per hour winds. In November 1989 a tornado with winds over 250 miles per hour swooped down on Airport Road, cascading through one of Huntsville's busiest intersections at Whitesburg Drive in rush hour traffic destroying shopping centers, churches, apartment buildings, schools, killing 18, destroying 119 homes, and tossing automobiles into heaps of jangled metal.

The German community was shocked in 1982 when one of their own, Arthur Rudolph, 13 years after his retirement from the Space Program at Marshall, was given the choice to voluntarily leave the

One of the outstanding architectural features of the Dallas Mill was its spiral fire escape, but nothing could escape the flames that engulfed the old unoccupied building the late night — early hours of July 24, 1991. Photo by Daniel R. Little

The Tornado of 1989 left few reminders in its path. The most striking was the part of the Alter at Holy Spirit Catholic Church on Airport Road left untouched on tall columns "Faith, Hope, Love" standing above the rubble. Huntsville Madison County Public Library

country or face a court trial and deportation. The United States Office of Special Investigations accused him of alleged war crimes "involving his work on the V-2 rocket which was built underground by forced labor from a nearby concentration camp, approximately 20,000 workers dying of malnutrition, hangings and other atrocities." His family and friends spent years trying to clear him of the agreement he claimed was forced upon him. One wonders if the Special Investigators would have gone after von Braun, who died of cancer in 1977, had he still been living.

In 1987, about 200 members of the community discovered that "that nice, unassuming" Steven Streit, to whom they had entrusted their savings and those of the Whitesburg Baptist Church, had swindled them in an investment scandal then called the "largest single securities fraud in state history." In 1992, popular Huntsville ophthalmologist, Jack Wilson, was murdered. The killer was paid to do it by Wilson's wife, whose twin sister was also implicated but acquitted. National TV and paperback sensationalized the case. Ken Englade, best-selling author, characterizes Betty Wilson as "alluring as a Southern Magnolia and as deadly as a Black Widow Spider."

The *Huntsville News* ran a story June 23,1992: "City Official Tied To Wilson Case." Reporter Greg Heyman's story connected Betty Wilson romantically to the city's risk management officer, the first African American to hold that position. Some contend that race prejudice was a factor in the jury's guilty verdict and sentence of life without possibility of parole.

To attract the talented citizens that missiles, space sciences, and their offshoot industries demand, Huntsville's last three mayors: Joe Davis (1968-1988), Steve Hettinger (1988-1996) and Loretta Spencer (1996-present) have had one overriding goal: to provide the governmental structure and leadership which best promotes diversification of the economy while expanding the federal presence and attracting more space and defense-oriented companies. They have also focused on quality of life and civil rights issues. The mayors were beneficiaries of a legislative enactment in 1963 calling for a strong mayor with full administrative powers.

Tall, slightly hunched over, with a John Wayne sort of half frown/half smile and swagger, Mayor Joe Davis kept his mild-mannered, fatherly, unflappable persona before the voting public for 20 years. Never brilliant or even buoyant, his leadership was tentatively progressive. Davis, who had served as administrative assistant to the previous mayor, Glenn Hearn, appointed a young man to be his administrative assistant in 1977 who had originally joined the city staff as an urban planner. Always close to the planning process and author of numerous studies, Ralph Gipson was Davis's representative on the City Planning Commission from 1976 to 1986.

The Davis years were deep into urban planning. What did the city want to protect, preserve or promote? Out of these questions came the Twickenham Historical Preservation District, the hospital district, an active Airport Zoning Commission and the decision that Research Park

Architect Harvie Jones contributed countless hours to historical preservation. He enjoyed leading tours downtown and through the districts pointing out architectural delights and surprises. Guided tours by leading citizens are now sponsored by the Convention and Visitors Bureau. To the left of Harvie is Hall Bryant another community volunteer. Courtesy, Author's collection

The Huntsville Hospital Complex extends over a half mile along Governor's Drive. Courtesy, Adalene and Ted Bledsoe

It is opening day at the new Huntsville-Madison County Public Library. From that day in April, 1987 to today, the library has continued to expand its service, usage and circulation under Director Donna Schremser. The Friends of the Library provide volunteer support. Photo by Daniel R. Little

would remain strictly and solely for research and not commercial or industrial purposes.

Mayor Davis never underestimated the crucial role of citizens—on municipal boards and commissions or as members of such groups as the Chamber of Commerce, civic clubs, and professional organizations—in shaping public opinion, forming goals, and making things happen. Historian Dr. Frances Roberts and architect Harvie Jones are prime examples of volunteers who contributed mightily to the town. Both served prominently on the Twickenham Historic Preservation Commission, the Huntsville Historic Preservation Commission and Constitution Hall Park Board. Jones also served on the Beautification Board and Roberts on the Burritt Museum Board.

One of the more powerful boards established as Davis began his mayoral term was the Industrial Development Board. The legislature allowed the board to construct and lease plant buildings and property to encourage new industry.

The Huntsville-Madison County Public Library Board, headed by Jane Roberts, assisted by such civic leaders as Harry M. Rhett and Guy Spencer, raised the money for the new library fondly called Fort Book. Its architect, William Herrin, designed open spaces for flights of fancy and fantasy.

When Davis and Gipson promoted the zoning, in 1971, of Governor's Drive as the Medical District, encompassing the Huntsville Hospital and the UAH Medical School, they were among the "forerunners in the nation to set aside a zone for medical district facilities with necessary land-use restrictions and regulations." Their forethought changed the skyline of Huntsville. Several blocks of gleaming white buildings, tied together by skywalks supporting a

The Huntsville International Airport is a growing transportation hub for cargo and passengers with ample parking and a hotel on site. Courtesy, Huntsville/Madison County Convention and Visitors Bureau

$60 million light rail tram system, dominate the southern entrance to downtown.

The hospital has become a major medical facility serving about 300,000 patients in a year. Stability of leadership under Joe Austin and Ralph Boston, with Alvin Blackwell, the president of the hospital's governing body for over 25 years, and Dr. Carl Grote, Jr., a "one-man medical band," has buttressed the facility's phenomenal success.

There was a wrenching need for an airport that could keep pace with development and for an interstate connection with I-65 that would ease transit east and west and connect with north and south. Bob Dunnavant noted that Huntsville was "the only U.S.A. city over 100,000 not on an interstate." Both were slow in coming, the wait troublesome and detrimental to the region's progress. Yet the rewards since their completion have exceeded the most optimistic expectations.

In 1967 the Carl T. Jones International Airport opened between Decatur and Huntsville, close to Madison and Triana. The region served by the airport gained a hub of high-tech industry, a valuable economic tool and connection to the world. When I-565 was completed in 1992, it returned to citizens priceless minutes spent in clogged traffic. The local lament was that it took longer to get to the airport than to send a man to the moon.

Spurred by the leadership of Ed Mitchell, the Jetplex became a U.S. Customs Port of Entry in 1980; six years later the Airport Authority opened an international intermodal center, facilitating movement of air, rail, motor, and water-transported cargo. Products from abroad could go through customs, be inspected by USDA inspectors and sent straight to market. Huge 747 cargo planes land and take products to Europe regularly. Port Director Richard Tucker, summarizes its mission: "to transport the world to its customers and its customers to the world."

The airport and I-565 swelled population and trade throughout north Alabama. Madison County Commissioner Dale Strong commented, "We're no longer rural Madison County. We're urban Madison County." By 2000, fewer than 1,000 acres of farmland were left to be farmed by only 242 farmers. Those magnificent fields of cotton ringing the city keep dwindling.

Huntsville went on an annexation binge in the 1980s; in 1986, alone, expanding by over 32-square miles, taking in 12,000 acres in Limestone County and 4,500 in Madison, with an additional hop over Monte Sano into Big Cove for another 4,100 acres. The *Times* described the annexation frenzy as "historic" and "hastily-called" by city officials "without any kind of comprehensive plan for developing and zoning the area."

Big Cove development, by contrast, followed an orderly process. Jeff Enfinger and his associates, John and Jimmy Hays, purchased the farmland acres for luxury homes tied into a 54-hole Robert Trent Jones golf course. Beginning in 1986, Enfinger told the *Times*, "We master planned this area with the city of Huntsville planning department. We built in conjunction with the city a new water system and sewer system in the valley."

While Huntsville was on its annexation spree, the citizens of Madison were put to the test: Would they vote to be annexed by the Space City that was swooping up their left flank? If tempers are any indication, 1986 was a long, hot summer followed by a chilling fall as competing citizen groups championed their causes. The 600 Madisonians who had signed a petition to initiate the annexation question gathered into a Committee for a Better Madison with Barry Shoulders as spokesman. Since the original group did not take a position for or against, Shoulders jumped to the pro-annexation Madison Residents for a Future. Those opposed called themselves Citizens FOR Madison.

The Huntsville City Council passed an ordinance in June endorsing annexation. Councilman Tommy Battle pledged "We in no way want to

Interstate 565 cut a wide swath through Huntsville. Here the road is displacing homes in the Dallas Mill Village off of Andrew Jackson Way. Fire destroyed the mill before the road was completed. Courtesy, Author's collection

destroy the culture, heritage and history of Madison." Loretta Spencer, Huntsville Planning Commission Chairman, argued that westward growth was inevitable. "That's the main entry into Huntsville." Advocates argued that Madison's school system would be improved, a stand that would come back to haunt them in 1997 when Madison citizens voted to establish their own independent school system and then upgraded their schools to compete with and even exceed the nationally esteemed Huntsville Independent School District.

As the tussle neared the November 25 vote, Intergraph told employees that annexation is in "the best interest of the company," and the Huntsville-Madison County Chamber of Commerce broke its neutrality, calling for annexation. Madison Mayor Burwell Wilbanks took umbrage, defiantly boasting "the people of Madison are not for sale." Wearing their "Nowhere Else But Madison" T-shirts, following the lead of farmer and landowner Don Spencer who led an emotional anti-annexation campaign, the citizens of Madison voted overwhelmingly, 2,245 to 699, for Madison's "independence."

Healing started instantly. Huntsville continued courting Madison, and Madison, filled with a fresh pride, met mounting challenges of growth. Huntsville had presented the large picture of efficient city services and extensive city planning for Madison, but could not overcome the personal pictures voters carried into the polls of small-town virtues.

No vote, however, could stem the tide of Madison's own population growth forcing the town to expand its city limits by 325 acres, 300 of them into neighboring Limestone county. In 1993, Madison Mayor Chuck Yancura boasted that his city was fifth fastest growing in the nation. By 2002, REALTOR.com classified Madison as suburban, with 67 percent of the population having a median age of 32 years with a median household income of $44,000; slightly older residents averaged $67,300. These facts translate into affluent neighborhoods, most of which were built since 1980. "The work force is professional, well-educated and mobile."

In 1991 Madison County Commissioner Rob Colson led an effort to establish a 21-member Madison County Task Force on Local Government Cooperation to study the feasibility of "fully or partially combining government functions such as law enforcement, education, tourism, jails and public works." Huntsville Mayor Steve Hettinger lent his support, calling, to no avail upon the state legislature to "let us vote on establishing a charter commission to draw up a consolidation plan."

Both Hettinger and Loretta Spencer accommodated the city's needs and temperament. Continuing the synergism established in Mayor Davis' lengthy 20-year tenure, they had to combat a "good ole boy" network that had evolved. *Huntsville News* writer David Bowman put it: "Hettinger was reform-tending, and Spencer was gender-bending." Their idealism was invigorating, their optimism contagious. But it was not always easy. The city's reputation as an "oasis of affluence" attracts those who seek or need its social welfare protections. Ironically, the number of homeless drawn to the area is a measure of the city's affluence. As Lee Sentell of the Convention and Visitors Bureau explained, "We're growing so rapidly, the tide is lifting all boats."

Hettinger's "first wake-up call" on social issues occurred when a group of homeless people came to City Council asking for a place to sleep where they would not be arrested or evicted. "We realized it was important for us to recognize that we did have a homeless problem." He named a Mayor's Homeless Commission to address the issue. Homelessness had become a way of life for some. Huntsville's parks became encampments, its overpasses and culverts temporary shelters. Citizens looked for solutions through their churches as well as governmental and social organizations.

Why are they so happy? Cecil Fain, Huntsville's beloved principal and coach, was being honored on Cecil B. Fain Day, September 7, 1991. Civic leaders and citizens gathered to pay homage to a person who helped thousands of youngsters to succeed in life. From left to right, Mayor Steve Hettinger, Woodrow "Pud" Chisam, Cecil Fain, Mike Gillespie, chairman of the Madison County Commissioners and Congressman Bud Cramer. Photo by Bob Gathany

When Hettinger took office in 1988, he faced new political realities as well. He was the only city official elected at large; the council had been ordered to redistrict into five single-member districts. Following federal mandate, state representative George Grayson, Huntsville's first black legislator since the 19th century, though frustrated by his own legislative delegation's refusal to act, secured a court order which shifted political power into the hands of distinct parts of town reflecting racial and class differences. For the first time in the century the north side of town elected a black council member, Richard Showers, and school board member, Dr. James Dawson. The south side of town, in elections for county commissioner, elected the first woman and Republican party member in the century. Redistricting was both liberating and limiting. It gave minorities electoral arenas they could win in, but tended to restrict their attention to their constituency rather than to the common good.

George Grayson, the man who led the redistricting battles, used the 1988 mayoral campaign to secure minority demands. He presented Hettinger and his opponent, Tommy Battle, a four-page listing of affirmative-action items covering minority hiring and promotions, contracts, housing, business needs, public transportation and appointment of a black municipal judge. Battle refused to sign; Steve Hettinger did sign, and was elected.

As mayor, Hettinger fulfilled many of these demands not because of any promise or secret agreement but because he believed in open government and equal opportunity. He appointed a minority businessman to chair the Planning Commission. He appointed a black to be head of the city's Animal Control office. He hired a black female attorney in the legal department. He made efforts, ("We have tried, tried, tried in the police and fire departments") to recruit minorities. When the Huntsville Housing Authority voted to demolish Binford

Court, the city's historic World War II black housing project, and move to a more progressive "housing voucher" system, a biracial "community crusade," given strong editorial support by the *Huntsville News*, to provide fine new replacement housing coupled with social service won the day. Hettinger secured a federal grant to build 200 units in Binford Court and another grant to initiate a pilot "core loop" shuttle bus to serve the poor, handicapped and elderly.

The 1992 mayoral campaign got ugly. Fraught with innuendoes and character assassination, the race came down to a run-off between Hettinger and Dr. Jimmy Wall, former city council president and well-known dentist in town. Wall got hold of the Grayson document and made political hay of it, publicizing it broadly in pamphlet and press:

A personal message from Jimmy Wall to the people of Huntsville.

These things I believe:

God is a real source of strength, of hope in our lives; Our children are our most important accomplishments; Government at all levels exists to serve the needs of the greatest number of people…

The secret agreement signed by Steve Hettinger and George Grayson…are presented for your information. You can decide for yourself whether or not this previously undisclosed agreement was a proper arrangement to be made just prior to an election. You can be certain I have never, and will never enter into any secret agreements in my efforts to become your next mayor.

What happened next is bizarre, and like the Watergate scandal

A place Mayor Steve Hettinger could relax and enjoy the political arena was at Aunt Eunice's Country Kitchen. Courtesy, Huntsville Times

The Sapp Shelter for Women and Children ribbon cutting represents the concern and generosity of Huntsvillians for the less fortunate, especially homeless and abused women and children. A kick-off contribution by the Sapps of $220,000 was augmented by over $1 million in contributions. About 100 women and children can be served by the new facility run by the Downtown Rescue Mission. From left to right: Adalene Bledsoe, Pat Sapp, Dr. Darwin Overholt, Gene Sapp, and Mayor Loretta Spencer. Courtesy, Huntsville Madison County Public Library

started as a "tempest in a teapot," but ended in three men, including George Grayson, going to prison on charges of extortion. An effort to secure claims against the city for black clients led Attorney Joe Lampley, political activist Michael Jennings, and Grayson to conjure a blackmail scheme to get Hettinger to push the claims through. In the heat of the runoff campaign, word got to Hettinger and his aide Richard Liles that a so-called handwritten addendum Hettinger purportedly had signed—stating that unless he received 40 per cent of the vote from District 1 in the general election and 60 per cent in the runoff, the agreement he had signed with Grayson would be "null and void,"—would be exposed to the press unless Hettinger agreed to support a $1.7 million settlement of claims against the city.

Hettinger never was totally clear whether he wrote or signed such a provision. In the long run, it did not matter. Richard Liles contacted the FBI, wiretapped several conversations between himself and the others, finally agreeing to meet Grayson, Lampley, and Jennings before dawn in the Lucky's Grocery Store parking lot in Meridianville to consummate the bribe. There in the dark, the deal was struck. A single match burned the scrap of paper that contained the alleged addendum. Later that afternoon, the FBI arrested the three men on charges of attempted extortion. At the trial that followed, Grayson pled guilty and was sentenced to eight months. Here was a man whose leadership and intelligence had cast him into esteemed positions as Alabama A&M University professor and biology department chairman, representative in the Alabama Legislature, and role model for all who knew him. In his zeal and impatience for racial justice, he sidestepped the law and he paid for it.

Hettinger and Loretta Spencer in their turns tried to shape policies

Dr. Sonnie Hereford has produced a video, A Civil Rights Journey: A History of Huntsville's Civil rights movement as seen through the eyes of Sonnie Hereford, III, M.D. *Here Dr. Hereford stands on the front porch of his Lydia Drive home. Courtesy, Author's collection*

inclusive of all neighborhoods. They both formed large citizen committees made up of diverse representatives from all parts of town. Hettinger's long-range planning group was called Vision 2000. Spending countless hours, Dr. William Lucas, Dr. Jess Brown, Anne Forgey, General Louis Rachmeler, Gary Pledger, Frank Morring, Richard Reeves, Woody Bethay, Joe Moquin and Dr. Frances Roberts with their committees produced a document Hettinger called "the single best portrait of the conditions and needs of this community."

Spencer's New Century Committee headed by architect Billy Herrin, hit hard on drugs, race, public schools, police protection, jobs, traffic, city government and services, downtown development, medical facilities, recreational facilities, tourism and citizen concerns. About 350 citizens identified these issues with separate meetings called to discuss each.

The meeting on race lasted three hours and drew 120 citizens. School Board President Dr. James Dawson called for observable results. It was decided that citizens of all colors should be more willing to "take some risks to break down racial barriers."

The most ambitious effort to break down barriers came in the fall of 2001 with the joint University of Alabama in Huntsville and Alabama A&M series on the 1960s Civil Rights Movement. Reaching beyond racial barriers, its Chairman, Dr. Jack Ellis of the UAH History Department, called for fresh reappraisal and frank discussion. Well attended by blacks and whites of all ages, Dr. Sonnie Hereford called this series "one of the best things to happen in Huntsville since Civil Rights days."

Dr. Hereford expressed pride, too, in the growing crop of black millionaires Huntsville boasts, especially his neighbor Thornton Stanley, owner of Stanley Construction and Landscaping, who had been named the National Small Business Person of the Year by the Small Business Administration. It did not escape his attention, either, that an Hispanic, Irma Tuder, won accolades for her business, Analytical Services, which grew from one employee in 1992 to 200 in 2001 and was named the National Minority Small Business of the Year.

Krispy Kremes, hot ham biscuits from Aunt Eunice's Country Kitchen, homemade cookies: these are the enticements Huntsville's first female mayor uses to put generals, CEO's, congressmen and highway directors in the right frame of mind to see things Huntsville's, and her way. With a sparkle in her eye that can instantly ignite, Loretta Spencer speaks passionately about her role as Huntsville's chief executive officer and diplomatic representative to the rest of the world, which she encourages to beat a path to the city's door. The *Wall Street Journal* ran an article in July 27, 1998, "Defense Strategies: How Huntsville, Ala. Manages to Maintain Its High-Tech Orbit." It says, "Few here are better at schmoozing than Huntsville's energetic mayor...Ms. Spencer is locally famous for her deft personal touch to get the attention of those controlling the federal and state purse strings."

The mayor started her first full day in office out in the median on North Parkway picking up trash with dozens of volunteers, calling on the community to join in and beautify the roadways. Assisting Decatur secure the Boeing Delta VI Rocket Factory, she seeks regional solutions to economic problems and looks to the state and the federal government to pave the way.

Spencer has an uncanny knack for turning other's distresses into Huntsville's successes, and she does it in tandem with regional leaders. As military base closings drew closer to home, Spencer worked with the arsenal command and the congressional friends of military contractors to present North Alabama's claims for Redstone Arsenal remaining open and in fact, becoming the strategic, space and missile, space intelligence, aviation and missile defense center for the Pentagon. She campaigned to have the St. Louis aviation base-closing work to Redstone's benefit by shifting the jobs to the arsenal. A team went to St. Louis and opened arms to the civilians whose lives were uprooted.

As a result of the terrorist attacks upon the United States on September 11, 2001, Huntsville and its environs—especially the Arsenal which houses the missiles, strategic arms and intelligence, plans and preparations national defense depends upon—braced themselves under high alert. NASA and the research parks containing the hundreds of contractor companies supporting the national interest, plus the thousands of women and men whose brain power and dedication have brought Huntsville and the nation to preeminence were put on notice: They are high on the enemy's list.

Governor Don Siegelman announced "Huntsville is a possible terrorist target." The area is vulnerable because of the presence of 1,700 Army and 13,000 civilian jobs at the Arsenal and AMCOM, the active Brown's Ferry nuclear plant in Limestone County, and the "many area defense contractors making Huntsville a national defense knowledge center."

The chilling dawn of a new age of terrorist reality was met with resolve; the head-to-shoe inspections and vehicular searches at arsenal gates were accepted with resignation. Here was a workforce disciplined by training and group code to rise to the threat using the same analytical and problem-solving skills they applied to their job assignments. Acknowledging that their jobs must go on, creative minds up and down the organizational chart looked for ways to beef up security and fight terrorism.

Even before September 11, as a "model city of preparedness," Huntsville had received monies to prepare and equip first responders in case of attack by weapons of mass destruction. Many firms have entered the war against terrorism. Protection of the more than $2 billion defense investment in the area and furtherance of it's knowledge base is equivalent to waging war. That knowledge base is extensive.

Alabama A&M's State Black Archives, Research Center and Museum, housed in the 19th century Home Economics Building now restored, plays an important role in reclaiming the state's African American history and providing a Civil Rights presence. Courtesy, Eric Schultz/ Huntsville Times

UAH and A&M offer Ph.D. degrees in physics. UAH granted 139 doctorates in this and other fields over a five-year period. Its campus illustrates the emphasis on science and engineering. Buildings bear the following titles: Optics, Engineering, Material Science, Solar Energy Research, Wernher von Braun Research Hall, Johnson Research Center, Olin B. King Technology Hall, and the major research organ, National Space Science and Technology Center. "Yet," Eleanor Hutchens observes, "UAH is not an institute of technology but a full-fledged university with a College of Liberal Arts at its core."

In grant dollars for 1999-2000, UAH garnered $33 million, while A&M was close behind with $24 million. Alabama A&M hosted the 2002 Conference of Black Physicists, offering new career vistas to participants. Chamber of Commerce President and CEO Brian Hilson hailed the conference as a powerful recruiting tool. Another weapon in Huntsville's service is Dr. Judy Franz, the wife of UAH's President Frank Franz, who serves as executive officer of the American Physical Society, the nation's largest professional organization of physicists.

The Alabama Supercomputer, located in Research Park, offers scholars and researchers interconnectivity and resources unavailable outside the state. The National Space Science and Technology Center, also in Research Park, is a brain trust of over 450 scientists.

Children from across the city may attend magnet schools, including the Academy for the Sciences and Foreign Languages, and the New Century Technology High School. Sci-Quest, the hands-on North Alabama Science Center located in Research Park, is a partnership between public and private entities to give this region's youngsters one of the finest real-life science and math experiences possible.

In some cultures, the "I got mine! You get yours!" mentality prevails. But not in Huntsville. The Harvard-trained attorney daughters of the Thornton Stanleys and the John Cashins, Deirdre Stanley and Sheryll Cashin, attest to it. So does the national leadership that native Huntsvillian, the Reverend Joseph Echols Lowery gave to the cause of racial justice as head of the Southern Leadership Conference for 21 years, following Martin Luther King and Ralph Abernathy. Oakwood College's President Emeritus, Benjamin F. Reaves, known as "Grandfather Reads," has given youth learning tools to grow on. Gurley's irrepressible Sara Hall raised black Angus cattle, sold a few to purchase a Baldwin grand piano and then donated it to the Huntsville Museum of Art for others' enjoyment. Jane K. Lowe left a charitable foundation which is benefiting infants by presenting new mothers at local hospitals with a packet of material emphasizing early reading practices, containing a children's library card application and a coupon to be redeemed at the public library for a favorite children's book. Randolph's new school on Garth owes much to her endowment.

Sci-Quest, the North Alabama Science Center, provides learning at its best with hands-on science exhibits and experiments for all ages. Courtesy, Huntsville/ Madison County Convention and Visitors Bureau

Graduation at Alabama A&M is better than ever in the new stadium between Memorial Parkway and Meridian. Courtesy, Author's collection

Business leaders are sharing expertise and dollars. The tradition goes back several generations. Marion Beirne Spragins saw to it that von Braun and his team had the credit they needed to purchase homes; Walton Fleming worked to start the Huntsville Industrial Expansion Committee. Will Halsey and Tom Thrasher helped form the UAH Foundation which, with von Braun's support for a first rank educational institution, resulted in the designation of the extension center into the Huntsville Campus of the University of Alabama. David G. Harris, retired information officer for the army at Redstone Arsenal, called Halsey and Thrasher his "go-to guys when the Army had a problem." SCI Systems' founder Olin B. King has not only given a building to foster education, he has supplied seed money for young entrepreneurs.

Keith Lowe began his career with Intergraph as a co-op student and was employed there for 13 years. Establishing his own software company, he subsequently sold it for $34 million. In a *Times* interview he said he devoted much time to "trying to generate capital for new companies," using Pretium Capital Group, Biz Tech, a partnership between public and corporate enterprise, and the Alabama Information Technology Association. "Around Huntsville," he observed, people who have succeeded spend "a lot of time helping other people make it. They are quick with a check. And they are quick with advice." Judging by the plethora of banking institutions in the city, there is sufficient venture capital to sustain a dynamic, volatile economy with room for one more good idea.

Through brainpower, creativity and the determination to hold fast the dream and follow their star, the citizens of North Alabama are preparing to meet the future, forging new beginnings in space and beyond. However distant their explorations, Huntsville and the beautiful Tennessee Valley will always beckon them home.

CHAPTER VIII

Chronicles of Leadership

Huntsville is a city that has never lost momentum in its economic progress, from the early 19th century, when it served as the political and commercial hub of the Alabama Territory, through the mid-20th century, when it became a national aerospace center, to the 1980s, when it achieved a very successful drive of industrial diversification to become a hub of high technology, to today, when that hub reaches past the Tennessee Valley to the world and beyond.

Among the first industrial products in Huntsville were cotton goods, flour, shoes, lumber, copper stills, and pumps. The first cotton mill in the community, Bell Factory, opened in 1832 with 3,000 spindles and 100 looms powered by a waterwheel. By the turn of the century Huntsville had developed into a thriving textile center. The advent of World War I saw a further expansion of industrial activity.

But it was the development of Redstone Arsenal by the U.S. Army during World War II that signified the explosive transition of the Huntsville economy from cotton to missiles to a solid, diversified industrial base. When the Army consolidated its rocket and missile products at Redstone in 1950, and brought Dr. Wernher von Braun and his team of scientists to the city, it marked the beginnings of Huntsville's modern era of industrial development. The first industrial contractors were drawn to the city, forming the foundation for Huntsville's prominent aerospace role. In 1960 NASA's George C. Marshall Space Flight Center was established at Redstone, and Dr. von Braun was installed as its director. The Army installation at Redstone developed many of the principal strategic weaponry for the Western World.

The mid-1960s brought a substantive shift in the economic and industrial base of the city. The space program, which had so dominated the local economy, began to level off as its pioneering days passed and the rush for exploration of space stabilized. The city foresaw that shift, and began a well-planned, long-range effort to attract a diversified collection of industries whose fortunes would not rest on space travel. The fruits of that program could be seen by the next decade, when fewer than 25 percent of the employees on the payrolls of private firms in Huntsville worked in support of missile and space projects—dropping from well over 50 percent in a decade's time.

A key factor in the economic stabilization and subsequent growth of Huntsville has been the phenomenal expansion of its resident industries. Three-quarters of the industrial jobs created from the early 1970s to the mid-1980s resulted from the expansion of existing firms in the city. Today's pioneer high-tech companies in Huntsville are centered in the computer and electronics fields, with worldwide customers, and account for half of the city's industrial employment.

By the 1980s international trade had become a significant element in the economic strength of Huntsville. A community-wide effort, with the support of key state and federal government officials, led to the awarding of Port of Entry status to Huntsville in 1980, and the establishment of a U.S. Customs Office in the city. Foreign Trade Zone status was then achieved.

Agricultural acreage has yielded to automotive plants, major regional retail centers, upscale residential development, a vastly improved highway system and an economy whose mix of military, space, high technology, industry, communications and tourism offer residents the opportunity to lead vibrant, multifaceted, prosperous lives. The city has become a regional center for health care, education, the arts, entertainment, transportation, trade, and distribution, attracting and serving a growing population.

The organizations whose stories are detailed on the following pages illustrate the variety of ways in which individuals and their businesses have contributed to the growth and development of Huntsville. The civic involvement of the city's businesses, learning institutions, and local government, in partnership with its citizens, has made Huntsville a first-class place in which to live and work.

A busy Huntsville passenger and freight depot in the 1930s. Courtesy, Huntsville Madison County Public Library

181

ELCOM

Kevin Beebe grew up in Long Island, New York, far away from Huntsville, Alabama. Like most of us, he was exposed to the stereotypes that are associated with different parts of the country, including the South.

In 1987, Beebe was given the opportunity to pursue a career in management with Signetics, but it would require him to move to Huntsville. So he came to Alabama, evaluated the quality of life in the area, saw the potential for growth, and made the decision to move. This meant that he would take a huge leap of faith and, along with his family, start anew. However, in 1989 after being with the company for three years, Beebe was told that Signetics was doing away with his position. He was offered jobs in other locations, but after falling in love with the area, opted to make yet another life-changing decision. He would start his own company.

Beebe borrowed money from his parents and together with money from his partner, they began a semiconductor manufacturers' rep firm and incorporated ELCOM, Inc. on January 1, 1990. Opening the first two offices simultaneously, one in

The 2002 Huntsville Chamber of Commerce Small Business of the Year Award and Kevin Beebe.

ELCOM owners, left to right: Bob Jones, Dave Ciampa, Kevin Beebe, Rick Bortles, Kerry Erwin.

Huntsville and one in Atlanta—the company started with eight employees. The first manufacturer they represented was Beebe's former employer, Signetics (currently Philips Semiconductors). And so ELCOM was born!

Beebe created and nurtured the ELCOM culture. Today, the owners, Kevin Beebe, Kerry Erwin, Rick Bortles, Dave Ciampa, and Bob Jones along with its founding members Dave Andrich and Jeff Wilson, continue to nurture those original ideals—integrity, honesty, innovation, and being best in class. This also spawned a mission statement that helps define the company's direction. It states that ELCOM's goal is: "To contribute to their customers' and principals' success by providing a world-class conduit for the exchange of information and technology."

In 1994 ELCOM opened an office in Raleigh, North Carolina. ELCOM expanded again in 1998, this time into Florida and Puerto Rico. With each expansion came the porting of the mission statement and core values that Beebe had driven into the existing team. The result? ELCOM proved that it could be successful in instilling its business philosophy into new

areas as it grew. They also continued to cultivate entrepreneurship in every employee at every level to insure individual and team success.

ELCOM faced many challenges initially. One of the first was to establish a reputation for high quality and consistent "best in class" service. As a service provider, ELCOM's success or failure depended on their reputation and outsiders' perceptions of their ability to perform. This challenge could only be overcome with the passing of time. Dedication and persistence helped ELCOM achieve exactly what they were looking for—a reputation for being one of the best technical reps in the southeast. This has been evident over the years as they have received numerous awards from their customers and principals for outstanding performance, including Rep of the Year from several semiconductor companies.

Another of ELCOM's largest challenges was to build a strong technical sales force. They needed to find sales engineers that had the ability and background to sell its principals' products. These employees would also need to possess the know-how to create the demand for those products. Individuals of this caliber are difficult to find and are even harder to keep. They are sought after by competitors, creating the constant threat of turnover...a threat that has been minimized at ELCOM by building a strong team environment and a culture where all benefit from the success of others. ELCOM, through the years, has been able to bring together a team of highly networked, successful, technical sales people with a strong desire to overachieve.

Today, ELCOM views its greatest strength as its people. One aspect of the company's culture is goal achievement. Each year sales goals are set based on knowledge of the customers and the upcoming trends of the market. These goals are not taken lightly by any of the employees and it is through teamwork and tremendous effort that these goals are accomplished. As a reward for outstanding achievement, ELCOM provides employees with an all expense paid family vacation in May of the following year. Over the past 10 years these company vacations have included cruises, trips to Mexico, and Florida. While these excursions are company group vacations, no business is conducted, and employees are praised and congratulated for a job well done.

Philips Semiconductors was the first manufacturer to support ELCOM as a rep organization, joined in the early years by Linear Technology, TDK, and other industry leaders who brought technical diversity to their portfolio.

ELCOM now has a strong, well-balanced line card that includes names like Intel, Philips Semiconductors, and AMI Semiconductors. Their manufacturing partners have recognized them as the clear leader in the southeast among their peers. Intel, the largest and most technical semiconductor company in the world, chose ELCOM as their exclusive extended sales force for the seven southeastern states after interviewing over 40 rep companies. ELCOM has had up to 16 different manufacturers on their line card simultaneously, but over time has come to the conclusion that more is not always better. Now ELCOM

ELCOM team, 2001.

focuses more closely on fewer lines, with more balance, allowing them to be more proficient in representing their principals.

Working with customers in the Huntsville area such as Sanmina-SCI, VMIC, Avocent, Adtran, Verilink and Chrysler, to name a few, ELCOM has grown sales approximately 25 percent each year, excluding the downturn in the economy for 2001. Having its corporate office located in Corporate Research Park, the second largest research park in the United States, they are able to develop a strong knowledge of the local market. They are also able to educate themselves and clearly understand the products of their manufacturing partners. The team is capable of clearly communicating product features and benefits to the local engineering community, and handle the business aspects of the customer service process. These successes are mirrored in the other geographies that ELCOM services.

ELCOM has been active in the community and been a member of the Huntsville Chamber of Commerce since its inception. They were nominated in 2001 and 2002 for Small Business of the Year. ELCOM was chosen as one of three finalists in 2001 and won

the prestige of Small Business of the Year in the Business Services category in 2002. Interestingly, the 2002 Small Business of the Year award came just months after Huntsville was rated 71st by *Forbes* magazine for the best cities in the United States to start a small business.

Since the founding of ELCOM, Kevin Beebe wanted to have a company that brought value to the manufacturers, not only through sales, but also through demand creation. In his experience while working for a manufacturer, this value was not the priority for the majority of the rep firms with whom he had been associated. In its 12-year history, ELCOM has not only added value for design and creation, but has also helped their manufacturing partners establish better business practices. Their customers look at them as a technical resource, not just another group of salesmen. They are the problem solvers and it is their product knowledge and strong customer attention that differentiates ELCOM from their competition.

THE HUNTSVILLE MADISON COUNTY PUBLIC LIBRARY

The Huntsville Madison County Public Library's mission is to provide everyone access to materials, information, and programs—delivered by a courteous and informed staff. The Library has a long tradition of leadership in serving the community's informational, educational, and recreational needs. No other institution so uniquely touches the lives of its patrons. Established in 1818, before Alabama was a state, its first public library has provided continuous service to the community. The Library was incorporated with William Atwood's purchase of two shares of stock in the Huntsville Library Company. Those certificates are the earliest records of any library in the state, according to a history of the Library written by former librarian Bessie King Russell.

In 1823 the Alabama Legislature granted a charter to the Library, then located in John Nelson Spotswood Jones' law office. The Library's first books were offered to the patrons, or subscribers, in October 1819.

The Library moved from available place to available place, including the Madison County Courthouse,

Story hour in the children's room at the Carnegie Library.

the Hermathenian Society and the Cliosophic Society of the Green Academy. The Green Academy was located on the current site of East Clinton School and was open from 1823 until the Civil War when Union Soldiers burned the building down.

The Huntsville Literary Debating Society reopened the library with its remaining books in 1870. Eventually the Huntsville Circulating Library opened in the corner of Murray and Smith's Book Store on the west side of the Courthouse Square in 1891, and later that year moved to the YMCA on Eustis Street. Many local citizens objected to the controversial location, because the YMCA was opened only to men, except for the Library. But in spite of its location, local citizens made good use of the library's book collection.

Posing with the new bookmobile in front of the Carnegie Library, circa 1955.

The Library moved once again to the Gordon Building on Franklin Street, then to a room over the fire hall on Clinton Avenue. Yet another move took it to a room in the Hundley Building on the east side of the Courthouse Square. After so many moves, local leaders and library board members were ready to apply for a grant from the Carnegie Foundation. They made their request to the City Commissioners and funded with a $1,500 appropriation from the City of Huntsville and a $15,000 grant from the Carnegie Foundation. Huntsville's "permanent" library opened in 1916. In addition to this funding, part of the opening collection came from door-to-door book drives.

The Library's first outreach program came as the result of the construction of the Guntersville Dam in 1939. The Tennessee Valley Authority asked the Library to provide services to its workers, and the Library's first bookmobile, and one of the earliest bookmobiles in the country, operated in Madison, Jackson, and Marshall counties. The library reverted to a one county operation in 1952.

The Friends of the Library were incorporated in 1958, and one of their first projects included building support for a new library to serve the fast-growing and highly educated population of Huntsville. In 1963 the Library applied for federal funding to construct a new library to serve a city whose population had outgrown the Carnegie Library. The "million dollar" library opened in 1966. The Library expanded beyond it's central building to open branch libraries in northwest Huntsville—the Bessie K. Russell Library: and southwest Huntsville at the Charlotte Drive Branch Library, later renamed the Eleanor E. Murphy Branch Library.

The "million dollar" library became inadequate to serve a population of nearly 200,000 in the early 1980s, and planning began for an addition and renovation of the 1966 building. Through the vision of the Library Board, Mayor Joe Davis and the Huntsville City Council, led by President Ernest Kaufmann, a new Main Library was included in a major bond issue, which would also build a new baseball stadium. The city provided $8 million for the construction of the building, and the Library Board was challenged to raise an additional $1.9 million to furnish and equip the 123,000-square-foot building. The Huntsville Public Library Foundation was created to conduct this important capital campaign, and the $9.9 million "new" Main Library opened to the public in April 1987. The Library continues to receive substantial support through the fundraising activities of the Library

The Huntsville Public Library as it proudly stands today.

Foundation and the Friends of the Library.

The Library system also grew and new libraries opened in Madison, Gurley, New Hope, Triana, Hazel Green, and Monrovia. Special homework centers and computer labs are provided at the Oscar Mason Center of Sparkman Homes and the Dr. Richard M. Showers, Sr. Recreation Center on Blue Spring Road.

The Library also provides specialized services through its Sub-regional Library for the Blind and Physically Handicapped; the International Media Center, a collection of popular foreign-language books and audiovisual materials; the Ready Reader Van, which provides programs and materials for all Head Start Centers in Huntsville and Madison County; and regular Bookmobile stops to retirement centers and nursing homes. One of the newest services was funded through a grant from the Jane K. Lowe foundation—the Raise a Reader program provides a welcome

package to each new baby born in Huntsville hospitals.

The Library's long tradition of service continues through its Main Library, 11 branch libraries throughout Madison County, bookmobile and vibrant outreach programs. Today, the Huntsville Madison County Public Library boasts over 2 million book loans each year and more than 4,000 visitors each day. It is the busiest library in Alabama and one of the busiest of any city its size in the Southeast. Nearly 75 percent of residents hold library cards. The library collections and services it currently provides will have a lasting impact on its children and grandchildren. The Huntsville Public Library plays the pivotal role in supporting the information, educational and literacy needs of the citizens of Huntsville and Madison County.

ALABAMA A&M UNIVERSITY

AAMU is a land-grant university, and its support comes from the state of Alabama and federal funds appropriated to assist in carrying on the work stipulated by the Morrill Acts of 1862 and 1890. The University is under the control of a board of trustees appointed by the governor, who serves as ex-officio chairman.

The University was organized nearly 130 years ago as the result of a bill passed in the state legislature in 1873, along with the continued efforts of its first principal and president, William Hooper Councill, an ex-slave. The school opened its doors to 61 students on May 1, 1875, as the Huntsville Normal School with an appropriation of $1,000 per year.

Industrial education was introduced around 1878. It attracted wide attention, and the school was assisted financially by the Slater and Peabody Funds, as well as by private contributors. The work in industrial education was so successful that the state legislature authorized the name to be changed to the State Normal and Industrial School at Huntsville. The appropriation was increased by the state to $4,000 per year.

In 1891, the school became the recipient of a part of the Federal Land-Grant Fund provided by an act of Congress, approved August 30, 1890. The purpose of this fund was to further training in agriculture and mechanical arts in the various states at the college level.

The name of the school was changed again to the State Agricultural and Mechanical College for Negroes, and a new location was provided at Normal, Alabama, where the school would have ample room for the development of its trades and agricultural programs. In 1919, the institution became a junior college, and its name was

Gates of Alabama A&M University.

changed once more to the State Agricultural and Mechanical Institute for Negroes.

In 1939, by authority of the State Board of Education, the Institute was permitted to offer work on the senior college level. The first graduating class since 1920 received the bachelor's degree in 1941, and on January 14, 1948, the name was again changed to Alabama Agricultural and Mechanical College. On June 26, 1969, the Alabama State Board of Education, the governing body of the institution, adopted a resolution changing the name of the institution to its current name, Alabama Agricultural and Mechanical (A&M) University.

The University received a "Class A" rating by the Southern Association of Colleges and Secondary Schools in August 1946 and became a fully accredited member of the Association in December 1963.

The institution has had three principals: William Hooper Councill, 1875-1887; Peter H. Clark, 1887-1888; and William Hooper Councill, 1888-1890.

It has had nine presidents: Will-

iam Hooper Councill, 1890-1909; Walter S. Buchanan, 1909-1921; T. R. Parker, 1921-1927; J. F. Drake, 1927-1962; R. D. Morrison, 1962-1984; Douglas Covington, 1984-1987; Carl H. Marbury, 1987-1991; David B. Henson, 1992-1995; and John T. Gibson, 1996-present.

True, AAMU has been around a long time. Since its founding in 1875, the north Alabama institution has become known throughout the world for its manner of achieving academic excellence without exclusivity. Having always opened its doors to all, the 6,000-student university continues to offer students who need an academic boost an opportunity to excel beside internationally recognized student scholars. Indeed, for four consecutive years, the university placed students on the coveted academic teams of *USA Today*. It was also named one of the Top 50 schools nationwide for African Americans by *Black Enterprise* magazine. From its modest beginnings in what is now downtown Huntsville, the university is a land-grant institution that boasts Ph.D. degree programs in the sought-after areas of food sciences, physics, and plant and soil science.

High School Senior Day at AAMU.

Perhaps no better American success story exists than the Olympus in northeastern Huntsville that is fondly referred to as "the Hill." Founded by William Hooper Councill, an ex-slave with the daring to dream big in a hostile American South, the university is called "alma mater" by men and women throughout the world. The commitment to the education of all who enter its gates has made AAMU an institution with the most diverse faculty body in the state of Alabama. Such diversity has spurred collaborations and numerous research opportunities. For example, AAMU has more partnership contracts with NASA than any other HBCU in the nation.

Many companies also quickly tap into the school's vast capabilities and benefit from quality and cost-effective research by brilliant campus scientists and researchers from the schools of Agricultural and Environmental Sciences, Arts and Sciences, Business, Education, and Engineering and Technology.

Dean Arthur J. Bond, who founded the National Society of Black Engineers (NSBE) during his faculty days at Purdue University, leads the School of Engineering and Technology. In addition to programs in civil engineering and electrical, industrial and mechanical engineering technology, the accredited engineering school recently has introduced to the world its first graduates with full-fledged electrical and mechanical engineering degrees.

Moreover, AAMU faculty members are heavily involved in various aspects of research for numerous governmental agencies and subcontractors. In fact, the tremendous volume of research grants and contracts entered into by the university under its research faculty necessitated the development, also in 1999, of the Alabama A&M University Research Institute (AAMURI),

Alabama A&M University General Campus Scene.

spearheaded by Dr. Daryush Ila, an energetic and internationally known physicist. AAMURI adds professionalism to the business of pursuing, negotiating, and entering into contracts by University entities.

The opening of the new millennium marked a period of significant improvements in a number of areas. For instance, thanks to the assistance of a very dynamic admissions office and the support of several alumni throughout the country, AAMU's student population has escalated. At some points, AAMU has been one of the few state universities able to boast of an enrollment increase at the beginning of the fall semester. The admissions

Student in laboratory in the Department of Plant and Soil Science at Alabama A&M University.

office has made aggressive strides to recruit more valedictorians and salutatorians, inclusive of a significant overall enrollment increase. Moreover, the admissions staff has been challenged to surpass a student enrollment of 6,000.

While AAMU aggressively seeks out top scholars, it maintains its historical role of providing a quality education to all students. Thus, a structured retention plan is in effect that will significantly assist in managing enrollment and meeting the academic, social, and psychological needs of students. While these support areas are key, students also expect more tangible indicators of a quality student life, including, but not limited to, ATM access on campus, direct deposit of student refunds, Lyceum Series funding, and improvements in numerous other areas. And, while major developments are occurring on all fronts in athletics, AAMU's emphasis will remain on graduating the students it cheers on to victories. Moreover, along with its entry into SWAC and Division I athletics came several requirements and institutional commitments. AAMU has met and continues to meet these new challenges with zeal. The end result has made the SWAC's newest member one of its most formidable forces. In other words, AAMU has a "Bulldog grip" on the SWAC, and it hopes to become its powerhouse.

Over the past years, AAMU has witnessed extensive renovations to campus facilities, including select residence halls. Immediately following the close of spring semester 2001, renovations began on a number of the residences. But because capital funds used to restore the historic Normal's Hill district are restricted funds that cannot be used to ease the burden caused by voids in funding from the state, the University's capital plans must and will continue. Construction has been completed on the nearly 90,000-square-foot School of Engineering and Technology facility, which has been a dream for quite sometime.

Renovations and construction have ended on the J. F. Drake Learning Resources Center. The end result is an additional 15,000 square feet. The plans have also been developed for the Old Drake Dining Hall and Carnegie Hall, but there rarely are enough funds available to meet all the capital needs of "the Hill."

Much excitement has been generated about the newly constructed 240-unit Normal Hills Student Apartments. These buildings were funded and are operated by a private developer, and the facilities offer upscale accommodations for upperclassmen, graduate, and married students. The facility includes a clubhouse, tennis court, weightroom, and swimming pool. Other amenities include cable and computer connections.

AAMU was announced as the feature university during the month of May 2001 for the national radio broadcast of the Tom Joyner Morning Show. Through this effort and the efforts of alumni nationwide, AAMU raised $1,017,121.84. The Tom Joyner effort generated

more than $590,000, making AAMU the top Tom Joyner Foundation fundraiser.

The use of technology holds great promise for keeping AAMU competitive and more widely accessible. In terms of price and performance, costs are predicted to increase by double digits each year for the foreseeable future. Therefore, the use of technology becomes ever more critical for this institution, as it is incessantly squeezed by market pressures on student fees and possible changes in Alabama tax policy.

AAMU Food Biotechnologist, Hortense W. Dodo.

AAMU typically gathers large amounts of data in the process of conducting day-to-day business—enrolling students, recording grades, hiring employees, collecting revenues, and paying bills. Currently, information technology has evolved to a point that these data are, or easily could be, made readily accessible to decision makers. However, AAMU will endeavor to solve the problem of providing reliable information "relevant" to the particular needs of its decision makers.

Also, "the Hill" has made great technology thrusts; however, there is still much to be done. The Office of Education Information Technology Services has evolved into the "Office Automation/Systems Integration and Support (OASIS)." I.T. staff members will collaborate to bring AAMU into the new millennium with a strategic plan to enhance the I.T. function for all university programs and departments.

The first fruits of its labors are beginning to emerge with the Alabama A&M University Research Institute. Indeed, AAMURI is paying dividends in terms of increased revenues from research, grants, and contracts. The energetic staff members are enthusiastic about this new venture; faculty researchers are increasingly involved in its success; and there is every reason to be optimistic about the future of AAMURI.

AAMU is an outstanding institution, yet it will press on toward educational and institutional excellence. AAMU can, and should, become a Research I doctoral degree-granting institution, committing the effort, planning, and resources needed to make this a reality.

Indeed, this is an exciting time for involvement at any level with the nearly 130-year-old Alabama A&M University. AAMU scientists are working on projects as varied as the development of an allergy-free peanut, flight simulation software for the Department of Defense, and detecting human error through mathematical concepts for NASA. The list is endless, and people on "the Hill" are much too busy to boast for long. From the freshman student to the oldest living graduate, the excitement of "the Hill" is forever captivating.

THE HISTORIC HUNTSVILLE FOUNDATION

From a cotton-based economy, Huntsville and Madison County evolved into the birthplace of the U.S. space program and a location of prime importance to the activities of the U.S. Army.

Over the years, many structures were sacrificed in the name of progress. But in the 1970s, influential citizens recognized that, in certain cases, such demolition was an unacceptable squandering of a rich legacy. These leaders founded the Historic Huntsville Foundation in April 1974. Since then the Foundation has worked to preserve historically and architecturally significant sites and structures countywide.

In 1975 the Foundation began regular publication of the *Historic Huntsville Quarterly of Local Architecture and Preservation.* This scholarly journal received the Alabama Historical Commission's Distinguished Service Award in 2001.

The Foundation operates a warehouse of architectural artifacts and materials salvaged from historic structures for reuse in restorations within Madison County and provides complimentary information and consultation on the tax credits available for the restoration of historic income-producing property. An annual awards dinner is the Foundation's primary educational event, honoring those who have made notable contributions in the categories of Personal, Professional, Project Achievement, Education, and Continued Preservation. Activities throughout the year include members-only events in historic private homes and buildings.

The Foundation's most ambitious undertaking came in Spring 1984 when the membership voted to purchase Harrison Brothers Hardware, in operation on the

Harvie Jones Building (left) and Harrison Brothers Hardware, Foundation properties on the south side of the courthouse square.

courthouse square since 1897. The death of the last of the Harrison Brothers left this local landmark in jeopardy of closure and conversion to office space. The store is now operated primarily by volunteers and serves as a successful business enterprise, hardware museum, and tourist attraction. In 2002, Harrison Brothers Hardware was designated by the U.S. Department of the Interior as one of Save America's Treasures and awarded a $100,000 Federal grant for much-needed repairs and restoration.

In 1998 the Foundation purchased the 1896 building adjacent to Harrison Brothers and named it the Harvie Jones Building in honor of its founding chairman, the late architect Harvie Jones. The building was returned to a more historically accurate appearance and is leased to a restaurant and an architectural firm.

The Alabama Historical Commission has provided grant funds to the Foundation for the restoration of the Harvie Jones Building; the stabilization of the 1857 Memphis and Charleston freight depot; the survey and nomination of the Dallas, Lincoln, Lowe; and Merrimack mill villages and the historic areas of New Market and Gurley to the *National Register of Historic Places.*

All are welcome to join in support of the Foundation's efforts to preserve and protect the irreplaceable symbols of Huntsville and Madison County's heritage.

WOODY ANDERSON FORD

C.W. Woody Anderson is a travelin' man. And throughout his life's journey he has humbly amassed a fortune in success, admiration and respect of his employees, his colleagues and the citizens of north Alabama.

Born October 17, 1921 in Elkmont, Alabama, Anderson went directly from Elkmont High School to work for A&P Grocery Co. in Louisville, Kentucky. After being promoted to store manager, he found himself returning to Alabama in 1944 and opening his own grocery store in Athens. Three years later in 1947, Anderson traded carrot tops for hardtops, starting with a used car business in Decatur, and finally jumping into the new car business. On April 15, 1950 he took the helm of the Dodge and Plymouth dealership in Huntsville, and with the purchase of Huntsville's Ford dealership in 1961, the Woody Anderson engine was revved up to race him into becoming an auto dealer legend.

The dealership began modestly on a downtown site on Clinton Street and relocated to Washington Street in 1964. It established a high profile presence on 16-acres of land on the north side of town at its

Employees at the 1958 Christmas party.

current Jordon Lane site in 1984. While there, the dealership collected numerous awards, including the Ford Motor Company Distinguished Achievement Award and nomination for the prestigious Alabama Time Quality Dealer Award sponsored by *Time* magazine, ADAA and NADA. In addition, Mr. Anderson was continually honored by his industry peers. The former president of the Huntsville New Car Dealers Association, Anderson was also an outstanding member of Ford Motor Company's Dealer Affairs Committee, Advertising Council and the Ford Dealers Council.

As active as Anderson has been in the automotive industry, he has gained even more recognition for his many contributions to the local community and the state of Alabama. He was fondly saluted as the "Governor of North Alabama" for his achievements in the political arena, including his co-chairmanship of the

State of Alabama Personnel Board, membership on the State of Alabama ABC Board and his service to Governor George Wallace as a member of the governor's staff. His leadership skills have also made an indelible mark on his community, helping to organize the creation of numerous corporate and charitable entities, among them Peoples National Bank, Kings Inn Hotel, radio station WVOV, and the Century Club of the Boys Clubs of Alabama. Recipient of the Jaycees Distinguished Service Award and former chairman of the Madison County March of Dimes, Mr. Anderson has selflessly donated his time, talent and financial support to many deserving civic organizations including the Boy Scouts, Boys and Girls Ranch of Alabama and the Multiple Sclerosis Society. Lastly, as a sparkplug in Huntsville's real estate marketplace, he is the developer of the 130-acre Harrison Hills subdivision, owner of both the Holiday Inn/Madison Airport and

Left to right: Fred Sanders, Tom Guthrie, C. W. Anderson, and a Chrysler executive.

Aerial view of building on Jordan Lane in 1984.

Hampton Inn of Huntsville and owner of many commercial properties including the AmSouth Bank, Goodwill of Alabama, Sizzler Restaurant, Dunkin Donuts and Green Hills Grille buildings.

The landscape and inventory of Woody Anderson Ford was dramatically different when the dealership began in 1961. At that time, roughly $1,800 would put you in the driver's seat of Ford's most popular model of the day, the Falcon. The famed Mustang was introduced in 1964 for the sticker price of approximately $3,500. To drive off Anderson's lot in a Mustang today will cost upward of $25,000, and Ford's fastest selling SUVs—the Explorer and Expedition—are a world away from the modest little Falcon in both performance and price tag.

As Ford models have evolved in silhouette and performance, so has the dealership's daily operation. Margaret Hightower, the company's current comptroller, has been with the dealership since the beginning and recalls having to perform every duty, from inventory control to parts ordering, by hand and with the help of a cumbersome Burr-

oughs Bookkeeping Machine. In 1975 the company embraced computerization, updating to a comprehensive in-house system in 1984 when the dealership moved to Jordon Lane. Today the dealership has a strong online presence, where customers can search available new and used vehicle inventories, reserve rental cars, make service appointments and even AutoApply for credit from Ford Motor Credit Online directly from the Website www.woodyanderson.com.

Along with Ms. Hightower, there are several other loyal employees who have formed the core of Anderson's "People Fleet." Members of the original staff of 50 include sales professionals John Ballou and Tom Guthrie, both of whom are still active on the sales floor. Collier Bush, who began as a porter in 1963 and then served as wrecker driver, is one of the dealership's top sales people today; James Clark, who began as a crack mechanic more than three decades ago, can still be found taking care of business on a part-time basis; Jannie McCain has been at the telephone switchboard controls since 1963. And last but not least, is octogenarian Woody Anderson himself, who is still

drawn to his namesake dealership every morning to take account of the over 900 vehicles in stock.

Long recognized as one of the top 100 dealers in the country, Woody Anderson Ford naturally attracts the most dedicated and talented personnel. While new employees are always warmly welcomed into the Anderson Ford family, a now abandoned "tradition" is a humorous legend often shared with those coming on board. For many years, the Anderson's graciously hosted all employees and their partners at an annual Holiday Party held at the country club. The purported tradition fabricated by the tightly knit group was to inform all new employees that a ritual "dump" into the club's swimming pool was to be an expected rite of passage into the Anderson fraternity. Thinking himself clever, one year a new employee packed an extra suit in his car, drove to the country club and immediately threw himself into the water, bragging that he escaped being thrown in by jumping in himself. Amidst the shock that erupted into unrestrained laughter, the soggy young man was belatedly informed the truth. The dunking tradition was just a spoof. In the long history of Anderson parties, he was the only person ever to get wet!

Employees with 38–50 years of service. Left to right: James Clark (1952), Collier Bush (1963), Tom Guthrie (1947), Janie McCain (1963), Margaret Hightower (1961), amd John Ballou (1956).

APT RESEARCH, INC.

APT Research, Inc., a Huntsville corporation, provides independent engineering services in the areas of quantitative risk assessment; test planning; systems engineering; range safety; system safety; industrial and quality engineering; and explosives safety. The company's primary customers include the United States Army Strategic Missile Defense Command (USASMDC); the Department of Defense Explosives Safety Board (DDESB); the U.S. Air Force; the U.S. Army; the U.S. Marine Corps; and the National Aeronautics and Space Administration (NASA).

When APT was founded in 1990, Tom Pfitzer and Betty Augsburger envisioned a company that would offer top-notch safety engineering services while providing a friendly, challenging, and team-oriented work environment. In the company's first Policies and Procedures manual, they wrote: "APT is focused on becoming a nationally respected company supporting the U.S. Government with independent analyses and recommendations in safety, missile testing, and other areas." Pfitzer and Augsburger planned for a top-notch environment, too. "At that point in our careers," said Pfitzer, "we wanted more than anything to look forward to going to work in the morning." Full-time employees would share ownership in the company and participate in planning and operation. The decisions and efforts of all employees would help determine corporate success, and employees would "share the pain and share the gain." This approach worked from the start—it both motivated employees and enabled them to provide optimum service to customers. It also helped save employee jobs during a lean period to come.

Pfitzer, an engineer, concentrated on developing the company's technical capabilities. His experience included development of range safety programs at the installation level, operational and flight safety, and finding safe solutions for range users. Augsburger, whose background included eight years overseas, managed the business side. In 1992 and 1993, system safety engineers Philip Owen and Saralyn Dwyer joined APT. Owen's 30 years of experience included chief of safety at the Strategic Defense Command in Huntsville, and Dwyer had worked for a local defense contractor. Energetic and congenial, they helped establish the corporate tone of technical capability, versatility, and willingness to "pitch in" wherever needed to support customers.

The first APT Research customers were elements of the United States Army Strategic Defense Command. As more and more customers came, they spread the word on APT quality and enthusiasm. By 1994, APT Research was up to 10 employees and $600,000 in projected corporate income for the year. New work was coming in— but sometimes it was not arriving quickly enough. A month came when there was not enough money to meet payroll. Workers at the employee-owned company chose to take a temporary cut in hours to avoid layoffs or borrowing. They cut their hours by as much as 20 percent, and management took a 40 percent cut. After several months, the crisis passed. The company had survived without layoffs. In its first 10 years, this had been the company's major storm—and

APT Research received a Chamber of Commerce Technology Small Business of the Year award in 2001. The company was started by Tom Pfitzer, corporate president, and Betty Augsburger, corporate secretary-treasurer.

together, the employees had weathered it safely.

Smoother sailing was ahead. The company's business base grew to include the Department of Defense Explosives Safety Board; the U.S. Air Force; the U.S. Army; the National Aeronautics and Space Administration; and other government and private customers. Leaders within APT were selected to head corporate divisions: Bob Baker, Test Planning and Range Safety; Johnny Allen, Systems Engineering; Pete Yutmeyer, Explosives Safety; John Hall, Industrial Engineering; and Nina Donath, Software Development. APT added personnel in Albuquerque and Las Cruces, New Mexico; Washington, DC; and Yuma, Arizona.

With growth, the company followed a simple strategy to assure that APT Research continued to satisfy customers: "Ask them," explained Pfitzer, "and in a variety of ways," added Augsburger. APT managers held periodic face-to-face meetings with customers to obtain feedback not only on technical quality but also on the contractual, financial, and staffing aspects of APT service.

From 1994 onward, APT gross sales grew 30–50 percent per year. In 1999, the company purchased its own 8,000-square-foot building in Cummings Research Park to serve as corporate headquarters, and within a year was making plans for further expansion.

In addition, because APT management had aimed the sights higher than merely overcoming internal and marketing challenges, APT's success was helping to establish Huntsville as a center of excellence for safety. Both Huntsville and APT Research were achieving national and international recognition for safety-related achievements:

• At the 1999 System Safety Society Conference in Orlando, Florida, attended by over 300 international participants, the Huntsville Chapter won the "Chapter of the Year" award.

• APT President Tom Pfitzer received

Tom Pfitzer, APT president, presents a Huntsville System Safety Society Professional of the Year award to Philip Owen, APT vice president.

APT, an employee-owned company, purchased its headquarters facility in 1999. APT employees gathered in front of the building after a barbecue lunch on July 8, 2002.

the international award "Manager of the Year" at the same conference, and he later represented the United States in developing NATO risk assessment methods.

• At the 2000 System Safety Society Conference in Texas, the Huntsville Chapter repeated as "Chapter of the Year."

• In April 2001, 35 different representatives from the safety organizations of nine different NATO countries convened in Huntsville for training in software that APT Research had developed.

• APT hosted numerous national and international safety working groups where safety policies and standards used by U.S. and foreign government installations and organizations were developed.

In 2001, the Huntsville/Madison County Chamber of Commerce honored APT Research with the Technology Small Business of the Year award, based on innovativeness of service,

financial strength, number of years in business, response to adversity, growth in employment, and community involvement. Although APT had successfully met those criteria, another factor had perhaps been even more important—the employees really enjoyed working at APT, and it showed in their support to customers. An APT engineer wrote, "APT Research is a great place to work. Each employee contributes to several projects that benefit our country. We strengthen our nation's defense, enhance public safety, and develop analytical tools for other engineers."

In future years, APT Research plans to continue tying its future to Huntsville's—clearly a win-win situation. By helping make Huntsville a recognized center of excellence for safety engineering, APT has increased its own visibility as a leader in this area. And as APT's influence has increased in the safety community, more people worldwide have become aware of Huntsville's professional community and what it has to offer.

LUNA TECH, INC.

How does a passionate hobby become a multi-million dollar industry? Like many successful people, Tom DeWille, founder and guiding light of Luna Tech, Inc. credits the influence of an inspired teacher. Tom describes his high school chemistry teacher as, "...old school; he believed everyone should know some chemistry, and chemistry should be fun. I learned a lot, and managed to get through school without blowing up the chem lab."

While trying to make some pyrotechnic effects to shoot for his sister's birthday, he came up against a technical problem he couldn't solve. Tom finally decided to call a local fireworks company to see about purchasing the effects. The owner of the company, Loren "Uncle Red" Wisdom was so impressed with the technical questions Tom asked, and his knowledge of pyrotechnics, he hired him over the phone. At the tender age of 16, Tom toured for Uncle Red with Tom Pack's Circus doing pyrotechnics all over the South.

Tom's pursuit of bigger and better rockets led him into the army as a Nike Missile Repairman. Shortly after his duty with Uncle Sam was up, his old friend and mentor Uncle Red passed away. At his widow's request, Tom stepped in and finished the shows that Uncle Red had contracted. He then went to work for NASA, but continued doing fireworks on the side. Tom's restless intellect—always looking for better ways to do things— soon led him to branch out into theatrical lighting after attending a ballet recital where "the music and dance was exquisite, but the lighting was terrible!"

After leaving NASA Tom and Amanda McLean started a theatrical services company in 1972. This was the birth of Luna Tech, Inc. They provided lighting, power dis-

"OK, Now everyone say 'PYRO'!"

tribution, security, catering—whatever was needed. As Tom said of those early days: "If you had an empty field, a power pole, a sound system and band, we had everything else." Tom and Amanda worked other jobs to support the company in the early days— reinvesting most of the money they made into expanding and improving the business. It wasn't long before Luna Tech, Inc. was an established company with a rapidly growing international reputation for excellence and they could, as the old saying goes, "quit their day jobs."

Propelled by Tom's restless creativity, innovation became the hallmark of Luna Tech. Often, his vision for lighting simply couldn't be accomplished with existing equipment—so Tom designed and manufactured his own electronic controls and systems. During this same time, Tom became a member of the International Alliance of Theatrical and Stage Employees and

Motion Picture Operators of the U.S. and Canada, Local M900, and a certified rigger. When the Von Braun Civic Center was built, Tom hung, adjusted, and focused every stage-light in the facility.

Since Luna had the only lighting system for rent in the area, they were soon doing all of the rock-and-roll shows that came to town. This exposed Tom to the early attempts at stage, or what was to become known as "close-proximity," pyrotechnics. It wasn't long before his imagination was soaring with the possibilities of this nascent art form. And of course, Tom could envision better ways to do it. And just as certainly, the technology didn't exist to realize his vision, so Tom set to work designing and building it. His innovation didn't stop with electronics and hardware; soon his love of chemistry came into play. After ordering some flash

Aimee Townsel and Tonya League prepare pyrotechnic material for mixing in an industrial tumbler.

powder from a theatrical supply company that, to put it mildly, didn't perform to his expectations, Tom invented Pyropak® A/B two-component flash powder, considered by many to still be the gold standard of the industry. From this humble beginning grew the world renowned Pyropak® Precision Pyrotechnic Products.

At this time the notion of indoor fireworks was relatively new. The only nationwide law governing fireworks was based on outdoor shows and stated they had to be a minimum of 200 feet from a building. "You want to do what?" was a common reaction from local fire marshals. Tom discovered that fostering a new art form was going to be as much about education as it was electronics and chemistry. In addition to his myriad duties with Luna Tech, Tom spent a great deal of time travelling and offering his considerable expertise to municipalities formulating regulations to ensure that indoor pyrotechnics would be a safe and thrilling experience. Many of the safety instructions that Tom wrote to accompany Pyropak® products were incorporated into the new regulations. The National Fire Protection Association drafted him to be on the pyrotechnics committee, which drafted what would become NFPA 1126 "Code For The Use Of Pyrotechnics Before A Proximate Audience." Tom shot the first indoor pyrotechnics show in Japan. They were so impressed that he was invited back to design and shoot the pyrotechnics for the opening of the Japanese Government Pavilion at Expo '85. Tom was also the first westerner licensed to shoot pyrotechnics over the heads of the Japanese Royal Family.

After 30 years in business, and with over 6000 Pyropak® Firing Systems in use in the field, Luna Tech continues to introduce new and exciting innovations in close-proximity pyrotechnics. The company has also been featured in specials about fireworks on the Discovery Channel.

The folks at Luna Tech also take great joy in contributing fireworks displays to worthy community causes, like elementary school reading incentive programs and the Aids Action Coalition's annual fundraiser. After 30 years of setting new standards for indoor pyrotechnics, Tom DeWille, the "mad genius" behind Luna Tech, retired in 2002. Tom could have been speaking for all of its 40 employees when he said, "I feel very fortunate that I have been able to make a living bringing joy and wonder to people's lives." Stepping up to take the helm upon Tom's retirement, co-founder Amanda McLean promises to continue Luna Tech's ongoing mission to fill audiences with child-like wonder, whatever their ages may be.

Lanney Moore bottles Pyropak® Flash Powder.

MEVATEC CORPORATION

In 1988, when a business advisor from the Small Business Administration advised Nancy Archuleta to give up her business plans and "go home and bake cookies," she took at least some of his advice. She went back home, but instead of baking cookies, she built a successful business with $120 million in annual revenues. Today, the company she founded, MEVATEC Corporation, is a well-known player in the government professional services industry.

Starting out in 1985 building circuit boards and integrated electronic systems, Nancy quickly grew her company, Mesilla Valley High Tech Industries, to 40 employees. However, when a major contract assembling pager systems was moved to an offshore company by the customer in a cost-cutting effort, Nancy was forced to lay off all but two of her employees—bringing in family members to help run the business. Struggling to stay afloat in 1989, and sensing that the government professional services industry offered greater opportunities, Nancy decided to make a wholesale change in the company. Renaming it MEVATEC, she switched the focus to government technical services. Other changes soon followed as the company developed outstanding technical capabilities.

In August 1989, Tom Houser and Larry Fulton joined the company as part of a new management team. They remain today, serving as president and executive vice president, respectively. Tom serves as the chief operating officer and Larry as chief technical officer; program manager on the largest contract in the company; and head of the engineering and technical group. Nancy serves as the board chair and CEO. Part of the company's success is attributed to its ability to keep the

Nancy Archuleta, MEVATEC chair and CEO, who successfully guided the company through wholesale change.

original management team intact.

In April 1990 the company moved from Las Cruces, New Mexico to Huntsville where MEVATEC had acquired work on a $21 million software contract for the Army's Space and Missile Defense Command. Nancy and her family followed the company from their home in Las Cruces. Although annual sales had declined to $50,000 by 1988, by 1989 MEVATEC had sales of $350,000 and is projecting $120 million in 2002. MEVATEC has grown every year except one since 1989 and its growth has been well above the industry average in most years. Between 2000 and 2001, the company's growth rate was over 39 percent!

MEVATEC is a diversified service company in both markets and capabilities. There are three sec-

tors within the company: Engineering/Technical; Information Technology; and Management Services. Customers include: the federal government; state governments; and commercial industry. The Department of Defense is the single largest customer. MEVATEC is heavily involved in many programs including missile defense, where it is the fifth largest contractor. Activities include: system integration software development; system analysis; environmental engineering; test planning and support; and business re-engineering. With respect to the latter, MEVATEC entered the management consulting arena in 1995, quickly establishing a reputation for excellence in identifying and solving problems in government organizations and commercial enterprises.

In 1997 MEVATEC won the largest contract ever awarded to a small business by the United States Army. The contract was for technical support to the Space and Missile Defense Command in Huntsville and the ceiling was $833 million. This contract led to opportunities that strongly fueled the company's growth over the next five years. The same contract was re-bid in 2002 and MEVATEC once again was awarded the job. During the five years of the initial contract, MEVATEC established itself as an outstanding prime contractor with the ability to manage a large team successfully. The new contract has 100 subcontractors, giving the team strong capabilities in all technical disciplines. MEVATEC considers subcontract management to be a core competency and has invested in tools and developed efficient pro-

Corporate offices are located in this building in Huntsville, Alabama. It is a sharp contrast from the original headquarters in Las Cruces, New Mexico.

cesses to perform this management function successfully.

Although MEVATEC started out as a company eligible for sole source contract awards, it graduated from this program, identified as 8(a) by the federal government, in 1997. Nancy and her management team realized that the failure rate of graduated 8(a)'s was well over 50 percent. Analyzing the factors that caused these failures, they took steps to ensure continued success after graduation. Part of their strategy included standardizing proposal processes with experienced proposal developers so that the company could successfully compete for contracts. As a result, the win rate over the past several years has been approximately 70 percent compared to the industry average of 25 to 30 percent.

MEVATEC is proud of its work supporting NASA's Marshall Space Flight Center in Huntsville. Marshall has a celebrated history in such efforts as development of the Saturn V booster rocket that put men on the moon and they played a key role in building the International Space Station. The company continues to aggressively seek work at Marshall with Nancy's son, Gabe Nieto, as the vice president for all NASA work.

MEVATEC is probably best known for its unique culture, making it a very attractive place to work. Elements of this culture include: a 100 percent open-door policy; employee councils to tackle issues directly affecting them; budget authority delegated to lower management levels; outstanding fringe benefits; respect for individuals; respect for opinions and ideas; emphasis on open communications; and an employee stock-ownership plan that has seen significant increases in value every year since its inception. Although managers are held to high standards, they enjoy the freedom to take action and make decisions to an extent not typical in industry.

Huntsville is the corporate headquarters for the MEVATEC Corporation, with 12 other locations throughout the U.S.—employing more than 500 people. The company is engaged in a wide variety of activities ranging from counting fish in the Colombia River to supporting test design for future missile systems. All of this is in real contrast to the days when they assembled electronic circuit boards in an adobe building in Las Cruces, while the ceiling rained down dirt and paint particles whenever a truck went by!

The original corporate headquarters in Las Cruces, New Mexico.

NEXTEK, INC.

Huntsville, Alabama was recognized as the "Watercress Capital of the World" for most of the early part of the 20th century. Huntsville remained primarily an agricultural town producing other common crops including cotton, which is still significant today. That changed in the 1950s when the Rocket and Science team of Dr. Werhner von Braun moved here from Germany after World War II, first spending a brief period in White Sands, New Mexico. Redstone Arsenal, a munitions plant during the war, offered an ideal location for Dr. von Braun and his team of "Rocket Scientists" to hone their skills and bring space technology to Huntsville and to America.

It was then that Huntsville was renamed the "Space Capital of the World," and rightfully so. With the full support of President John F. Kennedy and Congress, Huntsville's Rocket Science group put men on the moon before the end of the '60s and brought space tech-

Nextek's founding management team, from left to right: Dr. Jim Chiang, John Roberts, Jim Harris, Phil Yates and Jim Trummer.

nology to the rest of the world. With this outpouring of technology, Huntsville became the home of many major contract firms supporting space and government programs.

As the space program narrowed in the '70s, and with an abundant supply of engineers and manufacturing talent, another industry was born in Huntsville called "Contract Manufacturing," or Electronic Manufacturing Services (EMS) as

it is known today. This industry is one of the largest and fastest growing industries in the world today. Electronic Manufacturing Services companies are engineering and manufacturing companies that design and/or build electronic products for original equipment manufacturers (OEMs). These products range anywhere from consumer electronic products to space or military products. Other product examples would be telecommunication, data communication, medical, and optical related products to name a few.

Since Huntsville became recognized as the "EMS Capital of the World," many tier one and tier two EMS providers established a home in the area. However, in the early '90s, the landscape of contract manufacturing began to change. The need for products to be faster, lighter and have more functions in order to be more competitive became apparent, but the average EMS provider was not postured to

Nextek's cleanroom facility for advanced electronic assembly.

accommodate these new "needs based products." The technology content of these products is very high and requires unique engineering and manufacturing expertise for successful production.

Two engineering executives from one of the tier one EMS providers in the area, both long term veterans since the birth of the industry, recognized this need and began to talk about a new company that would offer the customer base a total solution. Vice President of Program Management Jim Harris, plus President and CEO Jim Trummer, of Worldwide Engineering founded Nextek. Incorporated in 1995 to answer these global needs. Jim and Jim (or Jim², as they are known) brought along two additional founders to start the company. Vice President Product Assurance, Dr. Jim Chiang (a third Jim) to head up the analytical and material analysis laboratory and a tier one EMS provider and another

The Nextek manufacturing and engineering facility.

veteran of the industry, Vice President of Materials and Systems, John Roberts. Not long after incorporating, the four founders brought Chief Technology Officer Phil Yates from an advanced group of AT&T to head up the technology engineering side of the business.

Implantable pacemaker/defibrillator manufactured with advanced assembly technology utilizing Nextek's cleanroom manufacturing facility.

From its humble beginnings in a one room office in Huntsville to a modern manufacturing site in nearby Madison, Alabama located adjacent to the Huntsville International Airport, Nextek (which stands for "Next Technology") has been recognized as a world leader in advanced engineering and manufacturing technology. In fact, Nextek has been awarded the distinguished Service Excellence Award for Technology for four consecutive years for being the most technologically advanced EMS company in the United States for engineering and manufacturing of technology based products. Among many other recognitions received since its inception, Nextek was awarded the Administrator's Award for Excellence for 2001 by the U.S. Small Business Administration for its quality service in support of government related contracts. Since Nextek's founding, the company has manufactured unique products in virtually every industry sector. Products such as implantable medical devices; products to support avionics; aerospace and defense programs; unique high end computing; specialty optical; telecommunications or data communications; wireless; and test, instrumentation and data acquisition.

Nextek is not only recognized for its engineering and manufacturing technology base, which also includes a Class 10,000 cleanroom manufacturing facility, but also for its Material Science and Failure Analysis Laboratory which provides world-class material analysis capabilities. The company has established alliances with major engineering universities and NASA. Additionally, Nextek's Material Management group employs the most advanced systems available that yields consistent 100 percent accurate inventory control. Its

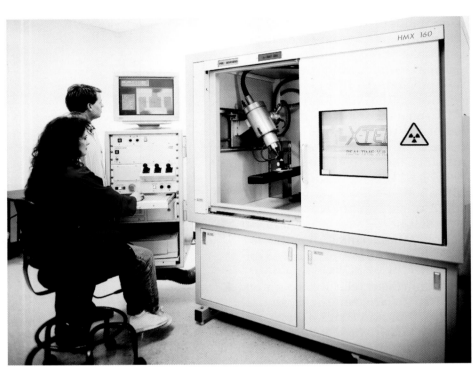

Nextek's custom three-dimensional X-Ray System can provide a three-dimensional image of an object in real time and show features that other X-Ray systems cannot image.

A three-dimensional X-Ray image of a microelectronic assembly.

Business System group employs an end-to-end Enterprise Resource Planning (ERP) system that is scalable to Nextek's continued growth and allows Nextek to manage its programs from the time customer's data is entered until the product is manufactured, shipped, billed and collected from the customer.

As Huntsville prepares for the new millennium, it continues to be a city recognized for technology and change, a city that cultures and nurtures new beginnings. In 2001 Huntsville was recognized by *Newsweek* magazine as one of the top 10 technology cities in the United States. Nextek is but one of many companies spawned from this city of progressive thinking and, like Huntsville, is committed to its mission of being a world leader of technology.

Backdropped by a blue and white Earth, the International Space Station (ISS) is now separated from the Space Shuttle Endeavour *following the undocking of the two spacecraft over western Kazakhstan. It is dated June 15, 2002. The shuttle is on its way home. Other missions will follow, and North Alabama will continue to play a large role in fulfilling mankind's destiny in space.. Courtesy, NASA*

OAKWOOD COLLEGE

Engraved in stone at the entrance to Oakwood College are the words, "Enter to learn; Depart to serve," indicating the school's commitment to the pursuit of knowledge and service to God and man. Its aim is Education, Excellence, and Eternity.

In brief, the college mission includes efforts to achieve spiritual vitality, educational excellence, nurturing environment, operational efficiency, resource development, institutional relations, and technology leadership.

Oakwood College was founded primarily for educating African Americans in the South. Under Divine leadership, (through Ellen G. White), the Seventh-day Adventist Church purchased the Peter Blow plantation which became the site for the new school. A former slave who lived and worked on this plantation was Dred Scott. His petition for personal freedom before the Supreme Court of Missouri, led to the famous Dred Scott Decision of 1857, which eventually resulted in the Civil War. The School, with an opening enrollment of 16 students in November 1896, underwent several name changes as it grew. In 1904 it was known as the Oakwood Manual Training School, changing to the Oakwood Junior College in 1917, and finally in 1943 became Oakwood College.

Recently the College discovered and developed an old slave cemetery on the campus, which has been entered in the *Alabama Registry of Historical Sites*. Adjacent to it is the new Oakwood Memorial Gardens Cemetery that officially opened on April 29, 2002.

Situated in a beautiful natural setting on 1,200-acres of prime land, Oakwood is an important landmark in the city of Huntsville, one of the nation's leading centers in high technology and space science.

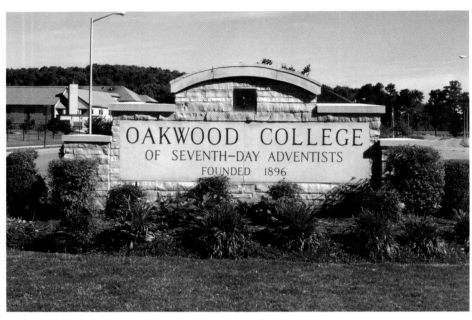

Main entrance to the campus.

Oakwood is accredited by the Commission on Colleges of the Southern Association of Colleges and Schools and the Adventist Accrediting Association of the General Conference to award associate and baccalaureate degrees. Departments with programs in Business, Social Work and Teacher Education are members of national accrediting associations.

The College also offers programs that are approved by the Alabama Board of Nursing, the Alabama State Department of Education, and the American Dietetics Association.

The academic program provides over 40 areas of concentration in 16 departments, namely: Adult & Continuing Education, Biological Sciences, Business & Information Systems, Chemistry, Education, English & Foreign Language, Communications & Art, Family & Consumer Sciences, Health & Physical Education, History, Math & Computer Science, Music, Nursing, Psychology, Religion & Theology, and Social Work. Oakwood is listed among America's best colleges by *U.S. News and World Report*, and rates among the top 15 to 20 colleges and universities in preparing Black applicants for admission to dental and medical schools.

Oakwood participates in cooperative programs with other institutions, including: Alabama A&M University; University of Wisconsin, Madison; University of Alabama, Huntsville; Loma Linda University, California; and Howard University, Washington, D.C. These programs enable students to complete degrees in Applied Mathematics and Engineering (Civil, Computer, Electrical, Mechanical and Industrial).

Its Business and Information Systems Department is housed in a new complex that is fully-networked, Internet and audiovisual ready with cutting-edge technology.

The college exists to prepare students for service. Approximately 1,800 students come from over 40 states and 30 countries. This provides a diversified campus, enhanced by a nurturing Christian environment.

Full-time faculty, also diversified, number over 100 with 53-plus percent holding earned doctorates themselves.

Oakwood alumni are loyal to their alma mater. The annual homecoming each Easter weekend, brings thousands of alumni and friends back to Huntsville and the college campus, resulting in multi-million dollar economic impact on the local community. Its alumni also continue to serve the nation and the world in numerous capacities as leaders and workers in varying careers and professions.

Through various ways and means, Oakwood provides valuable community services.

Students at Oakwood are prepared to develop a sense of service toward their community—local, national and global. Campus organizations such as the National Association for the Prevention of Starvation (which received much attention for their presence in New York following the September 11 attack on the World Trade Center) provide services as tutors, assistants in caring for children and the

The Aeolians, Julie Moore, director.

elderly, and volunteers for community improvement projects.

The annual UNCF banquet receives excellent support from the Huntsville community, and is directly responsible for the visits of many prominent guests to the campus and Huntsville.

Quality music is one of Oakwood's most valuable assets. The Aeolians, organized in 1946, has been the college's primary public relations medium. Following a

performance with the Huntsville Symphony, the *Huntsville Times* review stated, "The Aeolians could sing passages from the phone book, and still make you feel the presence of the divine." Loretta Spencer added, "As Mayor of the city of Huntsville, I feel that the Aeolians embody the heart, soul and spirit of our city. Huntsville could not have a better representation than that which the Aeolians present when they appear on television, at the White House, or in concert."

The Festival of Spirituals featuring Historically Black College and University choirs of Alabama and Tennessee has become one of the most dynamic and best-supported events by the citizens of the Huntsville community.

Oakwood's radio station WOCG 90.1 FM, The Light of the Tennessee Valley, provides news and public service announcements, as well as the best in the spoken word, and inspirational Christian music, 24 hours per day. It provides a warm welcome to the campus!

To learn more about Oakwood College visit it's website: www.oakwood.edu.

Business and Technology Complex.

THE UNIVERSITY OF ALABAMA IN HUNTSVILLE

It was an unusual scene. Members of the Alabama legislature sat in their chairs and listened as a man with a Germanic accent spoke to them about space travel and landing a man on the moon. The year was 1961. At that time, it must have seemed like a page torn out of a science fiction novel.

Dr. Wernher von Braun, who was director of NASA's Marshall Space Flight Center, told the group that not only were those dreams possible, but those dreams could be accomplished in Alabama by Alabamians.

Von Braun said only one thing was missing—a research university.

On that June day in 1961, von Braun convinced that legislative body to spend $3 million to help an extension center of the University of Alabama evolve into The University of Alabama in Huntsville, and what would eventually become an autonomous university that would

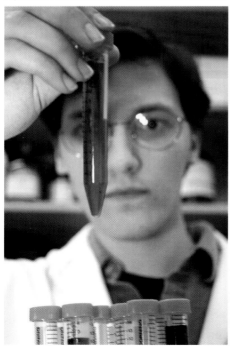

UAH students get plenty of hands-on learning experience in addition to classroom instruction.

Small classroom settings at UAH enhances students' education.

control its own destiny. The faculty at this emerging educational institution would conduct research and teach students the skills needed to put a man on the moon and allow travel beyond our solar system.

UAH was among the few universities in the nation that offered graduate degrees before providing undergraduate education. Among the early degrees offered in 1963 were master's degrees in mathematics, chemistry and physics. Undergraduate degrees were added a year later.

In 1969 the University of Alabama trustees gave the Huntsville campus autonomy from Tuscaloosa. This move would allow UAH to pursue its academic programs deemed critically important to the Huntsville community.

Since those early days, UAH has developed into a nationally recognized institution of higher education, valued for its research and prized for educational opportunities. The university thrives on the synergy between academia, government and business, and complements the research and development needs of local government

laboratories as well as private industry. At the same time, the university answers the community's need for advanced educational opportunities for students in science and engineering.

While UAH continues to excel in its technological capabilities, it also offers outstanding programs in liberal arts, business and nursing.

"The research of the university and its Ph.D. programs, with its concentration in engineering and science, has made us nationally and internationally visible," says President Frank Franz. "Our programs in Administrative Science, Liberal Arts and Nursing reach comparable levels of excellence within our region. We have focused upon building strengths that reflect the needs and interests of the broad-based community that we serve."

UAH's research is focused in information technology, propulsion, microgravity, material science, astrophysics, environmental science, biotechnology, and optics. These areas and the school's complete engineering and science programs allow UAH to provide strong support to NASA's Marshall Space Flight Center and nearby U.S. Army laboratories. The university was one of the founding tenants in Cummings Research Park, the second largest research park in the United States.

UAH research activities produce close working relationships between faculty and students. The university gives students opportunities to apply their education in real-life job situations through cooperative education. Approximately 90 businesses, industries and government agencies provide more than 300 students with hands-on experience and often-permanent employment each year. Several UAH students have also won state and national awards for their cooperative education activities.

The university has activities outside the classroom such as intramural sports, fraternities and sororities, choir and music ensembles and theater productions. While UAH's focus is on high quality education, it also has impressive athletic programs in 13 sports, including a two-time national champion ice hockey team, as well as competitive teams in baseball, softball, women's and men's basketball, cross country, volleyball, soccer and tennis.

Scientific research and athleticism have come together to win honors for the university, such as in the five national award-winning entries submitted by UAH students who used their engineering and athletic skills to design, analyze, construct and race a canoe made mostly of concrete. UAH students also have won national championships for the engineering, design, construction and racing of a moon buggy.

Incoming freshmen at UAH have the highest average ACT score of any public university in Alabama.

The university has more than 100 clubs and organizations, including the World Issues Society, Circle K, the Society for Ancient Languages, the Association for Campus Entertainment, the Student Government Association and professionally oriented clubs and societies in almost every discipline. Greek life ranges from social activities to service projects for local and national charities.

These days, *U.S. News & World Report* consistently ranks UAH among national universities. The university is also listed among Peterson's Competitive Colleges and is the only university in Alabama listed as "very competitive" in Barron's Profiles in American Colleges. The university has also been listed by Cullers Publishing as one of the

100 "best buys" in the United States.

The freshman students enrolled at UAH have the highest average score on their ACT for any public university in Alabama. More than 7,000 students take advantage of the 62 academic and professional majors offered by UAH and the 360-acre campus has grown to 32 buildings.

It took a unique community like Huntsville to create a university like UAH. In many ways, the university is a reflection of the needs of this high-tech community.

"UAH is the result of the special character of Huntsville," says Dr. Franz. "The interaction among the university, federal agencies and the community is crucial to our success. And the university's success is also crucial to the success of Huntsville."

UAH is a shining star on Huntsville's horizon, expanding the universe of opportunities for both students and the high-technology community that surrounds it.

As the world enters a new millennium, the men and women at UAH continue to look into the future to help provide a vibrant vision for Huntsville, earth and beyond.

Campus concerts featuring popular bands draw enthusiastic crowds.

VAN VALKENBURGH & WILKINSON PROPERTIES, INC.

Van Valkenburgh & Wilkinson Properties, Inc., a locally owned and operated real estate firm, specializes in fine homes and historic properties throughout North Alabama. The company also handles homes and commercial properties in the downtown, central city and southeast areas.

Often called by the initials in its distinctive logo, VV&W was established in Huntsville, Alabama in October 1985 to serve the needs of the Huntsville/Madison County area's unique historic and space-age community. Its establishment was an outgrowth of both the business and volunteer interests of its founders, Richard Powell Van Valkenburgh, Jr. and his wife, Nancy Wilkinson Van Valkenburgh.

The principals of the firm, like the city they call home, are a blend of the old and new in Huntsville. Richard is a sixth generation Huntsvillian; Nancy, who grew up in Claxton, Georgia near Savannah, came to Huntsville because of the Space Program.

Van Valkenburgh & Wilkinson Properties, Inc. located at 204 Gates Avenue in Huntsville, Alabama.

Richard Van Valkenburgh, president, standing in front of a property which is typical of the homes the company lists. Courtesy, The Huntsville Times. All rights reserved. Reprinted with permission.

In 1974, when many historic homes were being torn down in the name of "urban renewal," Nancy became one of the founders of Historic Huntsville Foundation, Inc., an organization formed to preserve sites and structures of historic and architectural importance in Huntsville and Madison County. She served as chairman during the 1977-1978 term. Richard served on the first board, and continued to serve on many committees, including twice as chairman of HHF's Harrison Brothers Hardware Committee and is the current chairman of the Foundation.

While working with volunteer groups and living in the family home where Richard grew up, in what is now the Twickenham Historic Preservation District, the couple saw that preserving their community's special atmosphere would require private as well as public investment. This led Nancy to become licensed in real estate.

Upon founding their company seven years later, Nancy brought her passion for older homes, while Richard contributed 10 years of commercial leasing experience and a background in building material sales. This was the first step in building a carefully trained team of 12 full-time licensed sales associates and four support staff. Less than a year after the October 1985 opening, the company built a new 5,000-square-foot Georgian style building at 2317 Market Place in Central Park.

In 1992 the company was named a Charter Member of the Historic Real Estate Program of the National Trust for Historic Preservation, one of only 10 in the United States. Since 1997, Van Valkenburgh & Wilkinson has been the only local firm included in *Who's Who in Luxury Homes*, a directory of the finest residential real estate firms around the world.

The accomplishments of Richard, Nancy and the company, in the selling of historic homes, were featured in the July/August 2000 issue of *Real Estate Business*, a nationwide trade publication. Richard

Richard and Nancy Van Valkenburgh stand in front of the office building constructed in 1883.

was featured in a special article about techniques for selling historic homes, including the oldest documented home in the State of Alabama. This sale was also featured in the *Wall Street Journal*, Forbes.com, and in the *Huntsville Times.*

The founders' emphasis on education and professionalism was also noted. Both Richard and Nancy hold the prestigious Certified Residential Specialist and the Certified Residential Broker designations. Their oldest daughter, Victoria V. Norris, is an attorney. Their two younger daughters are associates with the firm and are two of the youngest people in Alabama ever licensed to sell real estate. Both Julie V. Lockwood, and Sarah Lauren V. Kattos, became licensed while still attending Birmingham-Southern College, from which all three graduated.

Nancy's sister, Sarah W. Hereford, is a CPA and serves as vice president of finance. Sibyl Wilkinson,

Nancy and Sarah's mother, has an extensive accounting background, and has served as office manager since the company's inception. Six of the full-time associates hold the Certified Residential Special designation; all are actively pursuing continuing education toward that or other designations.

Richard Van Valkenburgh is the 2002 president of North Alabama Real Estate Information System (NARIS), the Multiple Listing Service of the Huntsville Area Association of REALTORS®. He is a director of the Alabama Association of REALTORS®, serving as Education Trustee. Both Richard and Nancy have served as president of the Huntsville subchapter of the Certified Residential Specialists.

In addition to being among the most productive and hard-working people in North Alabama, the entire team at Van Valkenburgh & Wilkinson is known for giving time and service to church and civic endeavors. Music, art, education, preservation, museums, sports, and health organizations have benefited

Julie V. Lockwood and Sarah Lauren Kattos, daughters of Richard and Nancy. Together they carry on the family tradition.

from their collective and individual work.

On September 7, 2000, Van Valkenburgh & Wilkinson cut the ribbon at its "new" 1883 building, becoming the second family to own the building since it was built by the Goldsmith family in 1883. The move to 204 Gates Avenue in the Twickenham District was an outgrowth of a Chamber of Commerce meeting encouraging the revitalization of downtown Huntsville. Discussions evolved, and it was apparent that Van Valkenburgh & Wilkinson was a perfect "fit" for adaptive use of the lovely Italianate building.

With the move to its Twickenham location, the family found themselves on the same city block, and just around the corner from the 1819 home, now an office, of Richard's great-great grandfather, Joseph Bradley. They were a block away from the location of the hardware store on the South Side of Court House Square founded by his great grandfather, John Van Valkenburgh in 1864. That hardware store grew to a new location on Jefferson Street and then 816 Wheeler, where it was known as Van Valkenburgh Brothers Huntsville Building Material Company until it was sold in the early 1970s.

The distinctive oval VV&W logo is patterned after bronze plaques placed in city sidewalks laid by Richard's grandfather, Joseph Bradley Van Valkenburgh, in the 1920s. The logo is a reminder of the company's commitment to serving North Alabama with the most innovative techniques while still preserving a heritage of service to the community. It is a reminder of the debt to the past and the obligation to the future—preserving the best of the past while working for a brighter future for all.

WHITESBURG BAPTIST CHURCH

Early in 1956, far-sighted planners of the Madison Liberty Association determined the need for a church ministry in the rapidly growing southeast area of Huntsville. Four acres of land bordering Whitesburg Drive were purchased for the new church, and organizational meetings commenced.

This was about the same time that the city of Huntsville was awakening from being a sleepy cotton mill town, to find itself at the very edge of space exploration. The population of Huntsville was 48,093.

Building and planning future growth has been a constant companion to the Whitesburg Baptist Church family. It is apparent that a building program was planned before the first worship service was conducted at the Fort Raymond Jones Armory, on August 14, 1957.

The first building, constructed in April 1958 was rapidly outgrown, as was the second in 1960. By 1964 the third addition, an interim Sanctuary was again outgrown. It would be 1968 before a fellowship hall and additional educational spaces were ready for use. That same year

Original building.

an additional four acres were purchased on Sanders Road.

In 1976 with a membership of 2,791, the church purchased the existing facilities and two acres from another church located on a tract between the two four-acre sections.

Construction on the multi-purpose building, which houses the 3,000-seat sanctuary, began in spring 1980. In 1984, the church purchased a 60-acre tract of land one-half mile south of the present location. In fall 1999, the north connector was completed and ground was broken for construction of the first phase building at the southern campus

Dedicated in December 2000, the

latest WBC expansion offers a concept that is unique in the Huntsville area. This beautiful 75,000-square-foot building houses a double gymnasium with an elevated walking track; aerobics room; fitness room; indoor playground; grill; atrium; dining room; chapel; brides room; youth rally room; craft room and many classrooms.

To accommodate the current need for space, the church expanded to three Sunday school hours and two Sunday morning worship services in 2002.

Born from a need to serve, the church makes every effort to meet the spiritual, physical and emotional needs of its family. This philosophy became the heartbeat from which its slogan "The Caring Place" evolved. Not an empty slogan! Through caring, the church has become one whose multi-faceted ministries touch the lives of its members and reach into the community and across North Alabama.

Nursery, preschool, kindergarten and Mothers-Day-Out became the standard after which other organizations have modeled their own programs.

Music and music education is available to every person. Choir training begins in kindergarten and continues through the senior

Grand opening of South Campus with Mayor Loretta Spencer.

adults. The Excel School of Fine Arts offers private lessons and helps to supply members for orchestra and drama productions.

I Love America, a major God and Country production, depicting God's love for America, was an annual Fourth of July event for 15 years. After three years in retirement, it was reinstated in 2001, and celebrated its 17th birthday in 2002. This patriotic musical drama has reached the hearts of untold thousands through the years. Mission teams have presented a modified version in many cities across America and to military personnel assigned to duty in foreign countries.

The recently established food pantry and clothes closet have helped many families through times of crisis. This all volunteer ministry further reflects the caring spirit of WBC members.

The growing list of ministries continues: Christian Academy; Bible College; Youth Rallies; Single Adults; Divorce Care; Newlyweds; Recreation Activities; Inner City Outreach; Home Bound; Craft Classes; Hispanic Worship Services; Korean Worship Services; and Monthly Newspaper.

New 3,000-seat Worship Center.

With its strong commitment to missions, WBC is a prominent supporter of the annual fund drives for Home Missions and World Missions, thus the tentacles of Whitesburg's caring literally extend to every country in which Christianity is embraced and lives are touched.

"As a growing body of believers, Whitesburg Baptist Church desires to know Jesus Christ and to make Him known."

Through a partnership with TIME (Training in Mission Evangelism), a mission team goes out at least once each month to "Sow the seeds of Jesus Christ in a lost world." These teams have gone to 27 foreign countries, taking along medical supplies, food, eyeglasses, clothing, Bibles in the native language and whatever is needed at the destination. The more recent teams have visited Brazil, Israel, Kosovo, Romania, South Africa, Spain, Togo, and Ukraine.

A mission team is comprised of people from the church who give of their time and money to participate. In addition to ministers, the team usually includes medical professionals, musicians, puppeteers, carpenters, painters, and teachers.

Under the 24-year leadership of Dr. Jimmy E. Jackson, the church has become more firmly grounded in every area. He gives all the credit to God. He said, "I know God called me here, and I know that God has His hand on WBC. The church is healthier spiritually and stronger financially than anytime in its history. God has blessed this church and I believe He has a special calling on it, and I am privileged to be here. There are other major ministries to be developed over a period of time and I hope to be here for that. I plan to be around for 10 or 15 more years. I can envision great things."

His vision is that of a "full church ministry," and feels that it will reach that status. Dr. Jackson believes that for WBC, "The best is yet to come!"

The 45-year life of the church reflects growth from 83 charter members to a current 6,000, while the population in Huntsville has in-creased to 280,000. Four pastors have served WBC: Reverend Wayne Hart, 1958–1965; Reverend Charles Carter, 1966–1971; Reverend S. M. Mulkey, 1973–1976; and Dr. Jimmy E. Jackson, 1978–present.

For more information visit: www.wbccares.org.

I Love America—The Living Flag.

WYNNSON ENTERPRISES, INC.

Wynnson Enterprises, Inc. was founded March 11, 1983. The company consists of a small machine shop and executive offices located at 12039 Hwy 231-431, north of Huntsville. Established by Joyce Oberhausen, Wynnson Enterprises is an exclusively woman-owned corporation. Her previous business endeavors included Precision Specialty Corporation, a national defense-contracting company established in 1966. A pioneer in the Huntsville area, the company serves the military spare parts program. Its products are primarily used in missile ground support systems. Joyce was also co-owner of Military Aircraft Sales, Inc. She is on the board of directors and has security clearance for Quality Control Electronics, her son's company. In addition she owned and operated Wynnson Enterprises Military Packaging Company and Wynnson Galleries, constructed in 1991. This site consisted of an art gallery, interior design, florist and gift shop.

Painting and International Art magazine cover, original oil painting in background, by Joyce Oberhausen.

Joyce Oberhausen, owner, right and Heather Edwards, administrative assistant.

Joyce Oberhausen is an extremely accomplished woman who values, among other things, peace, art, women's rights, the Republican Party, family and spirituality.

Imagine an oil and porcelain artist who used to travel the world, running a small machine shop that carves out parts for aircraft, tanks and missiles. "People always tease me," Oberhausen said with a laugh. "Being an art lover, they can't believe I'm running a machine shop. But it's almost like an art," she said as she described the work of machinists. Using a blueprint, "They take a blank piece of metal and make all kinds of designs and configurations," and like the work of an artist, "It all has to be perfect!"

Her artwork has been on permanent display at Wynnson Galleries, along with her private collection from throughout the world. Ms. Oberhausen has traveled extensively promoting various organizations founded by President Dwight Eisenhower. Her purpose was to create a better understanding between peoples of all nations. The United States Government and many other countries have supported her efforts. Joyce has journeyed with fellow artists all over the globe to fascinating places in the United States, Mexico, England, East and West Germany, France, Czechoslovakia, Austria, Denmark, Finland, Mainland China, Hong Kong, the Soviet Union, and other places. She feels that sharing her art contributes to a common goal—that of creating "peace among nations."

Joyce was selected as one of the first judges of the International Porcelain Art show in 1998. She is a founding member of the first Women's Museum in Washington D.C. and was awarded the Defense Department Certificate of Appreciation during Operation Desert Storm.

Mrs. Oberhausen, who is a Life Fellow of the International Biographical Association and a member of the International Order of Merit has been featured in many IBC publications and has been honored with medals, diplomas and awards. She was also a delegate at the 1989 Congress in Washington D.C.

The many honors, prizes and awards presented to Mrs. Oberhausen in business include: Life and Achievements of Personalities in America; Community Leaders of America; Hall of Fame for Outstanding Achievements as an Aircraft Executive; International Director of Distinguished Leadership Hall of Fame; *Who's Who: in Finance and Industry; in Society; Intellectuals; of Professional and Executive Women; of American Women; Emerging Leaders in America; The International Who's Who of Intellectuals; The World Who's Who of Women;* Commemorative Distinguished Life-Long Achievements Medal of Honor; World Biographical Hall of Fame; Commemorative Medal of Honor; Outstanding Achievements and Dedication to Personal and Professionals Goals; Personalities of America; 2000 Notable American Women; Excellence in Business and Art, *Most Admired Woman of the Decade, Book of Dedication* and the *International Biographical Association Directory.*

Mrs. Oberhausen contributes to the arts as co-founder of the National Museum of Arts; and member of the United Artists Association; American Society of Professional and Executive Women; Historical Society; International Porcelain Art

In 1994, left to right: Joyce, Terri and Georgan Oberhausen, (back row) Joe Rawlinson, Jolie Carter and Renee Christopher.

Guild; National Association of Female Executives; Porcelain Portrait Society; Chamber of Commerce; Better Business Bureau; Alabama Sheriffs Association; lifetime member of international Biographical Association; member, Metropolitan Museum of Art; national member, Smithsonian Association; Huntsville Art League and Museum Association; Heritage Club; Association of Community Artists; People to People International; National Trust for Historic Preservation; International Teacher Porcelain Artist; Republican Senatorial Inner Circle;

International Platform Association; International China Painting School, England; American Artists Publications; Alabama Artists publications; Presidential Task Force; American Association of University Women; and is a charter member of the National Women's History Museum, National Defense Industry.

Nominated by Jeremiah Denton and accepted to the Republican Inner Circle Club in Washington, Mrs. Oberhausen was invited and attended the 1989 Inauguration of President Bush. She continues to support the Republican Party and the current President Bush. Oberhausen was presented The Order of Merit from Republican Presidential Legion of Merit, and is a Republican National Committee member.

Her leadership style may be described by some as "pushy," but she gets the job done and believes you should treat people, as you would like to be treated. "I try to delegate. I have people in key positions of responsibility and I get involved when there is a real problem. I think my success comes from a strong work ethic, which my father instilled in me." The Huntsville Chamber of Commerce nominated her for Small Business of the Year on June 10, 1997. She was also

Wynnson Enterprises, Inc.

named Businessman of the Year by the *Wall Street Journal,* as well as having her name placed on the "Wall of Tolerance" by the National Campaign for Tolerance by Rosa Parks.

Driven by her ambition, Joyce believes that without a strong support team she would never have accomplished what she has. "You are only as good as the team behind you. We have supplied thousands of spare parts to the government over the years. Some parts as large as our parking lot and others as minute as a pin." This could not be accomplished without the work of a cohesive group of individuals.

Joyce Oberhausen enjoys the serenity of the mountains and pastoral views from her office window. She has not relented to the hustle and bustle of progress evidenced by the construction of bigger and better highways and new industry being developed all around her.

Having worked all of her life in government contracting, Joyce Oberhausen originally started as

production control secretary for a defense contractor. "I have never worked in any other industry. Wynnson Enterprises has supported rapid readiness of armed forces during wartime and peacetime. We will continue to supply all types of repair parts for the refurbishment and maintenance of military products in the field for soldiers." While she is involved in producing materials that are used in the military, somehow Joyce has maintained distinction with a creative outlet, giving her life balance.

For more than 35 years Joyce Oberhausen has been producing magnificent oil paintings and porcelain art in addition to her work as a business executive/owner in Meridianville, Alabama, where she lives. She is also an international art teacher and a member of the International Porcelain Portrait Society and the International Artist Association. She has had 20 original oils published and her limited edition lithographs have been shown extensively in regional,

All parts are inspected by the government, by QAR, and Wynnson's shop foreman.

national and international exhibits as well as private institutional displays. Mrs. Oberhausen has four of her original images as greeting cards.

Her work has been exhibited at The Tennessee Tom Trade Center, supported by Governor Guy Hunts; ADECA; Alabama Forestry Commission; Department of Commerce; Chamber of Commerce; SBA; and Alabama Office Advocacy. Sacred Heart Exhibition sponsored by Chapels of Redstone Arsenal (Huntsville, Alabama), presented Joyce with 2 awards: "Pathway To Heaven" and "Sheila's Lillies." *International Porcelain Artist* magazine published her work on its cover in 1997. In addition *Gallery* magazine, *Huntsville Times, Huntsville Finest,* IBSC publications and several others have published her work. The International Biographical Association published her poem: "Father's Day," written to honor her father who was a big influence in her life.

Joyce Oberhausen and Wynnson Enterprises, Inc., have been and will continue to be active supporters and contributors to local, statewide and global business, as well as civic and nonprofit organizations.

Joyce Oberhausen and machinist Glen Leaber, an employee of 15 years, standing in front of a rail pusher-set manufactured by Wynnson.

The Von Braun Center and Big Spring Park.
Courtesy, Huntsville/Madison County Convention & Visitors Bureau

THE HUTCHENS COMPANY

The Hutchens family has been a part of the Huntsville business scene since the Civil War. James Madison Hutchens was a carpenter and later a contractor in the post-Civil War period. His son W.T. Hutchens founded the Hutchens Company, as a plumbing business, in the 1880s. The company has been owned and operated by a continuous line of Hutchens family members ever since.

James Madison Hutchens (1834–1892) was born in Morristown, Tennessee and moved to Huntsville around 1857, making his living as a carpenter in the years prior to the Civil War. In 1858 he married Lucy E. Hodges and they had six children: William Thomas; J. Newton; Charles E.; India; Mary and Robert. The shots at Fort Sumter in 1861 shattered peaceful pre-war life in North Alabama; James answered the call to duty and joined the Confederate Army in 1862. He served in the Fourth Alabama Cavalry, Russell's Regiment, Forrest's Brigade. He was fortunate to survive his battles and returned to Huntsville after his service ended.

In the years following the war, James Hutchens played a signifi-

Vernon F. Hutchens, circa 1950.

W.T. Hutchens, circa 1895.

cant role in Huntsville's political and business life, serving six terms on the Huntsville City Council between 1872 and 1883. He became a leading contractor and builder during these years as well. His building projects included: Huntsville Cotton Oil Mill (one of Huntsville's first post-war industries); the first city school building; a major addition to the Huntsville Female College; and construction of Palmer Hall on the Alabama A&M campus.

James' eldest son, William Thomas Hutchens, was born in 1859. After several years working as a bookkeeper for his father's contracting business, W.T. (also known as Will) left that firm in 1887 and opened a plumbing business with partner John Montgomery. They advertised themselves as "practical plumbers, gas and steam pipe fitters" in the June 2, 1887 issue of the *Huntsville Independent*. This business was the beginning of what became the Hutchens Company. W.T. had several partners in those early years; his longest association from 1894 to 1910 was with A.J. Murdock.

In addition to his business accomplishments, W.T. was an active citizen in his community. In 1882 he was appointed Day Police Chief by the City Council, and later was designated Night Police Chief. In 1889 he was elected to the Huntsville City Council and was elected Mayor of Huntsville in 1893, 1895 and 1920. A life-long Republican, W.T. was appointed postmaster by President William McKinley in 1898 and reappointed to this position by Presidents Theodore Roosevelt and William Taft. He served on the Huntsville School Board and was president of the Library Board when the Carnegie Library building was erected on Gates Avenue in 1915.

The long-standing site of the Hutchens Company at the corner of Jefferson and Clinton Streets in downtown Huntsville was built in 1916. In the early 1920s, W.T. and his three sons, Morton, Willard and Vernon, managed the Hutchens Company. During this time the Hutchens Company performed plumbing, heating, electrical, sheet metal and roofing work as well as retail and wholesale hardware. Some significant contracting projects for the company were: The Tennessee Valley Bank Building (now the Terry-Hutchens Building); Huntsville High School (now the Annie Merts Center); the Times Building; and the Russell Erskine Hotel. They had phone number 11 and 12 in the early Huntsville exchange, and their letterhead listed "Electric wiring, Tinning, Heating and Plumbing, John Deere farm implements, Wagons, Buggies, Dry Batteries, Electric Lamps, Carey Roofing, Inspirators, Sewer Pipe, Mill Supplies, Steam Gauges, Pumps, Heating by Steam and Hot Water."

Vernon became sole owner of the company in 1946. The Hutchens Company maintained the contract-

The Hutchens Company, downtown Huntsville, circa 1950.

ing business and continued to be a primary source for retail and hardware needs for Huntsville and the surrounding area in the '40s, '50s and '60s. The retail store offered a wide range of items including: house wares; gifts; appliances; sporting goods; firearms; plumbing fixtures; roofing; and sheet metal supplies.

Vernon Hutchens married Elizabeth Alston Russell and had two children, Elizabeth Brandon (Betty), and Vernon Fisher, Jr. Vernon Jr. grew up working at the company. He obtained a degree in Electrical Engineering from Georgia Tech in 1955 and returned to Huntsville to join his father and Betty's husband, John McCaleb, in running the family business. In 1957 a second location was opened in the newly built Parkway City Shopping Center. With the development of Redstone Arsenal and the Space Program, this was a time of prosperity and growth in the area. The Hutchens Company was the first hardware store to locate outside of downtown Huntsville, and the hardware and contracting businesses grew with the city. At that time, air conditioning was added to

the line of products available from the Hutchens Company. Vernon Jr., remembers installing Janitrol and York brand equipment in those early days. The ground floor of the Terry-Hutchens Building and the S.H. Kress Building on Washington Street were some of the first Hutchens Company installations of "central air."

In the '60s, Vernon Jr., and John McCaleb saw the emergence of large discount stores and chose to concentrate on the contracting business. In the late '60s, the downtown store was closed, fol-

W.T. Hutchens with company truck, circa 1918.

lowed by the Parkway City Store and all operations were moved to the current Hutchens Company Building at 2508 N. Washington Street.

Vernon Jr., married Martha Sue Smith and had two sons, Vernon Fisher III and Thomas Albert. Vernon Fisher III, known as Fisher, graduated from Georgia Tech like his father, but initially chose a high technology career instead of the contracting business. After a 15-year engineering career in Southern California, he married Johanna Clements and moved to Huntsville in 1999. Fisher joined his father in business and is currently vice president of the firm. The second son, Thomas Albert, is a library assistant in the Heritage Room at the Huntsville Public Library and is the Hutchens Company historian.

The Hutchens Company, entering its 115th year in business, remains a viable and dependable force in the commercial construction field. Vernon F. Jr., president; V. Fisher III, vice president; Randall Cox, project manager; and Anna Freeman, secretary-treasurer, run the company, with 31 employees. They now specializes in plumbing, heating, and air-conditioning for both commercial and residential customers in Huntsville-Madison County. Job sizes range from small repairs to contracts over $1 million. Recent contracting jobs include: HVAC and plumbing renovations of several Huntsville city schools; HVAC and plumbing renovations on Redstone Arsenal; plumbing and medical gas installation at medical offices; and the plumbing and HVAC renovation of the Terry-Hutchens Building. This exciting and challenging project included installation of modern HVAC systems as well as replacement of the plumbing installed by Hutchens Company employees over 75 years ago.

INFINITY TECHNOLOGY, INC.

They named their company "Infinity Technology," adopted the song "Keep on Climbing" as their company anthem, and started off with very limited resources and capabilities. With this said it is easy to deduce that Alicia and Guy Juzang knew where they were going, that it would not be easy to get there, and that they would not be able to get there on their own.

Their God-fearing parents, brought up in Alabama, raised Alicia and Guy. Each acquired computer training during their education and were introduced to one another through a sales call Guy placed to Alicia's company. Little did they know after meeting in 1987, that 15 years later they would have a mighty faith; four children; own an aerospace defense engineering firm; have over 200 direct/contract employees; have a beautiful building in Cummings Research Park (second largest research park in the U.S.); and staunchly defend the freedoms and country they love so dearly. What makes this loom so large in their hearts are the lessons, experiences and relationships they encountered in the spring of 2000.

A culmination of tragedies, not the least being financial, plummeted them into the most traumatic experience of their lives. The company's banking credit line was exhausted, creating the reality that payroll for over 125 employees would be delayed, if not missed altogether for the first time in 10 years. Customers needed to know if their contract employees were going to be compensated, and vendors wanted to know when they were going to be paid.

Suffice it to say, Alicia and Guy had never faced such enormous consequences, stress, fear, and potential for devastation. However, within 10 days of that climatic

Juzangs accept SBA's National Subcontractor-of-the-year award.

moment, several miracles transpired and Guy calls them his "five new things" (Isaiah 43: 1-19). First, a consultant suggested he contact a business associate for financial help. The gentlemen lived outside of Boston, Massachusetts and had the exact same financial dilemma years ago with the company he owned. After hearing the predicament, he was determined to help Guy because not a single person helped him at his time of need. He invested enough money to help the company make approximately five payrolls. Then, through a succession of unlikely meetings with top executives, Infinity was offered a substantial credit line with Merrill Lynch, which has more assets than any other investment bank in the country. Moreover, ITI won a contract with NASA four times larger than any contract they had received prior to that date; they had major obstacles removed from attaining a top-secret clearance; and won the coveted National Subcontractor of the Year FY2000 award from the Small Business Administration— over 500 companies had competed

for the award. Alicia went to the podium to receive the award and after a few words of appreciation proceeded to sing the inspirational song by Wintley Phipps: "Keep on climbing."

Little did she know that what was once simply a beautiful song, would become a symbol of the greatest struggle of her life! Alicia believed that through her faith she was able to sing the song with so much emotion that she received a standing ovation. Afterwards, many people came up to her to express how that song had touched them.

Alicia Jones Juzang was born to Matthew and Bettye Jones and was raised in a rural southwest part of Alabama by parents who did not have many material possessions. However, she knows today that they offered much more than money could ever buy. They instilled in her the desire to put God first in her life and taught her to know that through God she could do all things. Alicia excelled academically from the first grade through college, where she received her Bachelor of Science degree in Computer Science. She kept on climbing when she went to work as a computer programmer/analyst for an engineering firm that specialized in radar technology.

Guy was born in 1955 in London, England. His father was in the midst of a 40-year career with the U.S. Air Force and his mother was a teacher/counselor. Guy's parents, William and Mary Juzang had nine children, so Guy also came from humble beginnings. His parents had an immensely positive impact on him as well as his other eight siblings as evidenced by their current careers. Amongst the eight are a judge, a medical doctor, a vice president of finance, three business owners, a child counselor and a vice president of marketing. After attaining an MBA, Guy joined IBM as a systems engineer. He continued to develop his computer and marketing expertise at Digital Equipment after working for IBM for about five years.

Corporate headquarters.

In 1989 Guy and Alicia founded Infinity Technology, Inc. (ITI) an aerospace defense-engineering firm. ITI has a subcontract with Lockheed Martin and has a leading role in developing the operational flight program for the new air dominance-mission critical air defense F-22 fighter jet. ITI has developed software and hardware for other defense systems like the Avenger (missile launcher); Ground Base Radar (GBR-now THAAD); E-Fog M, Apache Longbow; and Black Hawk/Huey Helicopters. ITI also

supports NASA with micro-gravity research-outreach and education (MRPO-OE), financial, educational, and administrative and services. The MRPO-OE services include: publishing developments in fundamental/fluid physics; materials science; combustion science; and biotechnology that results from the experiments flown on the space shuttle and the International Space Station. ITI publishes its results from these experiments for Congress, the general public, universities, and K-12 students via hardcopy publications, websites, conferences and demonstrations. ITI also fabricates hardware parts for the Army such as simulators (Avenger Table Top Trainer); racks (for munitions); grilles; bumpers and window frames. ITI gives back to the community by supporting organizations such as the U.S. Dream Academy, which helps at-risk children whose parents are in prison. ITI also provides student intern opportunities to work and develop computer, accounting, scientific and other skills, preparing them for the workforce.

Personnel at work.

LINDY INDUSTRIES, INC.

In the highly competitive industry of metal stamping, Lindy Industries Inc. of Huntsville has survived recession, rising steel prices and tariffs, loss of major clients, layoffs and a major lawsuit. Challenges seem to bring out the best in Margaret Hill, president of the company that produces precision metal stampings and assemblies for automotive, appliance, computer and other industry applications.

The story of what is now Lindy Industries, located at 15990 Chaney Thompson Road, began in 1953, when Hill's parents, David and Monica Collins, founded Lindy Manufacturing in Downers Grove, Illinois. An earlier enterprise started by Hill's parents, Yankee Pencil Company, was not successful, so the couple moved into metal stamping. They started out small, renting room in a large warehouse where they had to run a space heater to keep their hands warm enough to operate the machines.

"When they wanted to expand, it was pretty easy—they just moved the partition back five feet or whatever they needed," recalls Hill. Monica Collins also answered the phone in the early years. "She had a swivel chair at her desk, and she would turn around and run

David Collins and Richard Martul at the ground breaking for the 30,000-square-foot addition.

the punch press when she wasn't on the phone."

As the business expanded the couple built three additional stamping companies doing similar work: York Tool; Dabar; and Lindy. Hill's parents sold off York Tool and Dabar in the 1970s and kept Lindy Manufacturing, which still operates in Downers Grove. Margaret's brother, David Collins is president. Like Lindy Industries of Hunstville, Lindy Manufacturing designs and builds everything from simple compound tools to complicated progressive dies, depending on the customer's requirements.

Lindy Manufacturing opened its Huntsville facility in 1984 to manufacture metal parts for GTE telephones. GTE was looking for a supplier to purchase stamping equipment to produce parts in Huntsville. Hill recalls, "Dad saw it as too good of an opportunity to pass up, and we won the bid." Hill, who graduated from Trinity University in San Antonio in 1983, moved to Huntsville with several

other employees, including the nightshift foreman Richard Martul, from Lindy Manufacturing to start up the new venture. "I started working for Richard right out of college," recalls Hill.

For the first few years, Lindy Industries produced most of the metal parts in GTE telephones. When GTE decided to stop production of those telephones, losing its largest customer almost devastated the company. "What sounded too good to be true was too good to be true," says Hill. "I don't know if we would have survived without the link to Lindy Manufacturing." The company had to lay off employees and start searching for customers.

Hill realized that the company had to diversify its customer base, and mounted an aggressive pricing campaign to get new customers. "It was a real challenge to pull all that work in so quickly," says Hill. The company slowly started to recover and now 70 percent of its work is automotive—but with several different clients. After a couple of lean

Products manufactured by Lindy Industries, Inc.

Lindy Industries, Inc. 400-ton press.

years, the company enjoyed record sales in April 2002 and has been hiring new employees for its 60-member workforce. One of Lindy's goals is not to allow any customer to exceed 20 percent of its total sales. Lindy Industries became independent of Lindy Manufacturing in 1996.

To stamp and assemble automotive parts, Lindy put new systems into place, expanded its procedures and became a self-certified automotive supplier. Company employees did an excellent job learning how to meet the certifications needed for rigorous quality control, including international quality standards, QS9000 and ISO-9002 certifications. Lindy Industries maintains an employee training program in Statistical Process Control and continuous improvement techniques. Dale Hill, Margaret's husband, is quality manager for the company.

Lindy's top automotive customers now include Yorozu, Daimler-Chrysler and SW Manufacturing. Lindy also supplies parts to Ogihara America Corporation, which supplies automotive panels to the Mercedes Benz plant in Vance, Alabama. Although automotive stamping is relatively new to Lindy Industries, the company has already received a Master Quality Award from Yorozu Automotive Tennessee and the Chrysler Motors Quality Excellence Award.

Lindy supplies steel brake shoes to Haldex Brake and ballast boxes to Bodine Electric as well as appliance parts to GE. The company uses its 400-ton press to manufacture brake shoes from materials up to one-quarter inch thick. Most of the raw material is either hot rolled steel, cold rolled steel, or galvanized steel coil, which is run through a tool or die that has been designed

Lindy Industries, Inc. tool room.

and built by Lindy toolmakers. The material might go through several stations in the die, to punch a hole, create a tab, form a tab, or anything the part needs to become the finished product for the customer. Hill has great confidence in the company's engineers and tool and die designers who often come up with innovative solutions to customer requests, like rotating punches.

The design department has full CAD/CAM capabilities using AUTO-CAD linked to CNC milling and wire EDM operations via a local area network. Lindy designers offer prototype, tool and gauge design as well as piece-part design for manufacturability and cost reduction assistance. The tool and die shop develops prototypes and constructs new tools including progressive dies, draw dies, assembly tools and test fixtures. Lindy has 13 automatic presses ranging in capacity from a 30-ton Minster to a 400-ton Danly. Lindy also has the capability to clean parts, vibratory deburr, resistance weld, and assemble.

Hill's business philosophy is to keep moving forward. "I don't like to spend a lot of time and effort on mistakes. You figure out what went wrong and don't do it again. I like to focus on constant improvement."

The automotive industry is expanding in Alabama and the future is bright for Lindy Industries. "We feel real good about being here in Alabama. We have good people in place and automotive manufacturing is moving in our state—Huntsville is a great location."

NORTHROP GRUMMAN'S LAND COMBAT SYSTEMS

Northrop Grumman's Land Combat Systems—Huntsville focuses on providing innovative weapon systems that meet the emerging need for precision munitions in the U.S. and international markets.

Land Combat Systems—Huntsville was established in 1989 by Westinghouse Electric Corporation as the center for missile and sensor systems for the U.S. Army Missile Command at Redstone Arsenal. In addition to proximity to the Army customer, Huntsville had a great deal to offer the company's emerging missile business. It was a growing community with a strong technology base, a highly educated and experienced work force and a strong work ethic. With the planned investment in processes and equipment, the multi-talented team that was envisioned would successfully meet the challenges ahead.

From the outset, "best practice" manufacturing processes and innovative paperless work instructions and production control systems were designed and implemented. Every business system to be used by the team was evaluated and improved to ensure maximum efficiency and productivity. With new systems in place, and with the corporation's vast engineering and

Over 300 highly skilled, technical personnel produce 400 missiles per month.

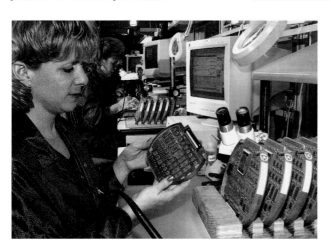

U.S. Representative, Bud Cramer, tells the Northrop Grumman team that the success of the Longbow Program is a testament to the teamwork in Alabama.

manufacturing resources to draw upon, the team was prepared to meet and exceed the high rate production program challenges.

Managers from the Electronic Systems Group in Baltimore, Maryland leased offices on Corporate Drive and began to establish a cadre of engineers to support the emerging Longbow Missile guidance section program. Concurrently, a second group began to identify possible locations for a state-of-the-art manufacturing facility dedicated to achieving the high rate production objectives of the Longbow program.

In 1990 Cummings Research Park was selected as the location for the manufacturing facility and construction began in mid-1991. The facility opened in January 1992 at 915 Explorer Boulevard and the manufacturing team began to prepare for production of the Long-bow missile guidance system. In mid-1992, the engineering center moved to 917 Explorer Boulevard. The team, having grown from three employees in 1989 to 62, was now

complete. Responsible for both product design and manufacture, the single team that was formed would significantly reduce potential design-to-production transition problems through teamwork and an emphasis on producibility.

The Army awarded the Longbow missile program contract in 1994, and the first guidance systems were delivered in 1997 at a rate of 25 units per month.

Northrop Grumman acquired Westinghouse's defense electronics business in 1996, and in 1998, moved the Brilliant Anti-Armor Submunition (Bat) program to Huntsville from Hawthorne, California. Recognizing the benefits and the quality of life in Huntsville, a large number of the Bat program team moved to Alabama. The melding of people from Maryland, California, and the local area has established a workforce, rich in diversity and talent.

Since 1996 Land Combat Systems—Huntsville has grown from 77 employees and approximately $100 million in sales to over 350 employees and more than $340 million in sales. The major focus continues to be supporting the precision munition needs of the U.S Army and increasing business and market share by providing reliable, affordable, high performance weapons. Key activities include high-rate production of the Longbow missile guidance system and the Bat submunition, and new engineering development of next-generation systems such as the Compact Kinetic Energy Missile and the Common Missile.

The Longbow missile is an advanced, millimeter wave radar-guided missile for the AH-64D Apache helicopter. Northrop Grumman is responsible for the design and manufacture of the guidance system. Approximately the size of a coffee can, each guidance section is a complete radar system. After the missile is fired, its radar tracks the intended target in spite of the presence of similar targets or clutter and guides the missile to a precise kill. In combat situations, the "fire and forget" precision not only increases lethality, but also enhances protection on the battlefield for America's warfighters.

Due to the success of an aggressive continuous improvement program, production rates have grown from 25 units per month in 1997 to 300 units per month in 2002. The cumulative effect of incremental improvement has played a significant part in the success of the program.

In March 2002 the Longbow team delivered its 5,000th missile to the Army. The Army plans to buy about 14,000 missiles through 2005 for use with the Apache and also intends to deploy the missile aboard its newest attack helicopter, the RAH-66 Comanche.

Bat is the Army's only long range, smart precision munition that can attack and destroy time-critical mobile and fleeting targets such as mobile rocket launchers and transporter erector launchers that could be used to field weapons of mass destruction. Bat's acoustic, infrared and millimeter-wave sensors, coupled with its ability to fly to its target upon detection and acquisition, provide the Army with a unique deep strike weapon. Initially developed for use with the Army Tactical Missile System, Bat is capable of being carried and dispensed from multiple platforms, including unmanned

Northrop Grumman occupies over 250,000 square-feet of floor space at Cummings Research Park and Redstone Arsenal.

aerial vehicles; aircraft munition dispensers, rockets and cruise missiles. The Bat production facility consists of eight buildings at Redstone Arsenal where the submunitions are assembled and tested.

Northrop Grumman continues to work closely with community and military leaders and makes it an ongoing priority to practice good corporate citizenship. In addition to supporting the growth initiatives of the Chamber of Commerce, the company continues to support a variety of social, charitable and educational programs through contributions and direct participation. Many employees serve as coaches, counselors and leaders in these programs, and Northrop Grumman supports these individual efforts as well.

Northrop Grumman looks forward to continued growth, building upon more than a decade of success both in the performance of its products and the achievements of the Land Combat Systems—Huntsville team.

The Apache Helicopters' Longbow Missile and the BAT submunition are highly effective precision weapons.

SIGMA SERVICES OF AMERICA, INC.

Sigma Services of America, Inc. was founded by Jeanne B. Weaver in Huntsville and incorporated in the state of Alabama. Sigma Services started working in the tactical weapons systems development doing program and test planning; and working in the smart weapon concepts and technologies. Sigma Services has expanded its capabilities to include visual graphics; multi-media presentations; web page design; and conference and event planning.

Jeanne, who remains the corporate president, started the company in 1987. Six months later her husband Tom Weaver, joined her. His background included Army research and development; major program planning; test and evaluation planning; facility requirements; Army and corporate management; and directed energy technology. The company is both female owned and operated, and veteran owned and operated.

Sigma began as a broad-based, problem-solving company with a flexible management structure.

Sharon Adams, vice president.

Jeanne Weaver, president.

The first management challenge faced by Sigma Services was to provide professional services tailored to clients' needs while permitting flexible employee work schedules. From the beginning, work schedules were tailored to family demands, continuing educational pursuits, and consulting desires to allow engineers and scientists to balance professional and personal objectives. Sharon Adams, who at the time was the office manager, brought her two-week-old daughter to the office for a few hours a day. At one time there was a crib in one office and a baby swing in another. This flexible management philosophy, although at times difficult, allows for the more nontraditional type of worker, the "part-time mom," and fosters a high degree of loyalty and dedication while encouraging creative responsibility.

Besides having degrees in Accounting and Behavioral Science, Jeanne is also a Registered Nurse. She was activated as an Army Re-

servist in 1990, served five months in Saudi Arabia during Desert Storm and was awarded the Bronze Star for exceptional Meritorious Service during Operation Desert Storm.

In 1993 the greatest challenge faced by Sigma Services to date has been survivability through the lengthy illness and eventual death of Tom Weaver, Sigma's vice president. Jeanne and Tom both openly accepted Tom's terminal illness and encouraged fellow employees to accept and assume additional responsibilities. Tom shared knowledge and expertise with Sigma's employees with the understanding and plan that they should carry on after his death. Tom willingly shared insight into multiple management and program areas, encouraging others to assume his responsibilities. After Tom's death, employees were offered an option to be bought out, but chose to invest, run, and manage the company themselves due to the confidence gained from the knowledge and insight Tom had passed on. The fact that communication remained open between management and employees, and the fact that employees directly influence management decisions, allowed Sigma Services not only to survive but also to prosper during this challenging time.

Sharon Adams, who had been with Sigma since its inception and has worked closely with Jeanne, became vice president. Together, Jeanne and Sharon looked to see what direction Sigma should focus on based on the capabilities of the staff. This led to developing and diversifying into two commercial areas, design and sales of gift baskets and custom matting and framing. The company grew and developed strong visual-graphics capabilities in the area of commercial art and graphics.

Sigma has provided services in support to Army Material Command (AMC); Smart Weapons Management Office; the U.S. Army Aviation and Missile Command Missile Research, Development, and Engineering Center (MRDEC); U.S. Army Smart Weapons Management Office (SWMO); the PEO-HELLFIRE; and the 185th U.S. Army Reserves. Sigma Services has also directly supported numerous businesses in the private sector, including the Huntsville Association of Technical Societies (HATS); Technical and Business Exhibition Symposium (TABES); the University of Alabama in Huntsville; U.S. Army Aviation and Missile Command (AAMCOM); Missile Research, Development (AMRDEC) for the TARA; and the Joint Aeronautical Commanders Group (JACG); the Diocese of Birmingham for an International Clerical Symposium; the Directed Energy Annual Symposium (DEPS); the Southeast Regional Reserve Officer's Association for the Army Nurse Corps; and Space and Missile Defense Command (SMDC), to name a few.

The philosophy of Sigma Service is seen in the corporate name and symbol. The Greek letter SIGMA was intentionally chosen to illustrate both the corporate style and objective. In science and engineering, this symbol stands for a "summation" or "total" of elements or components. Sigma Services is designed and managed to provide total service, in a broad range of disciplines, for its clients. The company believes that solving the client's problem, from the client's perspective, is a worthwhile business objective.

Jeanne and Tom Weaver, company founders.

Bring your daughters to work day 1995. From left to right; Cathy Thrasher, Ansley Adams, Sara Radulski-Weaver, and in front, Allie Thrasher.

Over the years Sigma Services has been honored by the community with numerous awards. Sigma was the Small Business of the Year Finalist from the Huntsville Madison County Chamber of Commerce; the Family Friendly Business Award Nominee Certificate of Recognition; and from both the Veterans, of Foreign Wars of the U.S. and the Disabled American Veterans, the National Commander's Employment Award.

Sigma has also received awards for its work such as the Service Award for Outstanding Project Planning & Performance Assessment by Smart Weapons Management Office; The Directed Energy Professional Society award for the fourth Annual Symposium for outstanding support; and Thomas C. Weaver was awarded the Outstanding Leadership and Support to the North Alabama Science Center; Jeanne Weaver received recognition for her contribution and participation as an author and as a session chair at the Portland International Conference on Management of Engineering & Technology (PICMET '97). Acknowledgements to the company were received from Lt. General Joseph M. Cosumano, Jr.; U.S. Army Commanding General SMDC, for extraordinary support to the Fourth and Fifth Annual Space & Missile Defense Conference; acknowledgement from BG John M. Urias for outstanding effort in support of the U.S. Army Space and Missile Defense Command's Security Awareness Day; an award for excellent support provided to the technology effort from Michael C. Schexnayder, associate director for Systems Research, Development and Engineering Center; and an award from MG Joe Rigby for dedication and commitment to excellence.

SYSTEM STUDIES & SIMULATION, INC.

System Studies & Simulation (S³) was incorporated in the state of Alabama in 1993 and began its operations as a provider of technical services for U.S. Army Team Redstone and the National Aeronautics and Space Administration/ Marshall Space Flight Center (NASA/MSFC), to meet the requirements in the high-tech area around Huntsville, Alabama. In 1997, S³ obtained SBA 8(a) Small Disadvantaged Business certification and continued its path of growth and diversification with Srini Srinivas as the CEO and Jan Smith as the president. S³ quickly established a quality base of diverse defense, intelligence, space, and commercial customers, significantly increasing the level of expertise in the technology community.

S³ has experienced remarkable growth, doubling in size and customer locations during the past two years and continuing expansion into 2003. The company currently offers comprehensive state-of-the-art technical engineering, programmatics, data management, information technology, modeling and simulation, training, and software development services to the Department of Defense (DoD), NASA, and the intelligence communities. S³ provides system integration, engineering, and technical assistance to multiple missile and weapons systems currently in use in the defense of the country. The company also supports NASA MSFC Payload Missions including the International Space Station. In addition to its headquarters in Huntsville, Alabama, S³ has personnel located in Ft. Hood, Texas; Ft. Campbell, Kentucky; Robins AFB, Georgia; Washington, DC; Ft. Monroe, Virginia; and the Arizona National Guard, Marana, Arizona.

A significant milestone in the company's history unfolded with

The technical diversity and superior quality of service have provided S³ with a remarkable growth in employee strength, locations and customers.

the move into S³'s new Corporate Headquarters in West Research Park at 615 Discovery Drive in April 2002 and continues with their growth around the U.S. by adding one to two field offices each year. The phenomenal growth achieved by S³ is the direct result of their ability to recruit and retain senior managers whose expertise mitigates risk for project support and qualified personnel who are experts in their field. By combining such varied expertise and working hard to maintain technical excellence, S³ is able to contribute greatly to the defense and technology growth of the country.

S³ was founded, and continues to operate, utilizing a condensed management structure. The corporate officers are supported by program manager/coordinators who focus and manage the tasks of each of the customers. This organization provides each program manager with complete delegation of responsibilities and empowered authority to implement each contract work plan. It also establishes access by the government or corporate customer to the full resources of the company and ensures that those resources are provided in an exceptionally timely manner. These program managers provide direct input into the operation and strategic planning required for the success of the company. The unique appeal to customers is S³'s approach to understanding the contract requirement and identifying the appropriate skill mix to address the requirement, within cost and schedule projections. The key to this success is in "planning the work and working the plan." Having achieved this objective, S³'s management, both corporate and project, maintains pro-active attention to changing requirements and applies the resources required to ensure customer satisfaction beyond their expectations.

S³'s strength lies in the experience, capabilities, and pro-active attitude of their employees. This employee base, when coupled with the responsive customer focus of management, enables the company to be adaptive to the diversified and changing needs of the customer. In order to recruit and retain a community-recognized quality technical staff, S³ offers a professionally supportive work environment, an attractive benefits package, and flexible family-friendly scheduling. S³'s excellent employee benefit package, one of the best in the industry, offers benefits for the employee and family, contributes to employee career advancement through advanced education, and supports peace of mind for quality retirement.

The size and diversity of S³ provides the project managers the ability to promote the integration of processes and procedures, and thus reduces cost for the customer. S³'s unique appeal to customers is their responsiveness, specialized technical skills, and its understanding of the requirements and the needs of the customer. "We assess how well we achieve our goals by how well we help our customers achieve theirs."

S³ combines a commitment to "do more than the customer expects" with exceptional personnel

S³ provides integration services to missile, aviation and space weapons that defend our freedom.

who provide the highest quality support possible. S³'s Core Competencies are focused in providing skilled services to missile, aviation, and space systems, simulation and modeling, and training to multiple government and commercial customers. S³'s services are tailored to project requirements and supported by state-of-the-art information technologies. Its business focus is to continue systems engineering and programmatics support to their current customers while diversifying their activities to other DOD, NASA and commercial customers. Their yearly goal is to establish at least two new field offices to serve new customers.

S³ assumes that all businesses operate with the same pro-active responsiveness, their program managers operate as good "stewards" of our tax dollars and ensure

that all products delivered are of the best quality and delivered within or ahead of schedule. Customer satisfaction stands alone and always ranks first in importance.

S³ enjoys an excellent reputation for quality performance with their customers and the community. In the Huntsville/Redstone Arsenal area, S³ continues to promote a cooperative spirit, pride, and tradition of technical excellence in working with both soldiers and civilians through Team Redstone. S³'s technical expertise enhances the strength of both National Defense and Security through their innovative and state-of-the-art capabilities. Recent work with Apache Longbow and Javelin training to U.S. Army and National Guard units are prime examples of their commitment to promoting strength in our National Defense.

S³ strongly believes in "Giving Back to the Community" in providing support and resources for both the technical community and to S³ employees in their support of local organizations. The technical support has aided the U.S. in strengthening its defenses, and the community work encouraged of its employees has greatly strengthened the people in the region.

The S³ approach is an excellent model in providing state-of-the-art technical services to a diversified field of customers. Proven expertise, diversity, their close working relationships with their customers, and the asset of their highly qualified employees have provided S³ with a solid foundation on which to continue this remarkable success for the future.

U.S. SPACE & ROCKET CENTER®

Imagine actually becoming weightless, flying to Mars and then landing a Space Shuttle—all in the same day. *The Complete Space Experience.* It can happen in only one place, the U.S. Space & Rocket Center, where the past, present and future of space exploration come to life.

A daylong adventure takes you through dozens of hands-on exhibits and more than a thousand artifacts as you examine the early stages of rocketry, the manned space program and beyond.

Space Shot™ allows you to experience more G-Force than NASA's astronauts during a shuttle launch, while traveling 140 feet in the air in only three seconds. Two seconds of weightlessness await you at the top. Small children can ride a cushion of air as they descend to Earth on the Lunar Lander in the Kids Cosmos Energy Depletion Zone. Also located in this play area are crawl tubes designed like a space station and child-powered Space Shuttle rockers.

A Space Camp® trainee in the 1/6 gravity chair.

The U.S. Space & Rocket Center, Huntsville, Alabama.

Join 14 passengers on a Mission to Mars, a motion-based experience to the red planet to "test drive" new rovers over rocky Martian terrain. Step inside the UFO-shaped G-Force Accelerator. It's designed to take 45 adventurers on a whirling trip that produces three Gs of force.

As an audience member, you may become an actor in "Outpost in Space: The International Space Station," a theatrical demonstration about living and working in an environment where gravity doesn't exist.

"Land the Shuttle" tests your aviation skill, as you pilot the orbiter to a runway landing. The computerized "Shuttle Adventures" experience takes you on a tour of the Space Shuttle orbiter, mission control and the astronauts. Then it's time to test your eye-hand co-ordination by blasting space debris out of the path of an orbiting satellite.

In the Spacedome IMAX® Theater, you'll feel the thunder of a shuttle launch or take an up close and personal look at the sun while watching one of the 70-millimeter IMAX® movies. Features currently include *Solarmax* and the newest IMAX® movie, *Space Station*, all showing on the 67-foot curved screen.

Walk alongside a 363-foot-long real Saturn V rocket, or gaze toward the heavens at the vertical Saturn V replica that stands 363-feet tall. Peer inside the Apollo 16 Command Module that took Americans to the Moon and learn about each Moon mission in the Apollo exhibit. Stand underneath Pathfinder, one of only two full-scale Space Shuttle exhibits in the world. See the SR-71 Blackbird reconnaissance aircraft. This spy plane flew at Mach 3 speeds of more than 2,200 mph and made a coast-to-coast trek in less than 68 minutes.

Currently there are two new exhibits that illustrate early rocket development history and programs related to the STS—Space Transportation System, more commonly known as the Space Shuttle. The early rocket development exhibit attempts to explain when the first thoughts of serious space exploration entered the minds of the dreamers who eventually became the scientists who made the dream of spaceflight a reality. There are many artifacts in the exhibit that are unique to their collection. No other facility has them. One such artifact is a shipping tube that went with the V2 rocket as it left the factory and was taken to the launch site. Also on exhibit is a verticant gyroscope used on the V2. The verticant controlled the vertical motion of the missile. The focus of the exhibit is a 43-foot long A4/V2 missile—the German scientists referred to the missile as an A4; Hitler gave it the V-2 name as a vengeance weapon.

The STS or Space Shuttle exhibit contains many components from the Shuttle vehicle. One outstanding element is the *Powerhead*, which controls the fuel supply to the shuttle engines. The unit and components are approximately 4 feet x 3 feet x 8 feet. This powerhead has flown on eight Shuttle missions. Also on exhibit is one of four fuel cells that provide electrical power while in Earth's orbit. An MMU (Manned Maneuvering Unit) is available for guests to sit in and have a photograph made.

Dr. Wernher von Braun's desk, chair and artifacts are displayed in the *Rocket City Legacy* exhibit. As one walks through the *Legacy* gallery, historical events are shown through artifacts and panels. A full-scale replica of the United States' first satellite, Explorer I, stands as a symbol of the beginning of the space race with the Soviet Union during the Cold War.

You can catch a glimpse of the future space explorers as they train at U.S. SPACE CAMP®, which is based at the U.S. Space & Rocket Center. Space Camp is a fun, educational program that's designed to

Spacedome IMAX® theater.

encourage young people to pursue more math, science and technology in school. SPACE CAMP®/AVIATION CHALLENGE® offers programs for youth ranging from 9–18 years of age. Teachers, adults, parent/child and corporate programs are also offered throughout the year. Campers participate in simulated Shuttle missions; fly high-performance simulated aircraft, aircrew land/water survival exercises and

Outpost in Space.

educational topics ranging from hydroponics, crystal growth, robotics, virtual reality and many other interactive activities. Since its beginning in 1982, over 407,000 students have graduated from one of the Center's camp programs.

Several gift shops offer items such as T-shirts, jackets, videotapes, books, patches, emblems, toys, do-it-yourself rocket models, astronaut food and flight suits. Full menus of breakfast and lunch items are available year-round in the Galaxy Food Court.

More than 350,000 people from all 50 states and numerous foreign countries visit the U.S. Space & Rocket Center each year. Over 11 million people have visited since 1970. The Space Center is open, except on selected holidays, from 9:00 a.m. to 5:00 p.m., central time zone. It's located at Exit 15 on Interstate 565, 15 miles east of I-65.

For more information, contact the U.S. Space & Rocket Center in Huntsville, Alabama, or visit the Space Center website at www.spacecamp.com.

A TIMELINE OF HUNTSVILLE'S HISTORY

1769 Cherokees defeated Chickasaws at Chickasaw Old Fields, which became Ditto's Landing between 1802 and 1807, and Whitesburg in 1824.

1802 Georgia ceded all her western land to the United States.

1804 John Hunt and David Bean spent the night at Isaac Criner's cabin on the Flint River.

1805 John Hunt brought his family to live in a two-room cabin by the Big Spring.

1808 (December 13) Robert Williams, Governor of the Mississippi Territory issued a proclamation creating Madison County.

1809 (August) Madison county land sales took place in Nashville, Tennessee.

1810 (June) LeRoy Pope established the town of Twickenham. (July 5) Twickenham became Madison county seat.

1811 The federal land office moved to Huntsville. (November 25) Twickenham's name was changed to Huntsville. (December 9) Hunts-

A baptism in the Big Spring, circa 1885. Courtesy, Ernest C. Smartt

General Joseph Wheeler reviews the buffalo soldiers, December 1898. Courtesy, Huntsville Madison County Public Library

ville became Alabama's first incorporated town.

1816 (December 11) Alabama's first bank was chartered, opening in 1817 as Planters and Mechanics Bank, later changed to Planters and Merchants.

1817 John H. Hickman built Madison's first courthouse. (March 3) Congress carved Alabama Territory from Mississippi Territory.

1819 (Summer) Huntsville became the territorial capital of Alabama. (June 2) President James Monroe visited Huntsville. (July 5) Alabama's first Constitutional Convention met in Huntsville. (October 25) The first state legislative session opened in Huntsville; William Wyatt Bibb became first governor, Thomas Bibb, second governor. (December 14) Alabama became a State of the United States.

1821 (February) Indian Creek Canal Company was chartered, fully operational in 1831.

1833 The Fearn brothers helped

establish Viduta on Monte Sano.

1835 George Steele completed the First National Bank of Huntsville. Clement Comer Clay of Huntsville became governor of Alabama.

1840 George Steele built the first of two county courthouses.

1861 (January 11) Alabama seceded from the union. (April 12) Huntsville's Leroy Pope Walker, Confederate Secretary of War, ordered firing on Fort Sumter.

1862 (April 11) Union troops under General O. M. Mitchell occupied Huntsville until August 31, 1862.

1863 (July 4) Union troops reoccupied city until war's end.

1865 (May 11) Confederates surrendered on Monte Sano.

1869 Rust School on Franklin was opened for blacks.

1874 William Hooper Councill was appointed principal of the Huntsville State Normal School for Negroes. Classes began in 1875.

1875 Leroy Pope Walker chaired the State Constitutional Convention in Montgomery.

1879 Harrison Brothers Hardware began as a tobacco shop; moved to present location in 1897.

1881 The O'Shaughnessy brothers began transformation of local economy.

1882 Confederate General Joseph E. Wheeler, elected to Congress.

1884 (April 25) Frank James was tried in Huntsville and found not guilty of federal payroll robbery.

1887 (June 1) Monte Sano Hotel was opened, guests arriving via the Monte Sano Railway.

1890 The Dallas Mills were started by Trevanion B. Dallas and Godfrey M. Fogg, of Nashville, began operations in 1892.

1891 Councill's normal school became the state's black land-grant institution in 1891.

1892 Huntsville Board of Trade was started. Hagey Hospital was incorporated to treat addictions. The West Huntsville Cotton Mill was opened by Tracey Pratt. Exchange of property from the North Alabama

Monte Sano Hotel, the jewel of the mountain, was built in 1887 and torn down in 1944. Courtesy, Huntsville Madison County Public Library

Madison, Alabama, circa 1917, prior to the installation of electric lines. Courtesy, Huntsville Madison County Public Library

Improvement Company to the North Western Land Association marked a new beginning for the city's economy.

1894 Huntsville Chamber of Commerce formed.

1896 The Seventh-Day Adventists founded Oakwood College.

1898 Fourteen thousand troops were stationed in Huntsville during and following the Spanish-American War.

1899 Merrimack Mill construction started; began operations in 1900 and was demolished in 1991.

1900 Street car tracks were laid. Monte Sano Hotel closed.

1901 (April 30) President Mckinley visited Huntsville.

1910 Huntsville Hotel burned.

1915 The Twickenham Hotel opened.

1930 The Russel Erskine Hotel opened.

1934 (July 17) Southern Textile workers strike began in Huntsville.

1941 (July 3) War Department announced that Huntsville was selected for a new chemical munitions manufacturing and storage plant. (July 8) The War Department announced the establishment of a $6 million Ordnance Corps Assembly Plant. (December 7) Japan attacked Pearl Harbor.

1943 The Ordnance plant was renamed Redstone Arsenal and the Chemical Warfare plant became Gulf Chemical Warfare depot.

1944 (Fall) Huntsville Industrial Expansion Committee began work.

1945 World War II ended.

1949 (November) Redstone Arsenal was selected to be the Army's missile and rocket arsenal.

1950 Wernher von Braun and the German Rocket team arrived in

Senator Sparkman, shown here with his wife on his left, and to his right Mrs. Tazewell Sheperd and Mayor A.W. McAllister. The senator worked tirelessly for his district, especially for Huntsville, where he made his home. Courtesy, Huntsville Madison County Public Library

Huntsville. The University of Alabama began classes at West Huntsville High.

1952 Senator John J. Sparkman became Adlai Stevenson's running mate in Presidential campaign against Republican Dwight D. Eisenhower.

1953 The first Redstone Missile was launched.

1956 The City limits included the mill villages. The Southern Depot removed its segregation signs.

1957 (October 4) Russia sent Sputnik into earth orbit, shattering American complacency.

1958 (January 31) America entered the space race with earth orbiting Explorer I. Congress passed the National Aeronautics and Space Administration Act establishing a civilian agency for space technology and exploration.

1960 Marshall Space Flight Center was created, with Von Braun the center director. The Nike-Hercules intercepted an Honest John Rocket, both Arsenal-built, beginning the antiballistic missile system which became the Army's Safeguard Systems Command in Huntsville.

1961 (May 5) Alan Shepherd became the first American in Space.

1962 Cummings Research Park was established.

A TIMELINE OF HUNTSVILLE'S HISTORY

1963 Desegregation began at public schools and the University of Alabama in Huntsville.

1967 Huntsville International Airport opened.

1969 (July 15) Apollo 13 historic mission to the moon carried three astronauts. Neil Armstrong walked on the moon. Dunlop Tire Corporation established its second American plant in Huntsville, helping diversify the economy.

1970 United States Space & Rocket Center began its educational and tourist mission envisioned by von Braun.

1974 Busing to achieve desegregation began in Huntsville.

1975 (March) The Von Braun Civic Center opened. The United States Strategic Defense Command was activated.

1978 *Enterprise* visited Huntsville atop a Boeing 747.

1980 Huntsville International Jetplex became a U.S. Port of Entry. In 1981 GoldStar became the first international occupant.

1980-1981 Intergraph emerged from M&S Computing, and be-

President Eisenhower and Wernher von Braun at the dedication of the Marshall Space Flight Center. Courtesy, Huntsville Madison County Public Library

Sonnie Hereford IV, whose father brought suit seeking the end of segregation, is seen here in his first grade class at Fifth Avenue School. Courtesy, Sonny Hereford III

came a publicly traded company pioneering in computer graphics.

1981 Jeri Blankenship became the first woman judge of a Madison County District Court. (April 12) Shuttle *Columbia*, America's first reusable spacecraft, made its first voyage into space. The Marshall Space Flight Center developed the external tank, solid rocket boosters, main engines, and conducted the tests for *Columbia's* launch. Weeden House opened as a

museum run by the Twickenham Historic Preservation District Association,

1982 Panoply started its long success story.

1983 (May) City Council approved acreage for a botanical garden.

1984 Cummings Research Park West opened. (July) *SCItanic*, a refurbished paddle wheeler owned by SCI Systems, Inc., overturned in sudden 75-mile-per hour winds. (August) Madison Square Mall opened. (October) Work began on I-565. Historic Huntsville Foundation purchased Harrison Brothers Hardware to be a living history museum and store.

1985 Mark Smith, an early SCI partner, left Universal Data Systems to form Adtran, Inc. Joe Davis Stadium was completed. District Attorney Bud Cramer founded the Children's Advocacy Center.

1986 (January 28) The *Challenger* explosion killed all aboard,

231

sending the space program into a tailspin as the country mourned. (September) MICOM tests of the Patriot anti-aircraft missile intercepting a Lance ballistic missile demonstrated its usefulness against cruise missiles. Alabama A&M began its first PhD program in optics. Huntsville annexed 32 square miles, but Madison voted down merger with Huntsville.

Wernher von Braun Day, February 24, 1970. Von Braun and his family view the parade. Courtesy, Huntsville Madison County Public Library

The antebellum Humphrey-Rodgers house has undergone war in the 19th century and removal in the 20th century, but it is now in safe hands as part of the Early Works complex. Photo by Daniel Little

1987 Boeing landed Space Station contract accelerating a housing boon in Madison County, including Huntsville and Madison. The Strategic Defense Command's budget was one-third the total national Strategic Defense Initiative (SDI), popularly known as "Star Wars." Steven Streit investment scandal, "the largest single securities fraud in state history." (February) Physicists at the University of Alabama in Huntsville, with University of Houston physicists, achieved superconductivity at 93 Kelvin. (April) The new Huntsville-Madison County Public Library opened. (November) State supercomputer, a Boeing Computer Services 38.7 million Cray X-MP, was installed at Cummings Research Park.

1988 City and county elections followed a court ruling that single-member districts be established.

1989 (November) A killer tornado struck one of Huntsville's busiest thoroughfares at rush hour.

1990 "Desert Storm" drew on U.S. Army Missile Command. Patriot missiles hit their mark with the public. (April) Marshall's Hubble Space Telescope was deployed by shuttle *Discovery*. The State Black Archives, Research Center and Museum at Alabama A&M opened to the public. An amendment to the State Constitution making English the official language of the state, led to problems in the Madison County Tax Assessor's Office when Wayland Cooley refused homestead exemptions to non-English speaking applicants.

1991 (July 24) A spectacular blaze consumed vacant Dallas

Mill building. International Airport completed its $50 million concourse and terminal expansion.

1992 A bribery and extortion attempt by George Grayson, Huntsville's first African American elected to the Alabama House of Representatives since Reconstruction, against Huntsville's Mayor Steve Hettinger who was seeking reelection. Interstate I-565 was completed.

1992-1997 An average of more than 10,000 people move into the Tennessee Valley region each year.

1992 (May 22) Murder of popular Huntsville ophthalmologist, Jack Wilson.

1993 (December) Jan Davis, the first Huntsville native to go into space and her husband go as a couple, another first. With them went the first black woman, Mae Jemison and another first was Mamoru Mohri from Japan. (September) Big Spring Jam first filled the air with music up to the present. (December)"Do-Or-Die Mission" by the *Endeavour* crew to repair the Hubble Telescope succeeded.

1994 (August) The arsenal's John J. Sparkman Center for Missile Excellence was dedicated.

1995 The University of Alabama Birmingham Medical School took over the University of Alabama Huntsville's Medical School. (June) Merger of the Saint Louis Aviation base with Huntsville's Missile Command, up to 2,000 workers to come. Huntsville Hospital purchased Humana Hospital for pediatric and Women's hospital, beginning new era in hospital expansion.

1996-1997 New Century Tech-

nology High School opened for the school year. This is a cooperative undertaking between Huntsville Independent School District, Calhoun Community College, business and local government to provide opportunities for students to work with high-tech companies.

1996 Gay Pride controversy became an election issue.

1997 Madison City formed its own separate school system. Cummings Research Park was named the "World's top research park" by the Association of University Related Research Parks. The Von Braun Center's South Hall was opened.

1998 (March) The Huntsville Museum of Art opened in Big Spring Park. (December) EarlyWorks, a Hands-On Museum, opened. Boeing was named lead contractor for the National Missile Defense Program. More than 70 percent of the work to develop a missile shield around the U.S. is to be done in Huntsville. John Glenn, the first American in

earth orbit became the "nation's oldest astronaut at 77" when he returned to space. In December, he came to Huntsville for a parade and appearance at NASA.

1999 (March–September) Three "hit-to-kill" missile systems had successful test flights. (December) Dedication of the Richard C. Shelby Center for Missile Intelligence, a $33 million complex on the arsenal. Physicians and support personnel opened "The state's first clinic for the under-privileged" called The Community Free Clinic.

2001 Toyota began construction of its truck engine plant in Huntsville. Diversification continued to build a healthy economy.

2002 Susie and Jim Hudson announce plans for Electric Avenue by Big Spring Park.

The Tornado of 1989 destroyed property in the millions of dollars, but it could not destroy the spirit or determination of the survivors who rebuilt their lives and communities. Photo by Daniel Little

Bibliography

Students of any facet of Huntsville history will want to begin their search for materials in the Huntsville-Madison County Public Library's Heritage Room. The room's vertical file is filled with facts not available anywhere else with an amazing variety of clipped newspaper and magazine articles and pictures. Genealogical information often spiced with historical data is found in the room's highly prized family files. Also helpful is a complete set of the unique potpourri of records compiled by Kathleen Paul Jones and Pauline Jones Gandrud, *Alabama Records*. There are also three volumes of photocopied newspaper clippings entitled *Historic Scrapbook*. The room contains complete federal census records for Alabama that are available to the public, 1820-1910. The map collection is thorough, with several sets of Sanborn-Perris Insurance Maps of Huntsville.

For territorial history, the *American State Papers Land Grants and Claims* are on microfilm as are the *Territorial Papers of the United States Senate 1789-1873* and *Mississippi Territory June 30, 1799-April 1, 1818, Records of the States of the United States*, Mississippi Territory, reels 1 & 2 and Madison County Personal Tax Rolls, 1802-1817.

For antebellum history, the Clay Papers provide political and social commentary and include the Mary Lewis letters which give one of the best glimpses into women's concerns. The microfilm Crutchfield-Fearn-Steele Family Papers are useful. For business, the records of the Fearn Donegan and Company Commission House yield insights. Also of interest would be the John Williams Walker Papers. The *City of Huntsville Minute*

Books on microfilm brings one into the deliberations of city government.

The Civil War is best viewed through the diary of Mrs. W.D. Chadick, the second wife of William D. Chadick, a Cumberland Presbyterian minister. The Zeitler Room adjoining the Heritage Room houses a fine Civil War, Reconstruction, and Black History collection with many references to local people and places.

For business history since the Civil War there are the W.P. Newman Papers, the Papers of the Dallas Mill, and the Isaac Schiffman Papers reflective of a multi-faceted involvement with cattle and cotton farming, real estate holdings, investments, automobile sales, and other family interests.

Recent history draws from such sources as the local newspapers and also Redstone and NASA publications. One should also consult the studies done by the Huntsville Planning Commission and those by TARCOG, Top of Alabama Regional Council of Governments.

An extensive photo collection is found in the Zeitler Room. Various citizens have followed the lead of long-time Chairman of the County Commission, James Record, and contributed to the collection. Containing over 10,000 photos, it is a city treasure called upon daily by local businesses, TV stations, and researchers.

Courthouse records are found either in the Historical Records Room of the Parsons Law Library or in the County Courthouse. The Historical Records Room houses original Huntsville newspapers from the time of the Civil War to the present.

No history of the area could be written without frequent or

extensive use of the following essential journals. *The Alabama Review, The Alabama Historical Quarterly, The Huntsville Historical Review, The Historical Huntsville Quarterly,* and *Valley Leaves.*

The following books and manuscripts are recommended as source material, for further reading and research.

Abernethy, Thomas Perkins. *The Formative Period in Alabama 1815-1828.* University: University of Alabama Press, 1965.

Akens, David S. *Historical Origins of the George C. Marshall Space Flight Center.* MSFC Historical Monograph No. 1. Huntsville: National Aeronautics and Space Administration, 1960.

Alldredge, J. Haden; Spottswood, Mildred B.; Anderson, Vera V.; Goff, John H.; and LaForge, Robert M. *A History of Navigation on the Tennessee River System: An Interpretation of the Economic Influence of This River System on the Tennessee Valley.* House Document No. 254, 75th Congress, 1st Session. Washington, D.C.: United States Government Printing Office, 1937.

Bailey, Hugh C. *John Williams Walker: A Study in the Political, Social and Cultural Life of the Old Southwest.* University: University of Alabama Press, 1964.

Bergaust, Erik. *Rocket City U.S.A. From Huntsville, Alabama to the Moon.* New York: Macmillan Company, 1963.

Bergaust, Erik. *Wernher von Braun,* Washington, D.C.: National Space Institute, 1976.

Betts, Edward Chambers. *Early History of Huntsville, Alabama 1804-1870.* Bicentennial reprint, Pictorial Edition. Huntsville: Loy

Printing Company, 1976.

Bragg, James William. "Frontier Entrepreneurs of Madison County, Alabama: The Bell Factory Enterprise, 1819-1842." M.A. Thesis, University of Alabama, University, Alabama: 1958.

Brantley, William H. *Banking in Alabama 1816-1860,* Vol. I. Privately printed, 1961.

Carter, Clarence Edwin. *The Territorial Papers of The United States,* Vols. V and VI. Washington, D.C.: United States Government Printing Office, 1937.

Chapman, Elizabeth Humes. *Changing Huntsville, 1890-1899.* Huntsville Alabama: privately published, 1972.

Clay-Clopton, Virginia with Sterling, Adam. *A Belle of The Fifties.* Memoirs of Mrs. Clay, of Alabama, Covering Social and Political Life in Washington and the South, 1853-66. Put Into Narrative Form by Ada Sterling. London: Wm. Heinemann, 1905. New York: Doubleday, Page & Co., 1905.

Cowart, Margaret Matthews. *Old Land Records of Madison County, Alabama.* Huntsville, Alabama: privately published, n.d.

Fiske, Sarah Huff. "Historical Edition 1900-1955." *The Huntsville Parker,* Vol. 8, No. 1. Huntsville. September 1955.

Hoole, Wm. Stanley. *Alabama Tories: The First Alabama Cavalry, U.S.A., 1862-1865,* Tuscaloosa, Alabama: Confederate Publishing Company, Inc., 1960.

Jenkins, Delia Maples Martin. *Variety and Spice.* New York: Vantage Press, 1969.

McDonald, Tom and Record, James (eds.). *Commemorative Album Celebrating Our City's Sesquicentennial of Progress.* Huntsville, 1955.

McMillan, Malcolm C. *The Alabama Confederate Reader.* University: University of Alabama Press, 1963.

Morring, Thomas Franklin. "The Impact of Space Age Spending on the Economy of Huntsville, Alabama." Masters Thesis, Massachusetts Institute of Technology, 1964.

Northern Alabama Historical and Biographical, Illustrated. Birmingham, Alabama: Smith and DeLand, 1888.

Nuermberger, Ruth Ketring. *The Clays of Alabama: A Planter-Lawyer-Politician Family.* Lexington: The University of Kentucky Press, 1958.

Record, James. *A Dream Come True: The Story of Madison County and Incidentally of Alabama and the United States,* Vols. I and II. Huntsville: James Record, 1970 and 1978.

Riley, Rev. B.F. *Alabama As It Is; or The Immigrant's and Capitalist's Guide Book to Alabama.* Atlanta, GA. Constitution Publishing Co., 1888. Revised ed., Montgomery, AL: The Brown Printing Co., 1893.

Roberts, Frances Cabaniss. "Background and Formative Period in the Great Bend and Madison County." Ph.D. Dissertation, University of Alabama, University, 1956.

Royall, Anne Newport. *Letters From Alabama 1817-1822,* Edited by Lucille Griffith. University: University of Alabama Press, 1969.

Ryan, Patricia H. (ed.). *Cease Not to Think of Me.* Huntsville: Huntsville Planning Department, 1979.

Ryan, Patricia H. *Northern Dollars for Huntsville Spindles.* Huntsville: Huntsville Planning Department, 1983.

Saxton, Melissa. "The Growth of Huntsville, Alabama—A Study." Huntsville: Randolph High School 11th Grade, 1973.

Spragins, William Echols. *A Brief History and Brief Genealogy of the Andrew Beirne, William Patton, William Echols, V, and Robert E. Spragins Lines.* Huntsville, Alabama: privately published, 1956.

Stubno, William Joseph, Jr. "The Impact of the von Braun Board of Directors on the American Space Program." M.A. Thesis, Huntsville, Alabama: University of Alabama in Huntsville, 1980.

Taft, Philip. *Organizing Dixie Alabama Workers in the Industrial Era* (Rev. and ed. by Gary M. Fink). Westport, Connecticut: Greenwood Press, 1981.

Taylor, Thomas Jones. *The History of Madison County, Alabama.* (Manuscript written in Huntsville from 1880 to 1886). Huntsville Public Library, 1940.

Testimony Taken by the Joint Select Committee to Inquire into the Condition of Affairs in the Late Insurrectionary States. Alabama, Vols. I and II. (Vols. VIII & IX in whole series of 13 vols.) Washington, D.C., 1872.

Thomas, Shirley, *Men of Space,* Vols. 1-7, Philadelphia: Chilton Company, 1960-1965.

Walker, Anne Kendrick. *Braxton Bragg Comer: His Family Tree from Virginia's Colonial Days.* Richmond, VA: The Diety Press, Inc., 1947.

Whitman, Willson. *God's Valley: People and Power Along the Tennessee River.* New York: Viking Press, 1939.

Index

238